Weird Calderdale

Strange and Horrible Local History

Paul Weatherhead

Tom Bell Publishing

ISBN 978-0-95488763-6

PUBLISHED BY

Tom Bell Publishing

Hebden Bridge

West Yorkshire

Contact the author: paulweatherhead@yahoo.co.uk

Contents

Church of St Thomas the Apostle, Heptonstall, from Wadsworth
(Larisa Moskaleva)

Acknowledgements

This research and writing of this book involved extensive trawling of historic newspaper archives, local history books, antiquarian journals, reports and pamphlets, and I am grateful to all the authors living and dead for recording the weird and wonderful events that this book explores. I'm also grateful to the many generous people who gave up their time to reply to my letters, emails, or agreed to be interviewed for this book. I would particularly like to express my gratitude to the following for sharing with me their ideas, expertise, memories and time: John Billingsley, Terry Binns, John Birch, Graham Birdsall, Calderdale Libraries, David Farrant, The Ghost Mistress, Bryan Green, Barbara Green, Halifax Antiquarian Society, Hebden Bridge Local History Society, Steve Hill, Ann Kilby, Stefnie Krzyszczyk, Bishop Sean Manchester, Steve Lacey-Marsden, Colin Lyall, Sir Patrick Moore, Larisa Moskaleva, Paul Pearson, Kai Roberts, Sub-culture Alternatives Freedom Foundation, Todmorden Antiquarian Society, Todmorden UFO Meet, Michael L.B. West.

Cover photos and artwork by Larisa Moskaleva

All photos and images are from the author's own collection or are in the public domain except where indicated.

Old Tom Bell (Larisa Moskaleva)

Introduction

I'd always felt a strange attraction towards the weird. Growing up, as I did, in Hebden Bridge in the 70s and 80s, that's perhaps a good thing. An offcumden friend of mine once said to me, not knowing I was a native valley lad, 'God help anyone who grows up in Hebden Bridge and thinks it's normal!' As a teen normality for me involved local news stories of alien abduction and shape-shifting witches which I followed avidly in the local press, and my interest grew, fed by publications like *The Unexplained* and the *Fortean Times*. All of this, and a fascination for horror and the macabre are what led to the book you're now holding.

The first edition of *Weird Calderdale* came out in 2004 and was followed by two more slightly revised editions over the next few years. I'd been planning a rewrite for some time, but in 2019 and 2020 the weird dystopia of lockdown descended upon us. It seemed a fitting time to revisit these strange events and explore some new ones. The chapters in this new edition have been greatly expanded and updated, and many new chapters of often previously undiscovered weirdness have been added. I hope you enjoy the trip.

Paul Weatherhead

Hebden Bridge, 2023

Contact the author: paulweatherhead@yahoo.co.uk

Author Website: paulweatherhead.com

Hebden Bridge (Larisa Moskaleva)

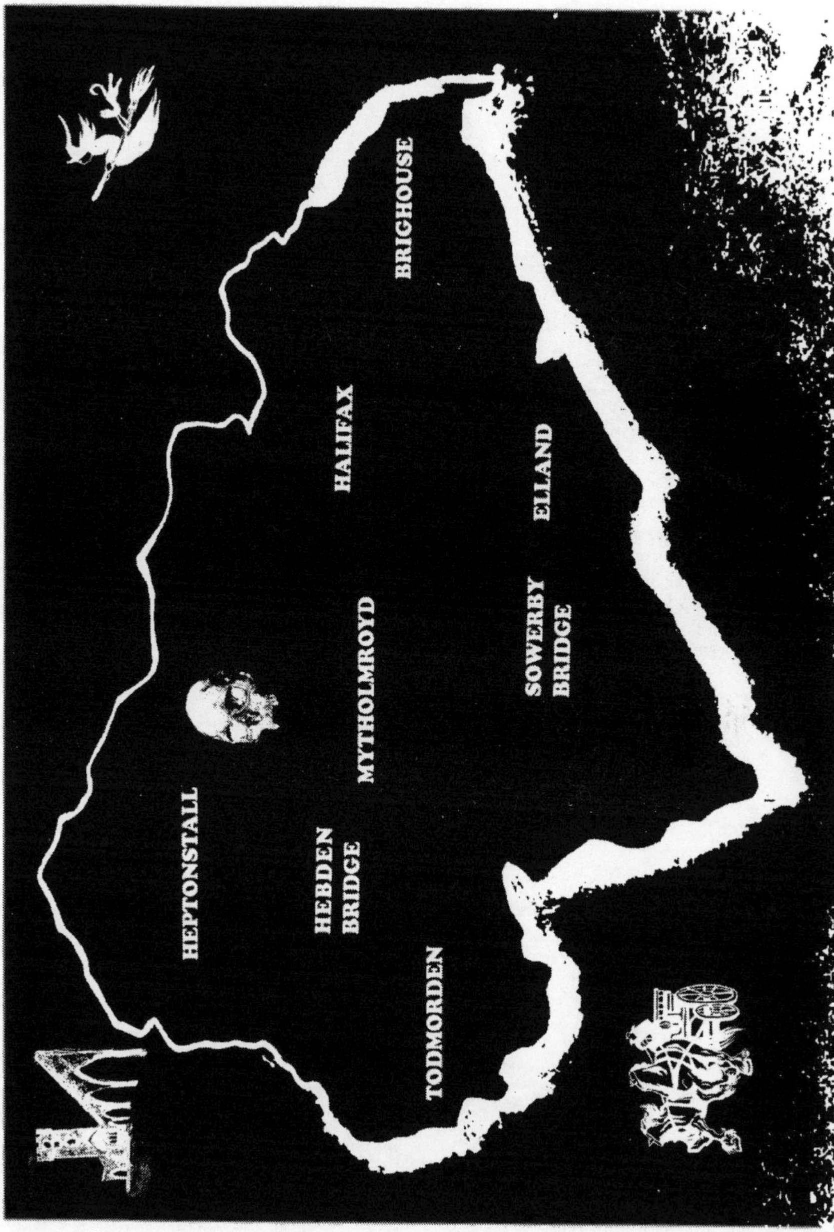
HEPTONSTALL
HEBDEN BRIDGE
TODMORDEN
MYTHOLMROYD
SOWERBY BRIDGE
HALIFAX
ELLAND
BRIGHOUSE

The Halifax Slasher ~ Razor Blade Terror

'He got hold of me with both hands near my shoulders and I thought he was trying to kiss me. He grimaced in my face and I noticed his flat nose and bad teeth. He seemed to brush both hands down my arms from the shoulders and I felt a sharp pain and screamed...'

(Margaret Reynolds, 1938)

In the winter of 1938, while Europe braced itself for war, the people of Halifax were in a state of nervous panic. Reports had begun to emerge of a razor blade wielding maniac leaping out from the town's many dark alleys and yards, slashing his helpless victims and then disappearing into the night with almost supernatural speed. Hundreds of vigilantes patrolled the streets in search of the mysterious assailant and Halifax and its neighbouring towns were gripped by a terrified hysteria as the seemingly motiveless attacks escalated and then began to spread across the whole country...

The First Attacks

The weather on the night of Wednesday 16 November 1938 was particularly dirty. A thick fog hung over the hills and mills of Calderdale, and the ground was muddy and wet underfoot. Gertrude Mary Watts and Mary Gledhill (both 21) were walking along Old Bank Lane to an evening class at Ripponden Technical Institute. They heard a noise behind them before feeling the sudden blow of a hatchet or mallet to their heads. They struggled briefly with their attacker before he vanished into the fog, leaving them shocked and bleeding.

The two young women ran and hammered on the door of a nearby cottage. They were looked after by a Mrs Helliwell, while her husband searched the streets for any sign of the assailant. He found no one. The police arrived and the friends' wounds were tended. Gertrude needed eight stitches to her head, while Mary needed three.

The women could tell the police little about the attacker as they had been hit from behind, and the evening had been so dark and gloomy. The man seemed to have been between twenty and thirty years old. He was wearing an overcoat and had a cap pulled down low over his face. The only other detail they could add was that he had a big mouth. Gertrude and Mary thought they had seen the man earlier in the evening, and that he had followed them prior to the attack. Other people also reported seeing a stranger in an overcoat in the area.

The reporting of this incident on Thursday 17 November 1938 in the *Halifax Evening Courier and Guardian* caused 'tremendous sensation' in the area and led to much 'womenfolk's uneasiness' as well as some all-night patrols of volunteers to try and catch the culprit.[1]

All was quiet for a few days, but this was to change for the town of Halifax on the 21 November. Mary Sutcliffe (21), a 'toffee girl' who worked at Mackintosh's toffee factory, was walking home along Francis Street and crossing Lister Lane after her late shift at the mill. Suddenly a man appeared from under a gas lamp with his arm raised as if about to strike her. Mary instinctively lifted her hand to protect herself and felt an odd sensation in her wrist. She ran home, and it was only then that she noticed the deep gash she had suffered on her arm. The wound, which required four stitches, had been a clean cut and the blow had been painless, so it was assumed that she had been slashed with a razor.

This attack is important for two reasons. Firstly, it was the first incident referred to in the media as a 'slashing'. Secondly, Mary was able to furnish the police with a description of her assailant. He was, according to Mary, aged between 25 and 35, five feet ten inches tall and clean shaven. She also noticed his rather prominent eyes. He was dressed in a trilby hat and a military raincoat. The Slasher's raincoat was to play a crucial part in the unwinding of the mystery. However, this was only the beginning…

The Attacks Escalate

The next attack was only a few days in coming. On Thursday 24 November Sunday school caretaker Clayton Aspinall was outside St Andrew's Methodist Church in Queen's Road, only a few hundred yards from the site of the Mary Sutcliffe attack. Without warning a figure rushed out of the darkness and aimed a blow at Aspinall's head. The victim threw his arms up to defend himself, receiving wounds on his head and two of his fingers. The assailant vanished behind the nearby art school and subsequent searches proved fruitless.

Mary Sutcliffe (Leeds Mercury)

Although Aspinall could not give a detailed description of the man, he remembered him as five feet nine inches tall and around 30 years old. He had a stoop and well-combed gingerish hair. He was also wearing what was coming to be the Slasher's trademark: a fawn overcoat. Nobody was in any doubt that the same culprit was behind the attacks on Mary Sutcliffe and Clayton Aspinall, and it was after the latter incident that the assailant got his striking nickname: The Halifax Slasher. The press speculated that whoever the assailant was, he was unlikely to be a stranger because he would need a good grasp of the labyrinthine ginnels and alleys surrounding Halifax in order to make his escape so effectively.[2] Furthermore, after the attack on Aspinall, the Slasher became nationwide front page news: referring to the fact that female students had been temporarily kept inside the art college for safety while searches were made for Aspinall's assailant, *The Daily Mirror* of 25 November's headline ran: 200 GIRLS LOCKED FROM SLASHER.

The seriousness with which the town took these assaults can be seen by the fact that police patrols were stepped up, outside forces brought in and a £10 reward offered for information leading to the arrest of the Slasher. Female students at the nearby art school were escorted home or sent home in groups, sometimes carrying makeshift weapons such as boxes of pepper or hat pins.[3]

However, nobody expected that the following night would prove to be the Slasher's busiest yet. The first of the night's four victims was Mrs Annie Cannon. Mrs Cannon (39) worked with a relative of a previous victim, Mary Sutcliffe at Mackintosh's toffee factory, and had been heard to express fears that the maniac might come for her, saying: 'I hope he doesn't get me.' As she left her outside toilet at about 6.20 pm and walked down the dark back street to her home in Highroad Well, a man stepped out of the darkness from behind the toilet door and struck her left shoulder before pushing her to the ground. She screamed and her phantom attacker made good his escape. A neighbour alerted by the screams saw a figure disappear into the darkness. Mrs Cannon was lucky to be left with little more than a slashed cardigan.

The second incident of the night took place in Ovenden, about half an hour's walk from the site of the previous attack. Mrs Alice McDonald passed a man who was apparently waving a white handkerchief. The man suddenly grabbed her arm and aimed a blow at her throat, but luckily her collar had been turned up against the cold and this protected her. She scratched at the attacker's face with the hat pin she had been carrying for self-defence and fell to the ground, noticing the bright buckles on the Slasher's shoes as he fled. Later attacks would also mention the razor being hidden inside a white handkerchief.

Shortly after the McDonald attack, there was some excitement in Sowerby Bridge. A man fitting the description of the Slasher was seen near a mill in the town but had escaped on to the roof of the building. Police surrounded the mill and a thorough search was conducted, though no sign of the elusive phantom was found.[4]

The third attack of the night took place at around five to ten. One Mrs Holden was startled by a sudden desperate hammering at her door. She opened it to see a man she recognized stagger in bleeding profusely from his left arm. Clutched in his hands were a bag of fish and chips and the ripped tab from a light-coloured raincoat. The victim, Percy Waddington, a 38-year-old grocery manager at the Elland Road branch of the Co-op, had just been to the pub and was returning with a fish supper. He had been walking along Elland Lane, close to his shop, when a mackintoshed arm had appeared from around a corner and slashed his left arm. Percy had fought back, however, and although he saw nothing of the man attacking him, he did manage to rip off the tab from the raincoat sleeve. This torn piece of material was the first solid lead the police had. Percy showed police where the attack had happened, and they found a pool of blood and a safety razor at the scene.

The final attack of this hectic night happened shortly after 10 o'clock in Green Lane, Halifax. Mrs Hilda Lodge popped out to buy some vinegar for the fish and chips that her husband had just brought home. As in the previous attack, an arm from an unseen assailant shot from around a corner and struck at her. She received scratches to her face and arm, but these proved not to be as serious as they first appeared.

It was at this time that a disturbing twist in the story took place. The citizens of Halifax had been showing admirable community spirit in the face of these attacks; they patrolled the town and women were escorted to their destinations after dark. However, when Sergeant Bland went to Mrs Lodge's house soon after the slashing, he saw around a hundred people in the street and heard a voice cry, 'They've got him!' Despite protestations of innocence, a man was being roughly manhandled by an uncontrollable mob. There were shouts of 'Kill the b------!' and 'Break his b----- neck!'. The police eventually managed to extricate the unfortunate man, a compositor named Clifford George Edwards, who had actually been one of the men patrolling the streets searching for the Slasher after the Hilda Lodge attack. In Sergeant Bland's own words: 'I got among them and got hold of Edwards. With the help of another officer I was able to get him away. The crowd was very angry and we had considerable difficulty in getting Edwards away.'[5] This was not the last time that an innocent person would narrowly escape a public lynching during the Slasher's reign of terror.

Percy Waddington (Yorkshire Evening Post)

Of course, the Night of the Slasher had a great effect on the nerves of Halifax's already on edge population. The police issued warnings for people not to go out alone at night. Streets were nearly deserted after dark, and anyone brave enough to be out at night often walked in the middle of the road rather than on the pavement to reduce the risk of a surprise attack from a hidden corner or alley. Unusually, the fish and chip shops were frequented by men as many women, who would normally have fetched the supper, were too afraid to go out.[6]

The difficulty of travelling on foot between these four locations in the short time span between the attacks could mean that either the attacker had a car, or perhaps more worryingly, there were two Slashers at work. Indeed, the headline in the *Halifax Evening Courier and Guardian* on Saturday 26 of November asked TWO SLASHERS AT WORK IN HALIFAX AND DISTRICT? But things were about to get much worse…

Hilda Lodge and children (Halifax Evening Courier)

Slasher Mania

Up to this point the police had been building up a composite picture of the Slasher. He was about five feet nine inches tall but with a stoop. His hair was 'inclining to ginger' and he sometimes wore a hat. He wore a fawn raincoat, now with one tab missing, and had bright buckles on his shoes. In the *Halifax Evening Courier and Guardian* the police stated that the Slasher is 'not a mental case. It is sheer devilment. There is more than one person concerned – probably three.' The reason why speculation moved from one slasher to two slashers to 'probably three' can be seen in the events of Saturday 26 November.

At 7.30 Leslie Nicholls, a 21-year-old baker and confectioner, was slashed by someone stepping from the shadows, but escaped with some cuts to his apron.

Sometime after 11.30 that night Mrs Margaret Reynolds was looking for her husband outside her home in Caddy Field when she came face to face with the maniac. This is what happened in her own words:

> He got hold of me with both hands near my shoulders and I thought he was trying to kiss me. He grimaced in my face and I noticed his flat nose and bad teeth. He seemed to brush both hands down my arms from the shoulders and I felt a sharp pain and screamed…

Mrs Reynolds' wounds required stitches, but she had added a few details to the Slasher's profile. He was now taking on the appearance of a villain from a Victorian melodrama with his gruesome grimaces and ugly physiognomy.

The excitement continued the next evening, Sunday 27 November. Beatrice Sorrell, a 19-year-old warehouse worker was walking from Gibbet Street to Pellon Lane when she saw a mackintoshed hand holding a handkerchief before she felt the slashing blow. Too stunned to scream, she ran to the nearby fire station for help. The firemen on duty noted that she didn't seem particularly distressed or out of breath. She pointed out the superficial cut on her arm saying only: 'Look what someone has done'.

The dog stands guard while his master, one of Halifax's volunteer searchers, lights a cigarette. A scene in the Pellon district last night. (By a "Mercury" photographer.)

Leeds Mercury

A journalist from the *Yorkshire Evening Post* described the scene in Halifax as he made his way to Beatrice Sorrell's house: 'Men with torches were falling over each other in their anxiety to be the first to lay hands upon the slasher… I approached a lady in a corner house, but she brandished a knife with a blade at least a foot long and did not desist until I assured her that I was not the Slasher.'[7]

Leeds Mercury

Lily Woodhead (21) was next in line for a visit. Shortly after 10 o'clock that same Sunday night she had just had a tiff with her boyfriend Frank Coupland and was walking down Twine Lane between Brearley and Mytholmroyd (about six miles west of Halifax) to catch her bus. Frank had refused to accompany her to the bus stop as was his custom and commented that 'she would be surprised if there was a slasher in the lane'. Suddenly, according to Woodhead:

> I saw someone jump over the wall and come towards me with his hands. One appeared to go towards my

throat, and I felt a stinging pain in my neck, and I received cuts on my hand. I fell to the ground and the man sprang at me, and I received the cuts while stumbling. I screamed out and then got up. The man disappeared over the wall.[8]

Lily was left scratched and bruised but not seriously hurt.

The attack was deemed unconnected to the other incidents by the police, although a corrux razor blade was later found; the same type of razor had also been found near the scene of the Percy Waddington attack in Elland.[9] It seemed obvious that the assaults were not now just occurring in Halifax, and nightly patrols by the police, volunteers and even scouts were extended to cover other parts of the district. There was considerable disruption to everyday social life; even Mytholmroyd's annual police whist drive and dance was postponed.

On that same Sunday there was another mob attack on an innocent passer-by. Fred Baldwin (15) was pushing his bicycle down Skircoat Green to Copley at about 10pm when he began to be followed by a group of five (possibly drunk) men. One member of this group, William Spencer, initiated an attack on the boy claiming he was 'him'. By the time the police arrived the crowd had grown to around fifty, some armed with pokers and other weapons fighting to get at the 'Slasher'. Fortunately, a neighbour recognized Fred and told the mob that she knew him, meaning he escaped with only a bad bruising. William Spencer, the ring-leader of the mob, later paid a visit to Fred's father to try and explain what had happened but received a hefty thumping for his efforts from Mr Baldwin.[10]

The following Monday Mrs Constance Wood was leaving her home in Long Lover Lane on her way to work as a weaver when she became the latest victim. She described the attack in the *Yorkshire Evening Post*:

> I had not got five yards away from my front gate... when a man came across the road to me. As there were lots of men about at the time I did not attach any importance to his appearance, but suddenly he made a rush at me and pushed me over on the ground, and as he did so he cut through my cardigan jacket and underclothes, right through my arm. I screamed and the man made off, disappearing the way he had come. He appeared to be wearing a light raincoat. I never heard any footsteps. I think he must have been wearing pumps.[11]

Men on their way to work heard Mrs Wood's scream and some chased a tall figure in a grey pullover but could not catch him.

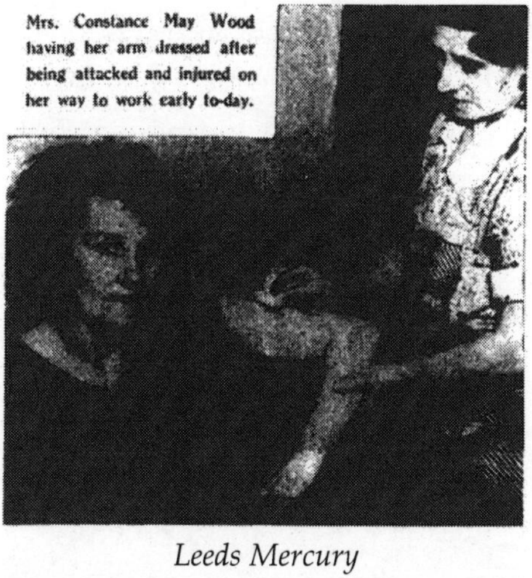

Leeds Mercury

It seems that the attack in Long Lover Lane was expected by some of the residents.[12] This is because the road is broad, long and poorly lit and has many alleys and passages adjoining it. Indeed, in the days prior to the attack on Mrs Wood a number of residents (including Mrs Wood's husband) had seen a suspicious stranger hanging around the area and peering into lighted windows. A near neighbour of Mrs Wood, Mrs Brooks, saw this 'lurker in the shadows', as the *Post* dubbed him, loitering in her gateway as she brought her son's bike indoors late one night prior to the attack. Mrs Brooks was terrified by the mysterious stranger and ran indoors up to her children's room. Sometime later she crept downstairs to hear someone trying her door handle.

By this time, the town was clearly in an escalating state of panic. Businesses began to suffer as people stayed away from cinemas and social events. The events that did go ahead had to provide free escort services to see women safely home. Workmen were carrying led pipes for protection. Shops were selling out of walking sticks, or 'slasher sticks' as they were becoming known. The screams of a dog being run over led to women panicking. Municipal by-elections were also affected as people refused to answer the door to canvassers and police advised voters to cast their ballot during daylight hours. An election meeting was cancelled as the candidate and his agent were the only people to turn up.[13] According to the Mayor of Halifax, Alderman John Radcliffe:

> There is suspicion everywhere. The slashings have not only frightened women, but have thrown suspicion on every man who is seen out alone at night. Many men have told me of the uncomfortable position they have found themselves in if they have chanced to venture abroad by themselves after dark.[14]

This is reflected in the headline for the national newspaper the *Daily Mirror* of 28 November: TERROR TOWN'S WOMEN GET POLICE ORDER: STAY IN. Halifax had gone from toffee town to terror town in the space of a few days.

Searchers in one of the dark courtyards of Halifax.

Leeds Mercury

Volunteers patrolled the streets of Halifax. Two such volunteers were Major Kington of the Duke of Wellington's Regiment from the barracks at Halifax and his wife. The Major's wife bravely walked ahead as a decoy to attract the Slasher, while the Major lurked behind with a golf club ready to brain the attacker should he appear.[15] Another courageous woman who offered her services as a decoy for the Slasher was a young Phyllis Davis from Burnley, who went on to become Fleet Street's first female crime reporter.[16]

One conclusion that seemed obvious to the press at the time was that the attacker must be a local man. This is because he needed a local's knowledge of the town's alleys and short cuts to make his escape so effectively. *The Yorkshire Evening Post* described Halifax as being 'riddled with ginnels and by-ways through which he can appear and disappear. The cover and opportunities at his disposal seem almost inexhaustible.'[17] Of course, if he was a local man, it followed that he could be a family member, a friend or a work colleague. No doubt the people of Halifax were eyeing each other with some misgiving as the attacks escalated.

Other conclusions that were drawn at the time concerned the physical attributes of the Slasher. For one thing, he was fast: no matter how many people attempted to run him down, he always managed to outstrip them and disappear into the backstreets of Halifax with an almost supernatural ability. Another point was his strength. As the *Post* put it: 'The Slasher has become a bogeyman. He is believed to be exceptionally powerful and active, and the marks of his grasp on some of his victims go towards proving this'.[18]

One of the most frightening aspects of the attacks for the residents of Halifax must have been their seemingly random nature. This led to speculation as to the motives of the Slasher. A police spokesman told the *Yorkshire Evening Post* on 30 November:

> This person is not out to maim or kill, but to terrorise, and he extracts a vicious pleasure from doing so. It is very much on the cards that this impulse will lead him to strike again. Another motive which may govern him is vanity. His success so far may delude him into the belief that he cannot be caught and he may be unable to resist in indulging once again in his vicious impulse. It may be that the vanity which helps to actuate him will prove his downfall.

The Slasher's supposed vanity notwithstanding, the attacks continued.

MONDAY, NOVEMBER 28, 1938

Daily Mirror

FOR BRITAIN AND THE EMPIRE

SHE SANG THE "LAMBETH WALK" IN CHURCH

TERROR TOWN'S WOMEN GET POLICE ORDER: 'STAY IN'

"ALL women must stay indoors," declared the Chief Constable of Halifax, Major A. H. Richardson, last night, a few hours after a girl aged eighteen walking down a dark street had become the eleventh victim in the "slashing" terror which is maddening the town.

"If women do go out," added the Chief Constable, "I advise them to have a male escort.

"I appeal to all able-bodied men to form themselves into street patrols. It is in this way that the public can safeguard themselves. The police cannot be in all places at once."

Screaming Woman

DEATH RIDDLE OF A BRIDE

PREMIER GOING TO ROME

The Daily Mirror 28 November 1938

However, the police had found the clue they had been looking for: the Slasher's raincoat. Back on the 25 November there had been an attack on Percy Waddington in Elland where the victim had managed to rip one of the tabs off the sleeve of his assailant's raincoat. This raincoat, minus missing left tab, was found on the Old

Earth Rugby Union ground in Elland. The raincoat was well worn; indeed, it had been patched with rubber. What is more, it contained a written number, perhaps from a cleaner, salesperson or a pawnbroker. There also appeared to be some scrawled initials that might further help to identify the owner. Pictures of the coat were printed in the papers and the reward for information leading to the capture of the Slasher was increased to £25.

Call in Scotland Yard ~ The Terror of the London Toughs

The *Halifax Evening Courier* headline for Tuesday 29 November read: SCOTLAND YARD CALLED IN TO HELP SOLVE 'SLASHER' SENSATION. Chief Inspector William Salisbury (known as the Terror of the London Toughs for his investigation of London's razor gangs) and Detective Sergeant Studdard were being brought to Halifax to help with a manhunt that was 'unparalleled since the days of Jack the Ripper'. Already help had been brought in from forces outside Halifax, not to mention the large number of volunteer patrols. The *Sheffield Star* claimed that 20,000 men had signed up for these vigilance patrols, and if true this would represent an amazing one fifth of the population of the entire town! And yet, despite the local police's best efforts, the attacks continued. No doubt it was a difficult decision to call in Scotland Yard. It was an admission of defeat by Halifax police, and the situation was clearly out of their control.

However, if anyone could make progress on the case, it would be Chief Inspector William Salisbury. Salisbury was in his early forties at this time and had wide experience of violent crime. He was one of Scotland Yard's top murder detectives and was well known for smashing the razor slashing organized crime gangs of Islington.[19] In Halifax, Salisbury and his assistant Studdard got to work studying over 400 reports, maps of the district, damaged clothes from the slashings, visiting the scenes of the attack and re-interviewing the victims.

Slash Attacks: A New Turn

ELLAND ASSAULT SEQUEL

Owner of Raincoat Traced

NO ARREST, SAY POLICE

There was a development to-day in the inquiries into the various slashing mysteries in the Halifax district.

A clue to which the police have attached considerable importance resulted in a man being interrogated by West Riding detectives. The police deny, however, that an arrest has been made.

The West Riding Police Superintendent, Mr. J. A. Gee, briefly announced that the owner of a raincoat discovered behind the wall of a playing field at Elland, three miles from Halifax, had been

Volunteers for the search for the slasher being directed to the assembling point by officers on duty at the Halifax police station.

Yorkshire Evening Post

Halifax and district continued to live on the edge of its nerves, and false alarms and wild goose chases were bound to occur. An example from Hebden Bridge illustrates this. The people of the Fairfield area of the town were very disturbed after an incident that was reported in the *Courier* of Wednesday 30 November. An 18-year-old man walking from Fairfield down into Hebden Bridge town centre passed an older man who seemed both wary and alarmed, as did the young man. The older man said 'I'll kill thi if tha comes near me!' The youth ran home and told his parents, and the story began to circulate that the Halifax Slasher was operating in Fairfield. Later investigation showed that the supposed Slasher was an old and respected native of Hebden 'whose fighting and running days had passed their prime more than half a century ago.' The story illustrates the air of mistrust and fear that people were living under. Any man in a raincoat in the wrong place at the wrong time could find himself being chased through the streets by an over eager patrol group.

Back to the attacks. The next victim had also been one of the first. Mary Sutcliffe's second assault was on Monday 28 November. It was only just dark when she went into her yard on Allerton Street and was slashed across her chest. As usual, nobody saw anything, though a van was seen driving away at unusual speed and a razor was found at the scene. Was Mary extremely unlucky or was she singled out in a carefully planned attack? It was even speculated in the *Sheffield Star* that the Slasher was going to hit all of his victims twice. *The Courier* of 29 November pointed out that many of the victims were Catholics and some must have wondered if religious hatred might have been a motive for the assaults. In any case, this second attack on Mary must have been a shock, as the victims up to now seem to have been chosen at random or had been in the wrong place at the wrong time. The *Manchester Guardian* called Mary's second ordeal the 'most cowardly of attacks' and commented that the 'most mysterious aspect is that no one apart from Mrs Sutcliffe saw her assailant'.[20]

On the same day that Mary Sutcliffe suffered her second assault, weaver Winnie McCall (17) fell victim to the Slasher. She was slashed about the forehead and temple by a mystery assailant and reported the attack to the police and Chief Inspector Salisbury himself inspected the wounds with a magnifying glass.[21]

Not long after this attack, Mrs Margaret Kenny was grabbed and slashed on the steps coming from Dean Clough Mill to Crib Lane. However, the assailant had not reckoned on the strength of Mrs Kenny. She said of the attack:

> I am fairly strong. I held on to him for what seemed to be two or three minutes. I dare not scream because I felt I had the chance of holding him until someone came. If I had screamed, he would have run away. But no-one came, and I realised that I should be badly hurt if I did not give the alarm. I screamed and immediately he released me and ran away.[22]

Mr Martin Egan heard her screams and ran to her assistance. Again, even the passing amateur footballers who gave chase to the attacker were unable to catch the Slasher as he vanished into the town's backstreets.

TOWN WHERE NO WOMAN WALKS ALONE

BY CLIFFORD SPEIGHT
"Daily Herald" Special Correspondent

HALIFAX, Monday.

CHIEF INSPECTOR JACK SALISBURY, of Scotland Yard, with a detective sergeant, will arrive to-morrow morning to help hunt down the "Silent Slasher."

Halifax is a town of terror to-night—a terror which reveals itself in silent streets, almost total absence of women walking alone and the furtive hunting of plain-clothes policemen.

There are innocent-looking motor-cars, too, patrolling the streets. They are manned by volunteers—citizens of this mill town who are determined to find the Silent Slasher and

And here is Miss Mary Sutcliffe, who has twice been attacked near her home—on November 21 and again yesterday.

Daily Herald

THE SLASHER STILL AT LARGE

SCOTLAND YARD CALLED IN

Halifax in State of "Nerves"

WORKMEN CARRY LEAD PIPES

Halifax police asked for the assistance of Scotland Yard officers in their search for the "slasher," whose series of attacks has spread consternation through the town.

Detective - Inspector Salisbury and Detective-sergeant Gray, of the "Yard," were expected in Halifax this afternoon.

Mr. Salisbury, who is 43, was

Mrs. Margaret Kenney, who was attacked by the slasher last night.

Yorkshire Evening Post

Slasher mania was spreading and it seemed unstoppable. Reports of slashings were coming in from towns and cities around the north, including Wigan, Giggleswick, Blackburn, Barnsley, Manchester and even as far afield as Glasgow.[23] But almost as soon as it had erupted, the whole business mysteriously petered out shortly after Salisbury and Studdard of the Yard arrived. The headline in the *Courier* of Thursday 1 December read: NO SLASHING ATTACKS IN HALIFAX AND DISTRICT YESTERDAY. That an *absence* of motiveless razor slashings was considered headline news shows just how under siege Halifax felt itself to be. In the same edition of the paper Halifax's Chief Constable A. H. Richardson called for the whole subject to be treated more rationally. And this marks the beginning of the end for the Halifax Slasher.

Slasher's Raincoat Traced!

The best clue the police had so far was the patched and torn raincoat found after the attack on Percy Waddington. The photographs of it printed in the *Halifax Courier* paid off; Wilfred Oliver, former employee of the Elland Co-op, recognized the coat as one that he had patched up himself.[24] And he knew who the owner was. It was Percy Waddington! It didn't take Percy long to crack under police interrogation. This is his statement:

> When I was walking near the Old Earth football ground I don't know what came over me, but I took out a safety blade from my pocket and cut my left hand across the back. I was frightened, and I went to a house nearby and kicked at the door…[25]

It was then that Mrs Holden had opened her front door to see Percy bleeding and clutching a torn raincoat tab and a bag of fish and chips.

The *Courier* headline of Friday December 2 read CARRY ON HALIFAX! THE SLASHING SCARE IS OVER. The report continued: 'The theory that a half-crazed, wild-eyed man has been wandering around, attacking helpless women in dark streets is exploded.' According to the police, 'There never was, nor is there likely to be, in this connection, any real danger to the general public.' Furthermore, the existence of a Glasgow Slasher was also denied and a woman was charged with making false allegations after inflicting wounds on herself.[26]

More confessions of false claims came from Lancashire.[27] More disturbing, though, is the case of a Sheffield school where the headmistress confiscated over twenty razor blades from boys after they had been cutting girls while playing at being the Halifax Slasher.[28]

Meanwhile, the Scotland Yard detectives had been busy re-interviewing some of the Slasher's 'victims', and the confessions of self-inflicted wounds began to come thick and fast. Beatrice Sorrell, Winfred McCall, Leslie Nicholl… all confessed to being responsible for their own injuries.[29] But this was not quite the end of the Slasher.

The Slasher Trials

By Monday 5 December the *Courier* headline was: HALIFAX BACK TO NORMAL. PUBLIC LAUGHS OFF SLASHER SCARE. However, the ghost of the Slasher was not yet exorcised, for the new year of 1939 brought the whole episode back into the public consciousness as the Slasher's 'victims' became the accused and were put on trial. The trials themselves, as one might expect, were not without drama.

Percy Waddington faced trial in Leeds on Monday 9 January 1939. It will be remembered that he was the third victim on the Night of the Slasher, 25 November 1938. He also claimed to have torn a piece of the attacker's raincoat off, which became his undoing as the raincoat was traced back to Percy himself. During the hearings, Percy had been allowed to sit due to his being of a 'nervous disposition'.[30] Part of Percy's confession was read out:

> I do not know whatever came over me…. I took out a safety razor blade from my pocket and cut my left

> hand… I think it must have been in my mind for a long time because I remember getting the old mackintosh out of the shop, and pulling off the tab.[31]

Percy had already apologized and tried to account for his actions in his previous confession to police: 'I am very sorry I have caused the police all this trouble. I apologise to everybody. I realise I have been a fool, but I get very excited, and sometimes don't realise what I am doing.'[32] Percy's crime (he was accused of public mischief, as were other Slasher 'victims') had led to him being demoted from his position as sub-postmaster, but the Co-op stood by him, giving him a good character reference and promising to keep him on as manager at the store he had worked at since leaving school at fourteen.[33] The Chairman, Judge Stewart, said to Percy 'you have brought disgrace upon yourself, you have brought deep sorrow on your wife', but his sentence was relatively light: he was bound over for three years.

Monday 23 January saw the trials in Halifax of Winnifred McCall, Leslie Nicholl, Beatrice Sorrell, Hilda Lodge and Annie Cannon.[34] All except Annie Cannon pleaded guilty. Beatrice Sorrell had argued with her boyfriend and then bought a razor: 'I cut my arm because I was in a temper and had been reading in the papers about the girls being slashed.' Winnie McCall admitted cutting her forehead by using a sharp comb. Leslie Nicholl's excuse was by far the most imaginative: he hoped having his name in the paper as a 'false' victim would lead to him being targeted by the Slasher which would in turn enable him to catch the attacker and claim the reward. Hilda Lodge admitted to cutting herself with a broken vinegar bottle and pointed out that she had a medical certificate saying she was 'hysterical and neurotic'. All four were of previous good character and the Recorder made it clear that he did not usually punish first time offenders, but in this case the effects on the town and the authorities were so serious that all four were sentenced to four weeks imprisonment with Leslie Nicholls getting an additional £10 fine. On hearing the sentence, Winnie McCall collapsed and had to be carried from the court. The recorder commented on the sentences: 'if ever there were any more false allegations from hysterical women or stupid men he would view the sentences as far too lenient.'[35]

Compared to these four, Annie Cannon had a lucky escape. She had, it will be remembered, claimed to have been attacked on 25 November. However, Chief Inspector Salisbury confronted Annie on December 1 and cast doubt on her story. Annie then admitted that she had been in a state of nerves over a disagreement about a washing machine with her sister and her husband and that she had cut herself.[36] 'I have been suffering with my nerves for some time,' she said, 'and have been under the care of the doctor.' A lecturer and expert on textiles from Halifax Technical College, William Stewart, testified in court that the cuts on Annie's cardigan must have been made against a hard surface and not as Annie had described. It looked bleak for Annie, but it seems that Salisbury of the Yard had made an elementary error: he had not made it clear that Annie was not obliged to give a statement. Furthermore, Annie's defence, Mr Hylton Foster, also claimed that Salisbury had intimidated Annie in a tearful two-hour interrogation in which he had allegedly pretended to phone Sir Bernard Spilsbury, the well-known father of forensics famous for his courtroom appearances and his work on the Crippen case as well as other high-profile murders. To make matters worse, aspects of Annie's original signed statement to the police after reporting her attack had been altered. In light of all the above, the jury were instructed to find Annie Cannon not guilty and she was dismissed. She did not escape any form of punishment entirely, though. It seems there was some ill feeling directed towards her and her windows had been smashed.[37]

The trail of Lily Woodhead also had its share of drama. Lily claimed to have been attacked near Mytholmroyd on 27 November after an argument with her boyfriend, Frank Coupland. She was due to appear at Todmorden police court on Monday 16 December on public mischief charges but had gone on the run with her boyfriend. Her absconding was sensational and a warrant for her arrest was issued. She was finally caught in Sheffield on 13 January 1939.[38] The Prosecutor, Mr Billington, said of her that he did not know if 'the girl had done it to get publicity or because she was a silly, hysterical girl, or she hoped to get her young man back by making up the quarrel this way.' However, Lily was quite fortunate in that she was bound over for two years.[39] There is a happy ending of sorts: she and Frank married that January.

The Slasher trials leave us with some unanswered questions. Four of the 'victims' were given custodial sentences, two were bound over and one was found not guilty. However, Mary Sutcliffe, Margaret Kenny, Clayton Aspinall, Constance Wood and Margaret Reynolds were not even charged. This could be because Salisbury and Studdard wanted to focus on the 'victims' who they thought would crack first, and several of these seemed to have had problems with their nerves. It could be that the five mentioned above just refused to confess, though it would seem that the Yard men put quite a lot of effort into extracting a confession out of Annie Cannon, so it's not clear why they wouldn't want to charge the others. This is especially so since Mary Sutcliffe had made two separate attack claims.

One possible reason why all the 'victims' were not charged is police embarrassment and frustration. Salisbury and Studdard were used to dealing with real hardened East End villains and now they found themselves in a damp and miserable Halifax winter chasing after hysterical girls. Salisbury seemed to have been humiliated in court due to the irregularities involved in Annie Cannon's alleged confession and one could understand the Yard men wanting to get back to fighting real criminals rather than imaginary ones.

Similarly, Halifax police would surely want to draw a line under the Slasher scare and move on. They had invested huge resources into chasing a non-existent maniac, lost control of the situation and had to bring in Scotland Yard, and yet the solution to the mystery was under their noses all the time. Every time someone appeared in court charged with false Slasher claims, it was a reminder of this police failure and they would surely be glad to hear the last of it. Ironically, Percy Waddington's raincoat was identified on the same day that Salisbury and Studdard arrived in Halifax. There is every chance that the local police would have solved the mystery without the aid of Scotland Yard, as the Slasher scare was already starting to unravel.

The Real Halifax Slasher?

Another question that remains is whether there was, amid all the hysteria and false claims, a *real* slasher at work. During the Slasher trials, Chief Inspector Salisbury made a rather cryptic statement: 'The Slasher was a mythical person. In one case only, if there was such an assault, it was by a person who was known to the aggrieved party.'[40] Salisbury seems to be suggesting that one of the attacks was real, but it's not at all clear which one he's referring to. One might speculate that he was referring to the 'Barkisland Girls' Gertrude Watts and Mary Gledhill who were attacked in Ripponden on 16 November. This assault seemed to set the scene for the other attacks but was different from subsequent incidents in a number of ways.

Firstly, there were two victims. All subsequent attacks were on lone individuals. Secondly, the attack was from behind, whereas subsequent assaults were slashes around corners or featured the Slasher jumping out on someone. Thirdly, it's not clear whether the girls were attacked with a blade or with a heavy implement such as a mallet.

Indeed, one of these two women claimed in a 1986 interview that she was the Halifax Slasher's first victim.[41] Gertrude or Mary (she remained anonymous for the interview) described how someone jumped the girls from behind and slashed them with a knife or a razor. She said: 'I still have the scars and the hair has never grown on the part of my head where I was cut.' Since the attack, she was left afraid to go out alone at night and felt nervous if anyone was walking behind her. She continues: 'That was the beginning of the Slasher scare. After that other people also said they had been attacked by the man but I think my friend and I were the only genuine victims.' It's worth noting that contemporary accounts refer to a hatchet or mallet in the attack on the Barkisland Girls. Given the fact that motiveless attacks by strangers are extremely rare and the slight discrepancies in the details of the attack, one would be entitled to wonder whether this attack was as fictional as some of the later claims. It is, after all, rather odd to claim to be the first victim of an imaginary attacker.

Behind the Halifax Slasher

It is impossible to attribute the Slasher scare to one simplistic cause, but it's worth examining some of the factors that may have contributed to it. No doubt mental illness played a role in some of the false claims. As we have seen, Hilda Lodge, Percy Waddington and Annie Cannon had been suffering with their 'nerves'. Both Beatrice Sorrell and Lily Woodhead had had boyfriend trouble and the faked attacks may have been a cry for attention or an attempt to get back at their boyfriends.

The recorder at the trial of McCall, Nicholl, Sorrell and Lodge suggested that the motive for their false claims was their desire for notoriety.[42] It's certainly true that after the claims, the 'victims' would have been treated with care and attention by family, friends and work colleagues and achieved the status conferred by stoic victimhood. Furthermore, once the claim of the false attack has been made, events would have taken on a life of their own. News would spread quickly around the close working-class community, followed by interviews with the police, journalists and the arrival of the newspaper photographer. For a few days in the winter of 1938, the status of Slasher victim would become part of their identity, and the nationwide media frenzy as well as the local hysteria would have snowballed out of their control.

However, this begs the question as to what it was about Halifax in 1938 that made it fertile ground for such a mass panic. Looking at the newspapers at the time, it's clear there were local, national and global concerns that together created the perfect storm from which the Halifax Slasher could emerge.

As Michael Goss has pointed out, residents of Halifax would have been shocked by a horrendous local murder that took place shortly before the slashing scare began and this must have played on the minds of many.[43] The murder was that of 8-year-old Phyllis Hirst whose abused body was found in the Horton Green area of Bradford. The murder remains unsolved to this day, and at the time it sent shock waves of fear and incomprehension through Bradford and the neighbouring towns. The fact that the victim was an innocent child suggests a motiveless malignancy in the crime, and this was also central to the slashing scare that followed.

No doubt the people of Halifax would also have read about the strange crime of dress slashing that gained much coverage in the 1920s. This bizarre behaviour usually involved men approaching women from behind in crowded public places and using a razor to make cuts in their dresses, underclothes and sometimes even the skin. One of the most widely reported was fine art student Alfred Soly who was arrested for slashing the skirts of saleswomen in a Paris toy shop. He said in his defence that he could not look at a beautiful dress without wanting to destroy it.[44] There were also reports of dress slashers at work in London, Oxford, Glasgow and Manchester throughout the 1920s. However, by 1926, Halifax had its very own dress slasher: James Francis Leonard.

Leonard was a smart looking labourer of no fixed abode who was charged with 'damage, injury and spoil to girls' clothing'.[45] Leonard had used a razor to cut six women's clothes while standing or sitting behind them at various 'places of amusement' on different days. He was easily identified by the women as he had a very prominent nose which made his face memorable and easy to pick out in an identity parade, which is what happened to Leonard. He was given six months hard labour. Although Leonard's distinctive nose proved his undoing in the dress slashings, it probably saved him from being wrongly accused of the 1938 slashings. None of the 'victims' mentioned this very distinctive feature, so no doubt he was quickly eliminated from police enquiries. However, the strange nature of the crime may well have lingered in the memories of the people of Halifax.

Another contributing factor to the Slasher scare was the nationwide concern about knife crime. The 20s and 30s were the golden age of the 'race gangs'.[46] These gangs were associated with racecourses, extortion and bookie protection rackets. Their weapon of choice was the razor. Most media coverage of the gangs occurred in the 1920s, but resurfaced again in the late 1930s. This period coincided with the tabloidization of the press and these razor gangs made for sensational headlines accompanied by exciting images of tough looking gang members. Graham Greene's razor gang thriller *Brighton Rock* was first published in 1938 and this image of the knife wielding gangster in long coat and trilby hat or flat cap may well have contributed to the image of the Halifax Slasher. Although it may be easy to scoff at the hysteria generated by the Halifax Slasher panic, the crimes discussed above make the idea of a blade wielding maniac attacking innocent people from the shadows seem eminently plausible.

The elephant in the room in 1938 was of course the build up to global war. At the end of October 1938, news reports discussed how thousands of Jews were homeless in the no man's land on the border with Poland after being deported from Germany, which was indulging in an 'orgy of anti-Semitism'.[47] News also discussed how the British government was preparing for coming war and the expected German bombing raids. Although we have the benefit of hindsight, there can be little doubt that the people of Halifax were aware that conflict with Germany was on the horizon and this will have fed into the fears and concerns they had at the time.

At the same time across the Atlantic there was a much more famous case of hysteria that demonstrated just how on edge people felt during the build up to World War Two. This was the infamous panic caused by the radio broadcast of Orson Welles' adaptation of H.G. Wells' Martian invasion sci-fi classic *The War of the Worlds.* The radio play featured a fake radio news report of the invasion of Martian octopus like creatures with death rays. The fictional reports were taken literally by many Americans and caused widespread panic which was widely reported in the UK, including in *The Yorkshire Evening Post* of Halloween 1938. There were reports of

Americans fleeing their homes in terror. The faithful, fearing the end of the world, gathered for prayer meetings in Atlanta, Georgia. Hundreds of motorists scoured the New Jersey coast (where the radio adaptation was set) in search of the invaders, with some even claiming to have seen the aliens. Hospitals treated many for shock and there were reports of gas attacks. A woman ran into an Indianapolis church screaming: 'New York is destroyed. It's the end of the world. We might as well go home to die. I've just heard it on the radio.' A girl rang up the press to say she had witnessed everything, declaring: 'You can't imagine the horror of it. It's Hell.'

In its editorial for the 31 October 1938, *The Yorkshire Evening Post* discussed the Martian invasion scare and pointed out that the panic created was understandable, at least for Americans as 'the public of all nations has been liberally fed for years on the horrors of war.' Such a panic, of course, could never happen in this country, *the Post* continued:

> In this "tight island" we have a tradition of common sense and level-headedness, not to mention a saving sense of humour, which would make such an exhibition of "nerves" highly unlikely.

Highly ironic, in that a similar (though perhaps more understandable) exhibition of nerves was only days away.

Epilogue

And so the Halifax Slasher was quickly forgotten as 1939 drew on and other concerns began to occupy people's minds. Perhaps the saddest part of the fallout from the Slasher panic was the tragic death of Michael McKeiver (46), a coach builder from Moss Side, Manchester.[48] McKeiver had previously tried to kill himself by drinking skin lotion and eating soap and had spent time in a London mental hospital after attempting to cut his own throat, which had left him with a large scar on his neck. Colleagues had lately heard him talking wildly about the Halifax Slasher. Finally, he took a fatal overdose of aspirin telling his neighbour before he died that he had done it because he feared his workmates suspected him of being the Halifax Slasher due to the prominent scar on his neck.

Chief Inspector William Salisbury of Scotland Yard who was central to solving the mystery of the Slasher, went on to have an illustrious career solving war related crimes. However, he went on sick leave before retiring in 1943 citing 'war strain'.[49] It seems ironic that after his investigation of a mass panic caused in large part by people's 'nerves' that it should be his own weakened nerves that put an end to his successful career. Salisbury died in Leytonstone, London in 1955 aged 58.[50]

A phantom attacker scare very similar in nature to the Halifax Slasher occurred in 1956 in Taiwan.[51] The Taipei Slasher supposedly attacked 21 victims, usually women or children with a razor blade. This led to great panic until the victims confessed to cutting themselves or in some cases reimagining slight injuries as evidence of an attack. No doubt similar panics are bound to happen again.

In the Halifax Slasher episode, the majority of 'victims' were working class women of limited education, and that does seem to be the profile of most cases of so-called mass hysteria. Of course, well-educated, sophisticated men and women of the present day could never fall victim to an imaginary attacker, could they? Well, yes, they could. In 2016, American staff at the newly opened US embassy in Havana, Cuba began to report a strange, piercing high-pitched noise and experienced all kinds of symptoms such as nausea, dizziness, headaches, problems with memory and concentration and issues with hearing and eyesight. Some were evacuated for hospital treatment in America. It was suspected that the high-pitched noise was a sonic weapon, possibly developed by Russia and China and deployed by the dastardly Cubans against Americans in the new embassy.[52] Training and advice were given to new members of embassy staff about these sonic attacks which were causing a diplomatic spat between Cuba and the USA. However, when recordings were made of the 'sonic weapon', several experts recognized the sound as that made by crickets.[53] It goes to show that even well-educated, sophisticated elites can be just as susceptible to unfounded hysteria as anyone else.

There is one lesson that we can learn from the Halifax Slasher. We can say with certainty that sometimes, some people just make stuff up, and that should always give us pause for thought.

Haunted Valley ~
The Ghosts That Time Forgot

'His fears chained him to the spot, and, to add to his excitement, when this something came within the light of his lamp... he saw that it was perfectly white, and had a most brilliant red eye like a flame...'

(Halifax Courier, June, 1864)

From the bleeding phantom of a murdered highwayman, to the moaning spirit of an outraged maiden; from a headless horseman with headless horses to the spectral green figure of a lovelorn suicide.... Calderdale has its fair share of spooky legends. Some of them, such as headless Leatherty Coit of Elland and the Green Lady of Blake Dean, are quite well known. Others, such as Brown Dick of Blackstone Edge and the Broad Bottom Ghost have slipped into obscurity. Others still have been long forgotten for reasons that will become obvious...

Old Leatherty Coit

If you happen to be in the West Gate area of Elland at around midnight and feel a sudden violent rush of wind on an otherwise still night, it might have been Old Leatherty Coit, one of Calderdale's best-known spooks, flashing by you. Leatherty Coit (Yorkshire for 'Leather Coat') is a headless horseman who rides a carriage pulled by headless horses through the streets of Elland. He emerges from a barn whose doors creak open without any human help and the grim headless spectre thunders out amid howling wind down Dog Lane and on to Old Earth before returning whence he came.[1]

Old Leatherty Coit (Larisa Moskaleva)

The main source for the story of Leatherty Coit is Lucy Hamerton's 1901 book *Olde Elland*. She also introduces us to witnesses who had seen the ghost. The first are an anonymous husband and wife returning from visiting a sick relative. They felt an ominous rush of wind before Old Leatherty Coit himself and his ghastly horses flew by to the couple's utter horror. The second witnesses were two of Lucy Hamerton's uncles. Once, when they were children, they were playing outside in Northowram when they suddenly dashed into the house claiming they had seen a carriage flash by pulled by headless horses and driven by Old Leatherty Coit.[2] They were not too scared by this apparition we are told, which may be some grounds for suspicion of their tale!

Hamerton writes that Leatherty Coit is the spirit of a traveller murdered at the Fleece Inn, Elland. The murder left bloodstains that could not be scrubbed away by any amount of elbow grease. Folklorist Kai Roberts, though, associates the stubborn blood stains with a nineteenth century murder, which leaves the origin of Old Leatherty Coit still a mystery.[3]

Brown Dick of Blackstone Edge

This version of the legend in all its melodramatic Victorian glory is adapted from the 'Lancashire Burns' Edwin Waugh's dialect telling.[4] Most of the action takes place a little outside Calderdale, but I've decided to include it here.

One snowbound mid-winter evening, a party of travellers were sheltering from the weather by the warm fire of the White House Inn, Blackstone Edge. The wind whistled around the pub as if all the witches of Pendle were frozen and riding the storm on a mad boggart hunt in the air. Suddenly, the Inn door burst open and in staggered a man shivering violently, teeth chattering and as white as milk. He asked for water, and told the party that he had 'seen summat'.

The frozen traveller told how he had been visiting his dying uncle in Sowerby and was now travelling home across the moor. As he approached the White House Inn, he saw a tall figure in a fur cap

Brown Dick (Larisa Moskaleva)

20 yards ahead of him. Thinking he would like some company in this lonely and desolate landscape, he called out but received no answer. He did, though, notice that the figure's clothes didn't seem to be ruffled by the howling wind. As the traveller approached, the figure turned and showed its long white face was streaked with blood. Then the figure started to melt away into the moonlight before drifting across the moors towards the stone known as Robin Hood's bed. It was this sight which led to the terrified traveller bursting through the White House door.

The assembled party listened in amazement to the story. Some were sceptical; after all *they* had never seen a ghost. And even if ghosts did exist, they were not sure why clothes and fur caps should also have ghosts. However, two gamekeepers who were present remained quiet during the discussion, before one turned to the other and said: 'He's seen Brown Dick.' He then proceeded to tell the tale of Brown Dick of Blackstone Edge.

In the distant past, the White House Inn was kept by a widow and her beloved son Dick, whom she doted on and spoilt rotten, giving him everything he wanted and always letting him have his own way. Of course, being brought up this way meant that Dick (or Brown Dick as he came to be known) soon fell in with a bad crowd: Iron Jack's gang. Iron Jack led this violent bunch of highway robbers, thieves and murderers and they terrorised the neighbourhood. They robbed travellers on the lonely moor, burgled the surrounding farms and cottages, and people who crossed them sometimes disappeared, never to be seen again. Dick's mother, though, would not believe that her beloved son would ever be involved in such business.

Brown Dick was often away from home for a couple of nights at a time, but on one occasion when he didn't come back after a week his mother began to worry. More and more weeks passed and still her son did not return, leaving his poor mother more and more distracted. She placed two candles in the window of the inn every night to guide him home should he return, but he never did. If the howling wind across the moor rattled the inn's door, she would open it and call out her son's name to no avail. She even took to wandering across the desolate Blackstone Edge crying for him to come home.

One night, the Inn was dark except for the usual two candles flickering in the window, when three men burst in. They were carrying a fourth man who was grievously injured with a gunshot wound. The three men were travellers who had met Iron Jack and his crew and the gang had attempted to rob them. They resisted and a fight ensued in which Iron Jack was accidentally shot by one of his own men. The cowardly gang left their leader for dead and escaped into the night, leaving the three travellers to carry Jack to the nearest shelter, which happened to be the White House Inn. It was clear that Iron Jack's wound was so serious that he was not long for this world and so a parson and a doctor were sent for from Littleborough.

Iron Jack knew he was dying and confessed to many murders, but he said that the deed that troubled him most was the murder of Brown Dick. This had happened when the gang had completed a successful robbery and had headed over to Robin Hood's Bed to divide up the spoils by lantern light, for it's said that no matter how much of a gale is blowing on the moors, Robin Hood's Bed is always wind free. The gang, though, fell out about how the ill-gotten gains should be split and Brown Dick was murdered and buried there near Robin Hood's Bed.

Iron Jack refused to name the treacherous colleagues who had deserted him and soon expired. Brown Dick's remains were found where Iron Jack had indicated and they were removed to Ripponden church yard. His poor mother went mad with grief and could often be found sitting by his grave singing to her lost son. One day she was found lying dead over her errant boy's grave and was at last reunited with her darling son.

Now that Brown Dick had been laid to rest, some say that his mother's ghost walks the moors of Blackstone Edge despairingly calling for her wayward son.[5]

Of course, the White House Inn still stands out there on the moors, though in his 37 years of running the pub, landlord Pete Marney hasn't seen the ghost of Dick or his mum. However, he told me that some customers have had spooky experiences in the pub: 'people have sworn blind to have witnessed paranormal activity mainly in the loos and some have even been sober when making the claims.'[6]

The Ghost of Old Cragg Hall

The secluded village of Cragg Vale may be picturesque and peaceful now, though it has a dark past. Many know the history of the Cragg Coiners, the infamous band of eighteenth-century counterfeiters that were based in the village. The story that concerns us here, though, is the tragic tale of a murdered maid and her revenge from beyond the grave.

Old Cragg Hall was once occupied by the Sunderland family who had a wayward young son. Young Sunderland (according to the legend) seduced a pretty maid in the family's employ, but when she became pregnant, he cruelly murdered her in the porch and buried the body in Burnt Wood. However, the spirit of the murdered woman was said to appear at night and walk between the wood and the Hall, where it would place its cold and clammy ghostly arms around the neck of young Sunderland, who soon became mad with drink, fear and guilt. Villagers heard horrible moans and screams and saw strange lights in the vicinity and were afraid to walk there at night. The ghost, it was said, would walk for forty years, for that's how long the maid would have lived if her life had not been taken.

Old Cragg Hall (John Illingworth)

Finally, young Sunderland, tired of being tormented by the ghost every night, organised a huge banquet at the Hall and invited all his friends. As the guests indulged in the lavish feast laid on for them, they became aware of a woman in white sitting beside the host. And to the horror of the revellers, they also realised that they could see through this strange figure to the flame of a burning lamp behind her. The guests scattered in terror and never returned. The shock, the horror, the guilt, drink and madness were too much for young Sunderland and he died soon after.[7]

The best-known retelling of the legend is by local poet F.C. Spenser in his ballad 'The Maid of Old Cragg Hall' from 1882.[8]

Although the ghost only had an allotted time span of forty years, villagers were wary of it long after this time had elapsed. Even farmers were reluctant to start haymaking in the area where the woman's body was said to have been buried.[9] Perhaps they have nothing to fear, as Spenser's poetic retelling ends with the lines:

The days of her lawful life are done,
And peacefully, peacefully sleeps the dead.[10]

An Easter Ghost

At Easter 1843 crowds began to gather round a certain Halifax house, and more curious onlookers joined the throng each day. The house was said to have been unoccupied for 20-30 years and yet strange sights had been seen through its upstairs window: a bed was seen to fly around the room and a ghostly female figure had appeared there over the Easter weekend. It had been seen the previous two days and was expected to be seen again as Easter Monday came. The spectral figure was, according to onlookers, the spirit of a housemaid who had cut her own throat on Easter Monday around 40 years ago.

As Easter Monday came, the crowds clearly saw the figure of a young woman appear at the window. People in the throng (according to the *Halifax Guardian*) shouted: 'Here it is!' and 'Nah, will ta believe it, does to see it nah?' The 'ghost' in question turned out to be a servant in the house, which was not empty at all, and behind the upstairs window was her bedroom, shared with another female servant. She had heard the clamour of the gathering crowds and looked out to find a large audience gawping at her. It seems a few days ago, she had taken down the blinds from the window for washing and temporarily replaced it with a makeshift substitute that looked a little like a female figure.

The *Halifax Guardian* lamented: 'Who could have imagined that in the 19th century… crowds should have assembled in the centre of a populous town, and in mid-day to witness the feats of a Hobgoblin.' The paper concluded thus:

> It is a pity that a fire engine was not used to disperse the credulous men and children who could spend several hours in looking at nothing but a bare wall and windows. As for the women, they are more excusable; their curiosity is uncontrollable.[11]

Old Red Eyes ~ The Ghost of Todmorden Station

There was a great deal of alarm in Todmorden at the end of May 1864.[12] Rumours had circulated that one Saturday at midnight, the night watchman on the station platform had seen a ghost and that subsequently both the ghost and the watchman had disappeared. The following Sunday and Monday great crowds gathered round the station to enquire what had happened to the poor watchman and what he had witnessed that night.

Thankfully, the watchman turned up safe and well, but he *had* seen something. As he patrolled the platform that night, he saw a strange shape, white and silent, gliding towards him. As it was midnight, dark and lonely, he feared that there might have been a terrible rail accident (all too common at the time) and that he was witnessing a spirit bringing news of the catastrophe. In the words of the *Courier*:

> His fears chained him to the spot, and, to add to his excitement, when this something came within the light of his lamp… he saw that it was perfectly white, and had a most brilliant red eye like a flame…

The terrified watchman ran to get help from station staff before approaching this fearful red-eyed spectre. However, on closer inspection the 'ghost' turned out to be an escaped ferret.

An Evening with 'Spirit Rappers', 1869

One Sunday evening in November 1869 a rather sarcastic correspondent for the *Halifax Courier* attended a séance conducted by 'spirit rappers' or Spiritualists in a back room of a house in a secluded area of Halifax.[13] The Spiritualist movement was a growing religion attracting scientific, media and public interest. No doubt this partly explains the Victorian fascination with ghosts and the supernatural. The *Courier* correspondent was, as we shall see, rather underwhelmed by the whole experience.

The evening began with a hymn that had to be quickly abandoned as those present had not learned it sufficiently to impress the spirit world. Another hymn was attempted, but 'Goodness,' the reporter lamented, 'how cracked and scrapy most of their voices were!' During the singing, all attention was on the medium: a middle-aged man who sat with his eyes screwed shut, his head jerking violently, shivering and starting 'as if served with a tremendous abdominal hiccup.' The president of the group asked for silent prayer for a couple of minutes before a new hymn was selected.

Suddenly, the medium began to speak, softly at first but with more and more animation and expansive gestures. The reporter described his voice as being mock posh, and his revelations were so incoherent and ignorant that he wondered if this was the spirit of an idiot! Nonetheless, everyone gave the voice their full attention. It said: 'Has it was, his now, and hever shall be!' over and over again and spoke of the 'Great Hi Ham'. Asked if he had ever seen God, he replied that he lived 10,000 miles away from Him.

More contortions followed as the medium prepared to channel another spirit. This one had a broad Yorkshire accent and described himself as a 'Jumping Ranter' (a mid-seventeenth century dissenting religious group). He still jumped now, he said, whenever he could find a body. Unfortunately, his accent was so strong that the reporter could understand little of what he said. He did, though, comment on the pejorative term 'spirit rappers' sometimes used for Spiritualists. 'They'n cawl o Rappers, dun they? Well ne'er heed 'em, if yo keep on rappin' yo'll ne'er get maungey.' These sage words were greeted with great approval by all present.

At this point, a woman suddenly started shrieking and laughing loudly and hysterically. This went on for a full five minutes. The reporter speculated that she had been possessed by the spirit of a hyena.

When this had died down, the medium took control again and the mock posh first spirit returned to intone about the necessities of a Spiritualist education movement. Unfortunately, and to everyone's surprise, there was a troublemaker in the room. This young man suddenly piped up from the corner and demanded to know if the spirit had the permission of Jesus Christ to be in the room. The spirit replied through the medium (though the medium's voice seemed to have returned to normal all of a sudden) 'Has Christ sent you here?' The youth was unabashed and continued, saying 'You have done and said nothing tonight to prove you are anything different from what I should judge you will be at your work tomorrow – a very ordinary, ill-spoken labourer.' He then challenged the spirit to give some proof of its existence, but the spirit refused because unbelievers were present. One may think that unbelievers being present would be a good reason *for* giving some proof.

With things getting out of hand, the president intervened. He said that in the last year at their meetings many greater miracles than had ever been performed by Jesus Christ had been witnessed. These included water being turned into wine, flowers materialising in locked rooms and heavy weights being lifted by invisible forces. But at this juncture, the doubting Thomas and the reporter made their exit, leaving us a tantalising glimpse into the world of the spirit rappers in nineteenth century Halifax.

A Drunken Ghost

A regular pastime for many mischief makers in the nineteenth and early twentieth century was the practice of roaming spooky places after dark dressed as a ghost and scaring the life out of any unfortunates that happened to pass by. On 22 July 1876 PC Bell apprehended a Brighouse navvy Thomas King and charged him with being drunk and disorderly. King had been in the habit of 'playing the ghost' in Mill Lane and terrifying the locals. He was dressed in white the night he was arrested and it was assumed that a bit of 'ghosting' was his intention. He was fined ten shillings.[14]

An Elland Ghost

On a dark December night in 1880, a white robed figure was seen with widespread arms in a church yard in Elland, scaring witnesses witless.[15] The figure appeared again the following night also causing alarm, especially in those whose windows overlooked the graveyard. However, this time some brave local lads were ready for the ghost and determined to investigate. As they got to the churchyard, though, the ghost disappeared. The lads didn't give up and eventually found the ghost hiding in a shed. The 'ghost' turned out to be a young woman who was about twenty dressed in her white nightgown and cap and with a whitened face. She had apparently recently separated from her lover, though it's not clear why she therefore took to scaring the good people of Elland. She swooned when she was caught and was carried to safety, though had she been a male, the lads of Elland may not have been so gallant.

The Broad Bottom Ghost

The story of the Broad Bottom Ghost was told by Hebden Bridge born political activist and suffragette Lavena Saltonstall to the *Todmorden and District News* in the early twentieth century.[16] It concerns the area between Hebden Bridge and Mytholmroyd with the unflattering name of Broad Bottom, consisting of some woods, fields and a few houses. During the reign of Elizabeth I when Catholics were forbidden from holding mass in Heptonstall, they would worship here instead, in a house known as the Old Chapel.[17] The ruin is always locked, not that anyone would want to go inside due to it having a 'very weird aspect', though you might be tempted to peer in through a crack in a boarded-up window. Inside, everything is black and rotten, the floor has mostly fallen in and there are centuries of dust and cobwebs. There was said to be a mysterious locked chest fastened to the wall, the contents of which are unknown. Even stranger, rumours say that an underground passage connects the ruin to a wood and a gentleman's residence three quarters of a mile away.

The ruin has the 'inevitable ghost', according to Saltonstall. The spirit appears on a white horse and makes its way from the ruin to the top of the hill before plunging furiously back down to the valley bottom and across the canal and into a rag shunt at a nearby mill. Who the ghost was or the reason for the headlong gallop are lost to time.

One windy Christmas Day, Lavena and a party of students went for a walk past the ruin. They paused by the ruin's gloomy window and wondered what might be inside its mysterious kist. One of the party, for a lark, 'entreated of the ghosts and goblins to come forth'. The laughter of the friends turned to silence, though, when 'a very thin streak of light appeared above the kist top and the wall. It gradually grew bigger until it formed a bright patch of light about 9 inches square.' After a few seconds it disappeared, and the party of ramblers made a mad scramble over the wall and away. They all asked each other the same question: 'Did you see that? What was it?'

We are assured that no one could be in the ruin as the floor is rotten and greatly fallen in. Perhaps, then, rumours of an underground passage are true and some person unknown was traversing the passage. But this raises the question of just who was there and why? The author of this account of the Broad Bottom ghostly happenings, Lavena Saltonstall, certainly had a sharp wit when it came to destroying her political opponents with facts and logic in the letter columns of the local press.[18] The tone of her ghostly account is tongue in cheek and one might wonder if this young rebel was having a bit of fun and doing a bit of leg-pulling in her account.

In any case, there is a little epilogue to the story of the Broad Bottom ghost. According to R. Thurston Hopkins in his 1953 survey of hauntings *Ghosts Over England*, one of the students that had accompanied Lavena on her adventure at Broad Bottom returned to the scene a few weeks later. She again invited the presence to appear, and again she saw a strange light in the ruin. 'It was not an ordinary light,' she said. 'It looked just like a woman wearing a robe of some kind of lustrous metallic material.'[19]

The ruin at Broad Bottom

An Amiable Ghost

'On one of the windswept heights overlooking Hebden Bridge there stands a grey, stone-built cottage, the age of which it would be difficult to guess.'[20] Which particular cottage it is impossible to tell, but it is nevertheless the site of a fairly friendly haunting reported in *The Leeds and York Mercury* in 1907.

A young couple moved into this house in the very early twentieth century and were disturbed by strange nocturnal noises. There were tappings on the wall and ceiling, and the doors creaked and groaned to such an extent that the couple sometimes thought they were being burgled. Eventually, the noises stopped and the young couple forgot about them.

However, one night it started again. Still suspecting burglars, the husband was about to get up and investigate, when the noises suddenly ceased. He lay down again to sleep but couldn't. At about 2am to his astonishment he saw a yellowish light illuminating the bedroom and he became concerned that the house was on fire. This thought left his mind though when he saw a black figure emerge through the wall, glide to the stairs and then head down them. The dark figure's arms were held rigidly by his side and his eyes were set in a fixed stare on some unknown object. When the figure disappeared, so did the eerie yellowish light. 'No, I was not dreaming, and I had not been drinking,' he told the impressed reporter for the *Leeds and York Mercury* who investigated the ghost. The couple were also insistent that the noises were not caused by rats or mice and that the light was not a policeman's lantern outside the window, nor could it have been some kind of practical joke. 'I saw it,' emphasised the husband, 'it was no delusion.'

The reporter from the *Mercury* managed to locate the previous tenant of the cottage. She said that she too had seen the figure and identified it as the ghost of the occupant before her. She said she had never been afraid as the ghost was harmless and she'd often held conversations with it, but disappointingly she couldn't remember what they had talked about. The spirit did, though, tell her that it was revisiting scenes of its physical life but would not elaborate. Furthermore, this rather underwhelming spook 'had never said anything of note.'

The Green Lady of Blake Dean

Possibly Hebden Bridge's most well-known ghost, the Green Lady of Blake Dean, was supposed to haunt a graveyard in Blake Dean and the surrounds of Hardcastle Crags.[21] She was the ghost of a rich young woman who lived in a cottage near Blake Dean and was said to have fallen in love with a navvy working on the nearby reservoirs. The love affair didn't work out and she threw herself off the long-gone trestle bridge, the remains of which are still visible nearby. The ghost is dressed in elegant green finery, with pearl buttons and black leather riding boots. She haunts Hardcastle Crags on her black horse, usually on New Year's Eve.

An unnamed local farmer claimed to have seen the ghost several times in the 1950s, according to the *Burnley Express and News*.[22] He added that the spirit disappears if you show any fear, but if you're brave enough to speak to her, she will bring you good luck.

It's been suggested, though, that the whole tale was invented by a mischievous pub landlord.[23] This was Midgely Barrett, publican at the Packhorse Inn, Widdop, between 1915 and 1933, who was well-known for his tall tales.

The Moaning Ghost of James Street

There were fears in 1933 that Old Leatherty Coit had made a return to his old haunting ground. On Friday 5 May, in James Street, Elland, a dreadful ghostly moaning was heard. It gave a young woman such a fright that she was unable to sleep. It proved impossible to locate where the scary sound was coming from. The terrifying groans were heard again by residents of James Street on Tuesday 9 and Friday 12 May. The locals were much disturbed and several were scared by the mystery sound. Mrs Perks of James Street said the noise was impossible to define, but was a 'long low moan.' The police were informed but could offer no explanation.

On Tuesday 16 May 1933, some of the bolder residents decided to go on a ghost hunt and track down the phantom, but with no success. It seems likely that this ghost was a prankster enjoying scaring the residents. This kind of spooky prank was popular in the nineteenth and early twentieth century, as can be seen from the account of the Elland Ghost above.

Hellish Nell in Todmorden

Notorious medium Helen Duncan, known as 'Hellish Nell' in her Scottish hometown, has gone down in history for being imprisoned after she was charged under the 1735 Witchcraft Act in 1944. Duncan, described as a large coarse woman even by her admirers, was a controversial 'materialising medium', meaning sitters at her seances would see ghostly forms of their deceased loved ones emerge from the darkness, formed from the spiritual substance known as ectoplasm which emanated from various orifices of the medium's entranced body. Her mediumistic performances attracted the attention of spiritualists, scientists and of course the authorities.[24] Before her Old Bailey trial towards the end of the Second World War, she visited Todmorden on two occasions and one of the sitters wrote up an uncritical account for the *Todmorden News and Advertiser* which gives us a glimpse into the peculiar lost world of materialising mediums and those who put their faith in them.

Since its origins in the USA in the nineteenth century, Spiritualism spread rapidly to the UK and was especially popular in the north. The first spiritualist church in England was founded in Keighley in 1853.[25] By the mid-thirties there were around 2,000 Spiritualist churches in the country with around 250,000 members.[26] Calderdale was no exception, and in 1934, Todmorden spiritualists were excited to have one of Britain's best-known mediumistic stars come to visit them.

Helen Duncan's first Todmorden séance took place on Friday 17 December 1934 at 33 Wellington Road.[27] An audience of 18 people gathered to witness the spectacle and a 'cabinet' was created by using a dark cloth to partition off part of the room. Inside this area, hidden from the view of the audience, was a chair for the medium to sit on and a small table with a vase of flowers on it. The room was weakly lit by three dim red lights, giving the space an eerie glow. According to the sitter who wrote up the séance, these were 'ideal' test conditions.

Helen would have been in her mid-thirties at this time. She was extremely large with jet black hair and a powerful stare, and was at the height of her powers. Before entering the séance room, Helen was stripped and searched by 'two competent ladies' and dressed in a black robe which had been examined by those present.[28] These measures were taken to ensure there was no trickery involved and that no fake ectoplasm was hidden about her person. How careful or intimate these searches were, we are not told.

Helen entered the séance room and proceeded to her cabinet and the curtain was drawn. This was supposedly to allow the medium to gather her psychic energy and enter a trance state. With Helen hidden, the gathered spiritualists invoked 'the name and the spirit of the Master'. A few minutes later, a spirit form emerged into the rose-tinted gloom. This was Albert, Duncan's 'spirit control' who acted as a ghostly master of ceremonies. Albert had been a man of Scottish extraction who had emigrated to Australia and drowned in 1913. In contrast to Helen Duncan's heavy Glaswegian accent, Albert spoke, we are told, in precise BBC English and would offer rather ambiguous wisdom to the sitters such as 'If your love is as big as yourselves then I should like to have it.'[29] On this occasion in Todmorden, Albert materialised and said, 'How beautiful to hear the words of the Master' and would introduce the spirits before retiring into the darkness.

The first Todmordian spirit to manifest itself was that of a well-known local woman who had died several months ago. We're told that a dozen people present recognised the spirit and even the deceased woman's daughter testified that it was her mother. Several more spirits appeared in quick succession, all of them recognised as family or friends by those present. One of these beat its hands on its chest to demonstrate that it was solid. Another, rather bizarrely, invited one of the sitters to put his finger in its mouth, which he did. He commented that the ghost's mouth was wet, warm and toothless. A ghost of a little girl appeared and said her name was 'Sunshine'. The spirit of an elderly lady, one of the sitter's grandmother, came out of the cabinet and complained that she had no slippers before dematerialising in front of the curtain.

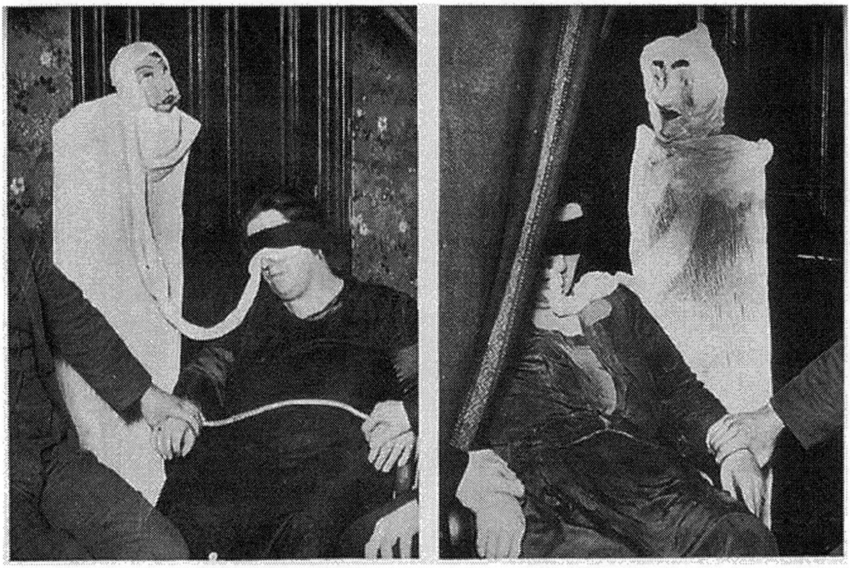

Photographs of Helen Duncan's 'spirits'

Next came one of Helen Duncan's regular characters, the spirit of a mischievous little Glaswegian girl called Peggy who provided light relief amidst the intense emotion of sitters meeting up with their departed loved ones. Peggy distracted the audience with comic chatter and jokes about one gentleman's baldness before singing 'O Danny Boy' and 'Bicycle Made for Two'. When a sitter attempted to join in with one of the songs, the cheeky wee ghost stopped and said: 'I'm singing this song not you!' Although no one in the Todmorden sitting had a camera, several of Helen Duncan's spiritualist manifestations were caught on film, as seen on page 67.

Peggy departed back to the spirit world and the more po-faced control spirit Albert returned for the next part of the séance: an ectoplasmic demonstration. There was no real agreement among Spiritualists and the various scientists who studied seances and mediums about what exactly ectoplasm was. It was a substance that was supposed to be both physical and spiritual, and it emerged from various orifices of entranced mediums. It would billow, shimmer and shine as it twirled around and formed into a spirit. There was something reproductive in the production of ectoplasm. The medium would often utter orgasmic moans or groan as if suffering labour pains. The sitters attending the séance might be told to sit with their legs uncrossed to allow 'reproductive matter' to flow from them to assist the medium. On this occasion, ghostly hands parted the curtains of the cabinet to reveal Helen Duncan in her trance and the sitters witnessed ectoplasm emanating from the medium and forming into a voice box. From reports of some of Duncan's other seances, we have an idea of what this ghost's ectoplasmic voice box looked like. Some describe it as like a 'large white potato', while others described it as a large pair of disembodied lips. Another still said it was a square box on a rod of ectoplasm, while cynics said it looked like Helen Duncan's fist under some luminous cloth. We are not told from whence Mrs Duncan produced the ectoplasm in Todmorden. One thing would have been clear to the sitters, though. Ectoplasm stinks.

The séance lasted a little under two hours, and in the words of the sitter who wrote the report for the local paper: 'All the sitters who recognised their friends and relations who had returned from the other side of life, testified to the genuineness of the materialisations.'[30]

Portrait of Helen Duncan

Helen Duncan returned to Todmorden to give another demonstration in June 1935.[31] This time the séance was held in Eagle Street Spiritualist Church, and again was a success, with the newspaper correspondent writing: 'What joy was given to those whose friends materialised before their eyes!' Again, Albert was master of proceedings. In his posh voice he berated the 'appalling grammar' of the entranced medium. Several spirits appeared over the session and most were recognised by the sitters except for one ghost who couldn't be identified by the relevant sitter as she had forgotten her glasses. And as always, Peggy, the charming little

Scottish girl with the cheeky sense of humour, made an appearance and made everyone laugh before spilling some water from a vase of flowers and making Albert cross.

Looking at the photos of the materialisations produced by Helen Duncan, it's hard to see how people were taken in by them. The painted doll faces look grotesque atop their coat hanger shoulders and white net gowns to be sure. But in the séance itself, with the heightened sense of expectation, the very dim red light and with luminous paint applied to the spirits, they must have been more convincing than under the harsh and unforgiving flash bulb. As for the ectoplasm, influential psychic investigator Harry Price, for whom Duncan had held a demonstration of her powers in his London laboratory, suspected it was regurgitated surgical gauze, as he found when he analysed a sample. When Duncan was given blue dye to swallow before a demonstration, no ectoplasm was manifested. In fact, Price said: 'I was impressed with the brazen affrontery that prompted the Duncans to come to my Laboratory… I was impressed with the amazing credulity of the Spiritualists who had sat with the Duncans for six solid months.'

Duncan had been exposed as a fraud on a number of occasions before her two visits to Todmorden. One of these exposures was the result of Harry Price's experiments, which he wrote about in a book called *Regurgitation and the Duncan Mediumship* in 1931.[32] In 1932, maids employed by Duncan admitted the medium had dummies and various masks for use in seances. One of them also told how she had been made to wash long lengths of stained, slimy muslin that stank of urine. In 1933, a year before she visited Todmorden for the first time, a trap was set for her at a séance in Edinburgh. During the séance in question, some noted that most spirits looked and smelled like Duncan with some white cloth draped over her. One of the sitters groped a male apparition to discover it had two large female breasts. When naughty little Peggy appeared, the trap was sprung. Someone turned on a bright light while an accomplice grabbed at Peggy. In the light it could be seen that the little girl Peggy was actually Duncan on her knees waving a white form around. Poor Peggy was subjected to a farcical tug-o-war between the sitter and Duncan before being stuffed up Duncan's dress. In her fury, Duncan waved a chair around in the air yelling 'I'll brain you, you bloody buggar!'[33] These events were widely reported, yet Duncan remained popular. Her fans reasoned that she was only human and may have resorted to fraud on those occasions, but at other times her performances were genuine because they had seen their loved ones with their own eyes.

Duncan's mediumship continued through the 1930s and 1940s until disaster struck. At a séance in Portsmouth in 1944, Helen materialised a spirit of a petty officer from the warship HMS *Barham.* The only problem was, although this ship had indeed been lost, the government had not yet released this information to the public. This was too much for the authorities, and Duncan was tried under the 1735 witchcraft act and sent to prison, serving 172 days. In fact, it was a sitter who mentioned the *Barham,* not Duncan, though that did not save her. Why Duncan was nobbled with the archaic Witchcraft Act is unclear and rather murky. What is clear, is that she made an impression on the people of Todmorden when she was at the height of her dubious powers.

The Sowerby Poltergeist

Bogdan and Doreen Tarandziej had heard stories about strange noises and inexplicable lights emanating from 59 Town Gate, Sowerby, but when the council house became available, they took it. It was their first home together, and they soon shared it with their baby daughter Kateryna and dog Lassie. However, by 1955, it seems that they were also sharing the 'neatly furnished little old house' with an unwelcome guest, the so-called Sowerby Poltergeist.[34]

Doreen described her experiences:

> Noises awakened us in the night. Gradually, they became worse… There were terrible 'rushing' noises. The jangling of pots in the kitchen early in the morning. Banging noises from the small back bedroom – and there was no one in there. We found doors opening after they had been fastened. And when we went to look – there was no one there. We never saw anything.[35]

Poor Lassie the dog seems to have been particularly sensitive. Doreen described how one night, with a fire burning in the grate, a sudden chill descended on the room and the dog started to whimper and darted under the sofa to hide. Doreen's father, George Georgeson, who lived on the same street, visited the house one night when the couple were out and described how the dog 'leapt and whined in terrible fright'. Georgeson also saw 'a sudden glow; a glow of golden light, coming from down the bedroom stairs.'[36] The Tarandziejs' neighbours, Mr and Mrs Smithson and their three children had also heard noises through the wall and thought that Bogdan was rearranging furniture.

The mysterious noises became too much for the Tarandziejs. As Doreen put it: 'Last autumn it became just too bad for us. Both of us are working. We could not sleep. We had to go.' The solution was that every evening, Doreen and the baby would go and sleep in her parent's house on the same street. There was not enough space for Bogdan, so he would catch a late bus to Halifax where he would stay the night in a lodging house before going to his work in a mill in Shelf the following morning.[37] The family would return to 59 Town Gate in the early evening and spend a few hours together before separating again before it got too late.

The couple complained about the strange noises to the council, who, it seems, debated the Sowerby Poltergeist in their committee meetings. 'The matter has actually been discussed in committee and is still under investigation,' a council spokesman told the press.[38]

It's at this point that an unusual ghostbuster entered the story: Jack Quain. Quain was a Sowerby Bridge electrician and also a well-known water diviner. Water diviners used forked twigs or pendulums to locate underground water sources, and their services were clearly still in demand in the middle of the twentieth century as Quain ran a water-divining business in Sowerby Bridge until his retirement. He was a regular on the local talk circuit, giving lectures and demonstrations of his water finding abilities. Quain's divining skills were not only in demand for finding water. It's certain that the Duke of Argyll enlisted his help on a hunt for stolen treasure.[39] It's also true that he attempted to use his trademark whalebone divining rods to locate Mary Hackett, a six-year-old girl who disappeared from Halifax in 1953. His attempt was unsuccessful and he claimed the girl was still alive, though in fact she had been murdered.[40]

So Quain, now in his late 70s, offered to stay alone in the troubled house in Sowerby and investigate the strange phenomenon. In the bedroom, Quain was suddenly thrown against a wall by an unseen force which was strong enough to snap his trademark whalebone divining rod.[41] Quain later said that he had 'killed' the poltergeist on this visit, though he did not say how. In any case, when he visited again with pathologist Dr J.W. Weston and his assistant Gavin Duncan, Quain said: 'All was dead as the dodo. Nothing happened at all. There was not a murmur.'[42] All the tests he carried out with his (presumably repaired or replaced) whalebone divining rod proved negative. Dr Weston, meanwhile, placed a lock of hair over the handle on the cellar door but it remained undisturbed. He also interviewed the neighbours to rule out pranksters being responsible. Whereas Quain announced that he had 'snuffled' the poltergeist, Dr Weston came to a different conclusion. He said that the poltergeist did not exist and that the phenomena were caused by 'warped and loose bedroom floorboards, a rattling window pane, draughts and winds.'[43]

Other investigations followed. Some mediums from Keighley visited the house and said they thought the troublesome spirit was Bogdan's late mother attempting to make contact.[44] In 1956 after numbers 59 and 57 had been left empty, parapsychologists Eric J. Dingwall and Trevor H. Hall investigated the properties and concluded that the 'poltergeist' activity had been caused by subsidence with underground water exerting pressure on the foundations and leading to the strange 'rushing' noises that had been heard in the house.[45] For some reason, this large underwater culvert remained undetected by professional water diviner Jack Quain, though these facts (Hall was a chartered surveyor) along with the rattling windows, warped floors and draughts may be sufficient to explain some of the strange phenomena the Tarandziejs experienced.

Some neighbourhood cynics, however, suggested the couple had fabricated the poltergeist in order to jump the queue for better council housing, though whether this is anything more than gossip is impossible to say.[46] In any case, it seems to have worked as the houses were demolished to make way for a new, and hopefully poltergeist free, housing estate.

The Blue Hand

A grave danger faced the terrified pupils of Central Street Infants School in the early 1970s: The Blue Hand. This ghostly hand scuttled around the school's corridors and was apt to pounce on unsuspecting children, especially if they were alone in the toilet. The spectral hand would gouge out the little one's eyes, before strangling the unfortunate mite and then dragging the infant to hell through the toilet. And the proof was there in plain sight: on the high ceiling of the cloakroom was what appeared to be a smudged handprint. There was no way an adult, let alone a child could reach the ceiling to put a handprint there. It had to be the Blue Hand. This is the story that my classmate, a girl who I will call Karen, told anyone who would listen. The fear this ghost spread lead to many a wet classroom seat as a visit to the toilet on your own was to take your young life into your hands.

When pressed on where the hand came from, Karen claimed that many years ago a crazed murderer had escaped from jail, broken into the school and hanged himself in the boys' toilets. His body was later dug up by a witch who had a spell which would turn a murderer's severed hand into a familiar to do her bidding. She cut the withered and now blue hand from the corpse and the spell worked. The hand could now scuttle around at her will, stealing, strangling and all kinds of other mischief. Unfortunately, the spell wore off and the hand turned on its mistress, gouging out her eyes before choking her. And then the hand scurried off back to Central Street school…

Of course, the teachers said the whole thing was nonsense and that the 'handprint' on the ceiling was actually a couple of muddy stains from a dirty ball being bounced in there. Karen got into big trouble when the teachers found out where the stories of the Blue Hand were coming from. What her punishment was I can't remember, but she was made to promise never to mention the Blue Hand again. And she didn't. Though she did inform anyone who cared to listen that if you put two pencils tip to tip on the floor and lie on top of them on your stomach, the Devil would appear…

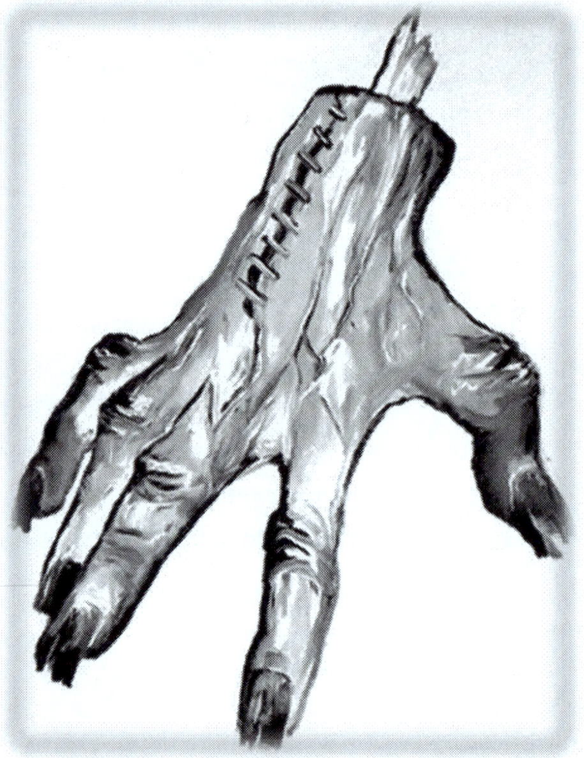

The Blue Hand of Central Street Infant School (Larisa Moskaleva)

The Adamski Mystery

'It was quite the most mysterious death I have ever investigated in twelve years as a coroner.'

(James Turnbull, coroner)

Zigmunt Adamski, a Polish born miner living near Wakefield, popped out to the local shop for some potatoes on 6 June 1980, the day before he was to celebrate the wedding of his goddaughter. He never came back. Five days later his body was found 30 miles away in Todmorden lying on a pile of coal near the railway station. His shirt was missing and his jacket was incorrectly fastened. He had curious burns about his head and neck which had been coated in an unidentified substance. The mystery of what happened to Adamski in his missing five days has never been solved. Speculation centred on revenge, illicit sex, family feuds and cold war skulduggery. And aliens…

The Mysterious Death of Zigmunt Adamski

On 11 June 1980 Todmorden policeman Alan 'Gobber' Godfrey was called to investigate a dead body found perched atop a coal heap near Todmorden railway station. PC Godfrey arrived at the yard with fellow officer Michael Agley and they climbed the 15-foot-high pile of coal to inspect the corpse, which had already been confirmed dead by medics who had arrived shortly before the police. The body was dressed in jacket and trousers, but curiously he was wearing no shirt; only a string vest was visible under the incorrectly buttoned up jacket. There was no wallet or other means of identifying the body in the pockets. 'I will never forget the sight that confronted me,' Godfrey wrote in his autobiography, 'the look on his face in death was of fear and pain. The eyes were open and staring into the sky.'[1] The dead man appeared to have corrosive burns on the back of his head and neck and a sticky substance, perhaps some kind of ointment, looked to have been applied to the wounds. There was no clue as to how the body came to be where it was; the coal was wet and slippery after torrential rain and no signs of anyone having clambered up the pile could be found. PC Godfrey suspected foul play, and he was not the only one.[2]

The dead man was later identified as Zigmunt (or Zigmund) Adamski (56), a Polish coal miner who had been missing from his home some 30 miles away in Tingley near Wakefield for five days. The mystery of what happened to Adamski and how and why he came to be found in such a peculiar state remains unsolved to this day. It was, as UFO researcher Jenny Randles commented, 'a mystery of epic proportions'.[3]

Adamski was a troubled man. He had a heart and lung condition. His application for early retirement from the coal mine he worked at had been refused.[4] His wife Lottie was also ill and confined to a wheelchair. Adding to his woes, he was caught in the crossfire of a family feud: Lottie's friend Laska Teodozia had left her husband after taking an injunction out against him and was staying with the Adamskis along with her son.[5] The difficulty was the allegedly abusive husband happened to be a close relative of Adamski.[6] To top it all, he was due to give his goddaughter Stefnie away at her wedding and had some concerns about this. His goddaughter had asked Zigmunt to give her away as her father had refused because he had separated from her mother and said he would only do it if he was allowed back in the family home.[7] Adamski may also have been on bad terms with him.[8] This, then, was the background to Adamski's disappearance.

On 6 June 1980 Adamski left home at 3.30 to buy some potatoes from a local shop. A neighbour casually asked him if he was going for a drink but Zigmunt replied that it was too early for him. He bought some groceries at the store.[9] And then he vanished, only to reappear dead five days later on top of a pile of coal in Todmorden.

The body was taken to Hebden Bridge mortuary and examined by consultant pathologist Dr Alan Edwards. The time of death was estimated to have been between 11.15 a.m. and 1.15 p.m. on the day the body was found.[10] This means that either Adamski had crawled up the coal heap before expiring, or that he had been placed there in the few hours after his death and before he was found. The mysterious corrosive burns seemed to have been suffered two days or so *before* his death, but the substance coating the wounds remained (and still remains) unidentified. As well as these wounds, he also had some superficial cuts on his hands and knees.[11] The cause of death was determined to be Adamski's heart and lung conditions. Dr Edwards didn't rule out the possibility that Adamski's heart failure was brought on by fright.[12]

However, what really baffled the police was the question of where he had been in the intervening five days. Adamski had no known reason to suddenly go to Todmorden and, so far as anyone knew, had no connections with the town. It seemed he hadn't been sleeping rough as his body was clean, there was only one day's stubble on his face and his hair appeared to have been cropped. His stomach was empty, indicating that he hadn't eaten on the day of his death.[13]

PC Godfrey finds the body of Zigmunt Adamski from a TV reconstruction (Strange but True)

Adamski's body was shipped to Poland for burial on 17 July 1980; surprisingly soon given the strange nature of his death. Although the official cause of death was given as natural causes, PC Godfrey continued investigating the case and discovered that Peter Sutcliffe, a part timer at the coal yard, had visited the scene between 1pm and 1.30pm and not seen the body. As the estimated time of Adamski's death was between 11.15am and 1.15pm, this suggests that the body was placed on the coal pile after death. Godfrey informed Halifax CID but was told to forget the case: natural causes were the cause of death. A senior CID officer even visited Godfrey to warn him off the case, telling him to 'leave well alone'.[14] Over a year later Godfrey would read in the *Halifax Evening Courier* that the full inquest had been held without him. The coroner, James Turnbull, returned an open verdict. But Godfrey had not been invited to the inquest despite being one of the first officers on the scene. A written statement was read out, though Godfrey denied that this had been written by him.[15] However, a few months after becoming involved in the Adamski case, the life of this Todmorden policeman would take an extraordinary extra-terrestrial turn. The alien adventures of Alan Godfrey will be examined in the next chapter. In the meantime, let's look at some of the explanations proffered as solutions to the Adamski mystery, starting with the most outlandish.

What happened to Adamski?

Theory One: Death by Aliens. Over a year after Adamski's death, *The Sunday Mirror* ran with the sensational headline: AMAZING UFO DEATH RIDDLE.[16] The article went on to outline some of the circumstances of Adamski's disappearance and death and how experts were baffled by the mysterious burns on his neck and head. One of the policemen called to the scene, the article continues, saw a 'flying saucer' only hours before the discovery of the body. This is obviously a garbled reference to Alan Godfrey, though in fact Godfrey's UFO experience occurred at the end of November, over 5 months *after* Adamski's death, as we shall see in the next chapter. Whether this was an error on the parts of the journalists or a cynical piece of tabloid sensationalism is unclear, but it certainly helped to link the Adamski mystery with UFOs. Furthermore, the newspaper article goes on to say, somewhat incredibly, that West Yorkshire police were 'seriously considering' the possibility that Adamski's death was UFO related, though there is no source for this dubious claim. So, what could be offered as evidence for an alien connection?

Firstly, it could be argued that the location of Adamski's body, face up on a tall pile of coal suggests he was dropped there from above. The problem with this is that it's not clear he *was* found face up. The leaked mortuary photo, which I have, shows coal residue on his face consistent with him being face down. Furthermore, the man who actually found the body, Trevor Parker, who worked in the coal yard, confirmed that he was face down and this suggests Adamski was probably turned over by the medics when they arrived on the scene.[17] In any case, there are many ways Adamski could have ended up where he did that do not need recourse to aliens.

Secondly, UFO buffs would have noticed a strange synchronicity regarding the name Adamski. Many readers of the *Sunday Mirror* article wrote to the paper to point out that the name Adamski is legendary in ufology, referring to *George* Adamski. George Adamski came to fame in the 1950s with his claims that he had been in contact with aliens from Venus and been taken aboard their spaceship, detailed in his best-selling book *The Flying Saucers Have Landed.* Compared to the more familiar alien abduction cases of subsequent decades, so-called contactees like George Adamski went voluntarily on their space adventures and came back to earth to pass on alien wisdom about living in peace and harmony.[18] Obviously, the coincidence of the two men sharing a fairly common Polish surname proves nothing.

Another coincidence used to suggest a UFO connection to Adamski's death is based on the fact that he was missing for five days. This is significant to some as it mirrors the missing time experienced in a famous American case, the supposed alien abduction experienced by Travis Walton. Walton was one of six loggers working in Arizona in 1975 when a UFO appeared and beamed Travis up, only returning him to earth five days later.[19] Aviation expert and UFO sceptic Philip Klass suggests the whole affair was a hoax and gives several plausible reasons for this.[20]

Nevertheless, it's still a flimsy piece of evidence and hardly enough to support the claim that Adamski's death was UFO related.

Another spurious reason for advancing a UFO connection can be seen in the incautious speculation of James Turnbull, the coroner at Adamski's inquest. Turnbull was quoted in the *Sunday Mirror* as saying:

> It is quite the most mysterious death I have investigated as a coroner… I tend to believe that there may be some simple explanation. However, I do admit that the failure of forensic scientists to identify the corrosive substance which caused Mr Adamski's burns could lend some weight to the UFO theory… As a coroner, I cannot speculate. But I must admit that if I was walking over Ilkley Moor tomorrow and a UFO came down I would not be surprised. I might be terrified, but not surprised. I cannot believe that all the thousands of reports of this sort of phenomenon – covering almost every country in the world and going back through the ages – result from human error.[21]

Of course, it's true that Yorkshire police forensic expert Leslie Albert King and a Wetherby based dermatologist could not identify the substances on Adamski's wounds.[22] However, nor did they give any indication that the substance was not of this world, only that they could not identify it. Given that it was judged Adamski had died of natural causes, we do not know how much effort was put into identifying the substance, nor how common it is for forensic experts to be unable to identify a chemical. We will consider another possible explanation of the burns and mysterious substance presently.

Finally, Jenny Randles pointed out that there were sightings of strange lights in the skies above Bradford, Halifax and

Todmorden in the days Adamski was missing.[23] Randles herself seems coy about making a direct connection between these lights and Adamski and with good reason. Lights have been reported in the sky many times, especially in the Todmorden area, as will be seen in other chapters of this book.

So, all in all we have a couple of spurious coincidences, unidentified (though not necessarily unidentifiable) ointment and some strange lights in the sky to link Adamski with UFOs. But it seems reasonable to argue that the main reason the Adamski mystery is linked with aliens at all is the sloppy journalism of the *Sunday Mirror*. Even PC Alan Godfrey, who later claimed to have seen a UFO and (under hypnosis) to have been abducted, has at times described the Death by Aliens explanation as 'a daft theory'.[24]

Theory Two: Death by Commies. Adamski disappeared at the height of the Cold War, which might lead one to wonder if he was the victim of a Soviet assassin. Back in 1980, the so-called umbrella murder would still have been fresh in people's minds. This famous assassination took place in 1978 and involved the murder of Bulgarian dissident Georgi Markov with a poisoned pellet fired from an umbrella while he was waiting at a London bus stop.[25] There was also the mysterious case of Father Borynski, a Polish priest known for his anti-communist sermons, who vanished in strange circumstances from Bradford in 1953. He is presumed murdered, though his body was never found.[26] Police considered the possibility of Borynski having been killed by a Soviet assassin named Bogdan Staschynski who was later arrested and imprisoned in West Germany for the assassination of Ukrainian nationalist leaders.[27]

Against the backdrop of these two famous cases, it might be speculated that Adamski was murdered by Soviet spies. Indeed, according to Graham Birdsall's investigation into the Adamski mystery, one of Adamski's neighbours who helped care for Lottie after her husband's death suggested that the case had something to do with the war years in Poland and that something unspecified from Adamski's past may have caught up with him.[28] However, there is no evidence (beyond Adamski's nationality) that this is anything but neighbourhood gossip, though the fact that the neighbour was in close contact with Lottie might have given her some inside knowledge. Against this is the fact that by all accounts Adamski was an unassuming man rather than an outspoken critic of communism or a high-profile dissident. It's hard to imagine why he would be on the hit list of an international communist assassin. Nevertheless, Adamski's goddaughter Stefnie Krzyszczyk told me that Adamski was adopted so there was some mystery as to his background and that she had sometimes wondered if he'd been involved in some clandestine operations. In any case the Polish community at the time were concerned about possible threats coming from the Polish government or the Soviet Union.[29]

Theory Three: Death by Sex. Perhaps, it could be argued, Adamski was having a clandestine affair. The day before the wedding, the family circumstances got too much for him and he absconded to spend time with his girlfriend. According to this theory, his heart gave out during sex and he was hurriedly dressed (hence the incorrect buttoning of his clothes and the missing shirt) and the body dumped at the coal yard. This theory had been advanced in some internet forums, but again evidence is lacking. Adamski's goddaughter Stefnie thinks this unlikely as he was a devoted husband to his wife Lottie.[30]

Theory Four: Death by Acupuncture. Detective Inspector of Halifax John Boyle, the detective who persuaded the Yorkshire Ripper Peter Sutcliffe to confess, claimed that Adamski visited an acupuncturist in Nelson, Lancashire on the day he disappeared.[31] This may explain the burns and substance found on his body. Researchers Hanson and Sankey in their investigation suggested that Adamski may have had moxibustion therapy that went wrong.[32] Moxibustion is an alternative treatment often used in conjunction with acupuncture that involves the burning of the dried herb mugwort on the skin. If Adamski was undergoing this treatment and it went wrong, it could explain the serious burns, the mysterious ointment (perhaps a salve related to the treatment) and his state of undress. Perhaps the stress of the burn caused a heart attack and so the acupuncturist, to avoid the negative publicity of a scandal, hurriedly dressed the body and dumped it where it was found.

There are, though, several problems with this theory. The first is that the burns seem to have occurred around three days before his death, suggesting that they were unrelated to whatever killed him.[33] The second is that according to coroner James Turnbull, the visit to a Nelson acupuncturist was 'highly unlikely and certainly not established'.[34] Finally, in my search of the academic literature I could only find one example of death associated with moxibustion and acupuncture and this involved a fatal asthma attack brought on by the stress of the treatment.[35] This suggests it's an extremely unlikely cause of death. One problem, though, is that many researchers on Adamski's death are understandably quite cagey about sources so it's often impossible to check them. However, if Boyle (cited in Birdsall) is correct (coroner James Turnbull's views notwithstanding), and Adamski visited an acupuncturist in Lancashire, it may be a missing piece of the puzzle.

Theory Five: Death by Lorry. One suggestion made by the CID was that Adamski had fallen asleep under a lorry and acid had dripped onto his head and neck and perhaps he then sought treatment for the burns.[36] However, the condition of the body suggests that Adamski had not been sleeping rough, under a lorry or otherwise. Another lorry related explanation is that perhaps Adamski was placed after death in a coal lorry which was later delivered to Todmorden. The problem with this is that the coal yard owner confirmed there had been no deliveries that day.[37] And of course there is the fact that his time of death was between 11.15 and 1.15 on the day he was found.

Theory Six: Family Feud. We know that Adamski was caught up in family feuds and this may be relevant to his disappearance and death. The most in-depth investigation into the mystery was carried out by former police officer John Hanson and UFO researcher David Sankey in 2008 and offers some tantalising hints at what may have happened, though details are kept sketchy and vague no doubt for legal reasons. We know that Lottie Adamski believed her husband was kidnapped as she told the *Sunday Mirror*: 'He was a good man with no enemies. He must have been kidnapped, by who or what or for what reason, I don't think I will ever know.'[38] One could ask why she would assume he had been kidnapped if he had no enemies. Indeed, Hanson and Sankey say an unnamed source told them Adamski had fallen victim to a family feud, possibly involving his male relative whose wife was hiding out with the Adamskis.[39] They believe Adamski died of natural causes while being held captive and was not necessarily murdered, though they claim to know the names of two or three people in Leeds who hold the key to the mystery. Adding to this, UFO researcher Graham Birdsall told me he had heard from an unnamed relative of Adamski that he had been held captive in a garden shed and in attempting to escape spilled battery acid on himself and subsequently died.[40]

Stefnie Kryszczyk told me that outside the court at the hearing into Adamski's death, Adamski's wife Lottie confronted Stefnie's mother and said that her husband (Stefnie's father) was responsible.[41] We know Adamski was concerned about giving his goddaughter away because it was the duty of another relative with whom he was on bad terms.[42] The relative who one might expect to give a bride away would be the father, Jan Smolen. In any case, the wedding went ahead without Adamski the day after he disappeared at the Polish Roman Catholic Church, Lansdowne Place, Bradford.[43]

Unfortunately, we can go little further than hearsay and speculation. Although a botched kidnap seems plausible and fits with some of what we know, there are some problems with this explanation. The first is the Todmorden connection: why was

Adamski taken there? Was he taken while still alive, or after death? What about his state of undress and the fact that he had been washed and shaved the day before his death? Another issue is that it would be quite a difficult feat to kidnap someone who doesn't want to be taken in broad daylight and hold them captive in a garden shed without arousing suspicion. Furthermore, garden sheds are not the most secure of buildings so one would think it would be quite easy to break free. This suggests that wherever Adamski went, he went voluntarily. Could Adamski have gone to see Stefnie's father or another relative after going to the shop and been prevented from leaving eventually leading to his death?

Another point worth noting is the police seem very touchy about the investigation. This is demonstrated in part by what PC Alan Godfrey experienced at the hands of some of his superiors, though it's hard to disentangle the effect his UFO experience had on this as will be seen presently. Researcher Mark Birdsall asked a police officer friend to look into the Adamski files. His friend agreed, but was obviously unsuccessful and ominously told Birdsall never to ask about it again.[44] Of course, this could be that the police just don't want UFO enthusiasts bothering them for access to this mysterious case. Or could it be they have something to hide?

Epilogue

With tragic irony, Adamski's employers changed their minds about his request for early retirement, but by this point he was already dead.[45] Adamski's widow Lottie returned to Poland five years after her husband's death where she died in 1991.[46] The case remains open and the mystery remains unsolved.

Invasion of the Bobby Snatchers ~ The Alien Adventures of PC Alan Godfrey

'I was driving towards it when I realized I was seeing something you don't expect to see in Todmorden at that time in the morning...'

(Alan Godfrey)

One fateful winter night in 1980, Todmorden bobby Alan 'Gobber' Godfrey was hunting for an escaped herd of cows when he claims to have been confronted with a UFO hovering over Burnley Road. His experience became a nationwide sensation. Later, under hypnosis, he described an alien abduction by some of the most bizarre extra-terrestrials in the history of ufology. But someone at the top wanted him gone, or so he maintains. Was it because of his UFO experience, or was there something else behind the alleged conspiracy to drive Alan out of the police force? Todmorden was fast gaining its reputation as the UFO capital of Europe...

May the Force Be with You!

In the early hours of 29 November 1980 PC Alan 'Gobber' Godfrey was on the night shift in Todmorden just over five months after the body of Zigmunt Adamski had been found (see previous chapter). Working through these miserable winter nights must take its toll. As Godfrey describes it: 'Such a late shift during long winters was often depressing and had an insidious effect on your metabolism.'[1] He was tired and somewhat sleep deprived; to make matters worse it was pouring with rain and he was fruitlessly driving round Todmorden investigating complaints by residents of a housing estate that a herd of escaped cows was wandering around.

One of the residents who had called the police about the cows was an old lady that Godfrey was friendly with and she offered him a cup of tea. She then told him a strange story. Just after she had phoned the police about the escaped cattle, she happened to glance out of her window at the cows and saw a glowing bright light like a car's headlights on full beam that lit up the window and then vanished. She noticed that the cows had also disappeared. She made Godfrey promise not to tell anyone (she was afraid of being thought senile) and Godfrey promised. Anyway, he thought it was probably just the glare of a passing car's lights.[2] He returned to the station and then just after 5.00 a.m. feeling rather fed up, he set off to have a final drive round town before having another look for the peripatetic cows.[3]

On Burnley Road his eye was caught by the bright lights of what he thought was a works bus. As he drew nearer it became obvious that whatever this thing was, it definitely *wasn't* a bus. 'I was driving towards it,' he said, 'when I realized I was seeing something you don't expect to see in Todmorden at that time in the morning.'[4] He described the object as a huge fluorescent diamond hovering above the road. He estimated it to be 20 feet across and 14 feet high and it had what appeared to be a line of dark windows two thirds of the way up. Although the object was stationary, Alan said the bottom was rotating anti-clockwise. He tried to call the police station but his radio would not work, though this was not unusual as there are some radio black spots in the Pennine hills. He had the presence of mind to make a sketch of the object as it hung there in front of him. At this point he said he had a vague memory of a voice in his head, his own voice or that of someone else, he couldn't tell, saying: 'You should not be seeing this. This is not for your eyes.'[5]

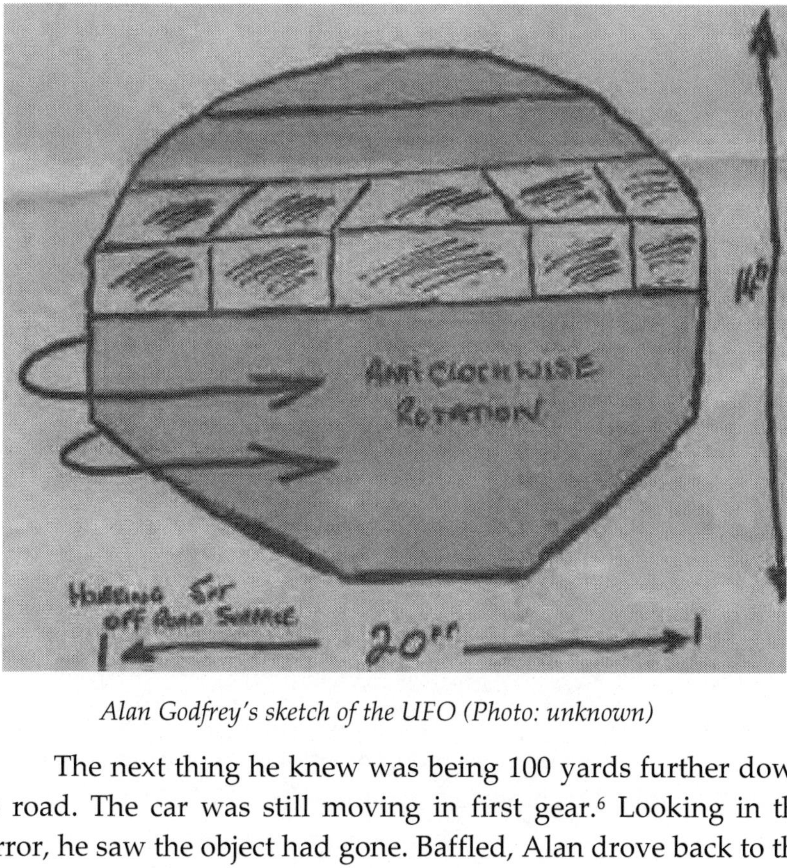

Alan Godfrey's sketch of the UFO (Photo: unknown)

The next thing he knew was being 100 yards further down the road. The car was still moving in first gear.[6] Looking in the mirror, he saw the object had gone. Baffled, Alan drove back to the centre of Todmorden and picked up a colleague, Malcolm Agely, and together they returned to the place on Burnley Road where Alan had seen the object, but all that remained were some blotchy patches on the road where the rain had dried unevenly and some peculiar patterns in the debris lying there.[7]

Godfrey and Agely then did something rather strange. They decided that there might be some witnesses to the UFO in Todmorden park, just opposite the site of Alan's experience. This is bizarre. What witnesses would be in a locked park in the early hours of a miserable November morning? Anyway, the two coppers climbed over the park gates and made their way through the darkness. They were suddenly shocked to see strange silhouettes in the gloom: the missing cows![8] Godfrey couldn't understand how these cows had made their way across a road and a river and past locked gates into the park. Back at the station Alan was persuaded not to report his strange encounter immediately.

As he reflected on his UFO experience a few things began to puzzle PC Godfrey. First, after the sighting he noticed that his boot had somehow been damaged, split along the sole. On the same foot there was a red patch on his skin which was later diagnosed by his doctor as psoriasis, but this explanation didn't satisfy Alan. After all, he had never suffered from this complaint before.[9] Even more puzzling, he began to have flashbacks of three conflicting 'memories' about the fateful evening. In one flashback he 'remembered' the UFO dematerialising as he drove through it. In another he reversed his police car away from the object, while in a third 'memory' he saw himself outside his vehicle in a field. Finally, it seems that a chunk of time, about 15 minutes, was missing from Alan's life.[10]

As Alan entered the police station the next day, it was clear that news of his encounter had spread. He was greeted by his workmates with: 'Hey up, it's Captain Kirk!'[11] He took this in good humour as he knew he'd have done the same in their shoes. He was, though, called in to see the inspector. Godfrey related his experience to his superior, and was thoroughly taken aback by what the inspector said in reply. He told Godfrey that on the previous night, the same night as Alan's encounter, three other officers had reported seeing a strange light in the sky nearby. PC John Porter, PC Howard Turnpenny and WPC Julie Baxter from Halifax had been looking for some stolen motorbikes on the moors between Halifax and Hebden Bridge. PC Porter noticed a pulsating steel blue light below the cloud that seemed to be following the officers as they drove over the moors. They got out of their cars and watched as the light swooped down and moved off in the direction of Todmorden.[12] This obviously left Alan feeling more confident about his own experience. The inspector told Alan to make a full report.[13]

Later, Alan was told by his brother that Leonard Smith, a caretaker at Ferney Lee Junior School, Todmorden had also had a strange sighting. He had been firing up the school boilers at around 5.15am on the same morning as Godfrey's experience when he saw a 'large sphere-like object' rising from the valley before it zig-zagged from one side to the other and then shot off. Again, Alan felt vindicated to hear this account.[14] There are, though, some inconsistencies in these accounts, which we'll examine in more detail later. In the meantime, on 5 December both the *Hebden Bridge Times* and the *Todmorden News* reported these sightings under the jokey headline: MAY THE FORCE BE WITH YOU!

'Gobber' Godfrey Undergoes Hypnosis

To try to get to the bottom of his strange encounter, Alan agreed to be hypnotically regressed back to the time of his UFO encounter to see if he could remember anything else. He underwent regression sessions with Dr Robert Blair, a psychiatrist and lecturer at Manchester University, and also with Dr Joseph Jaffe, a consultant physician and psychiatrist in Manchester. The two hypnotists were not told the object of the session, and all but the first session with Dr Blair were filmed.[15] The result was an account of one of Britain's best known and most unusual alien abduction encounters. The following summary combines information from the four sessions.

Alan was hypnotically regressed to the early hours of 29 November 1980, which by the times of the sessions was almost a year ago. In his trance, Alan first described seeing the diamond shaped object hovering above Burnley Road, before he was blinded by a dazzling flash of light and felt himself being carried upwards and into an entrance to the UFO.[16] Curiously, being beamed through the UFO's entrance was only mentioned in the first hypnosis session and not in any of the others. The next thing he knew, he was inside the UFO. He described the room he was in, paradoxically, as round but with corners.[17] He was surrounded by a very strange assortment of characters. First there was a rather Biblical looking gentleman who telepathically introduced himself to Alan as Josef. He was bearded and dressed in a white sheet or robe with a skull cap on his head. Josef seemed to have a calming effect on Alan, who seemed distressed during all the regression sessions. There were also some 'disgusting' three-foot-tall robot figures. These were metallic, with heads like lamps and one horizontal line for eyes.[18] Most surprising, and unique in the alien abduction literature, was the next occupant. Here is part of the transcript from one of the sessions with Dr Jaffe:

AG: There's a bloody dog down there!

Dr J: A dog.

AG: Mmm.

Dr J: Describe the dog.

AG: Well I think it's a dog – horrible – just looks like a dog – black, size of an Alsatian.[19]

Next, Josef telepathically tells Alan to lie down on a black leather sofa bed, and after some initial reluctance he complies without really knowing why. Some bracelets, thick but light and similar to the ones doctors use to measure blood pressure, are put on his wrist and leg. The robots somehow plug themselves into the bracelet and Alan says everything begins to flash and he starts to feel sick. Alan was visibly disturbed at this point and the session was stopped.

Later, when not under hypnosis Alan said cryptically: 'They have come for me before,' and 'they will come for me again – in ten years' time.'[20] Although he was reluctant to talk about it, and it was entirely missing from his autobiography, he said he'd had a strange encounter with a ball of light in his childhood bedroom. We'll return to some of the young Alan's unusual adventures presently. But first, as hypnosis plays such a central role in this story, let's meet the hypnotists. All *three* of them.

Meet the Hypnotists

One aspect of Alan's hypnotic regressions has been emphasised a great deal. This is the fact that Godfrey really seemed to be reliving his abduction and to be suffering great distress as he recounted the details. He grimaced, squirmed and whimpered.[21] On watching the footage of the sessions, seasoned UFO researcher Jenny Randles told Godfrey: 'As you are talking there you really believe this is happening to you, because if you are acting you deserve an Oscar.'[22] The two hypnotists were no doubt somewhat taken aback by Godfrey's revelations, especially in their first session with him. They had assumed the session was to help remember some detail from a crime he had witnessed, so no doubt a UFO, Biblical alien, robots and a space dog came as a shock. The first of the hypnotists, Dr Robert Blair, seems not to have believed a word of what was said and was clearly not very interested in the whole proceeding.[23] Dr Jaffe, on the other hand, said he was mystified by Alan's revelations. In his own words:

> This is quite the most mysterious thing I have ever witnessed in my professional life. I have no doubt that the patient was undergoing very real stress in telling this curious story. This case is worthy of the most detailed scientific investigation.[24]

However, Dr Jaffe was not the reputable therapist he seemed.

From the late 1970s until the mid-1980s, Jaffe had been treating a bicycle shop owner called Mr Waterson. The treatment involved getting him addicted to a cocktail of drugs the doctor called 'Jaffe Juice', the tabloids, which covered the scandal, called a 'zombie drug', but which is conventionally known as the anaesthetic methohexitone.[25] Jaffe injected his patient with this wholly inappropriate drug six times a week. Not only that, Jaffe was accused of using his secretary to further ensnare Mr Waterson by wearing see-through blouses and flirting with him. Mr Waterson was turned into a Jekyll and Hyde character (or into Jack Nicholson from *the Shining* as his daughter described him).[26] Jaffe was said to have milked his hapless patient of between £33,000 and £60,000.[27]

Jaffe was accused of brainwashing and conspiracy in the longest ever hearing of the General Medical Council in its 128-year history.[28] His patient accused him of ruining his business, his health and his mind. Fortunately for Jaffe (or, perhaps, suspiciously) all the files relating to the case were stolen in a burglary of Jaffe's office shortly before the complaints were made.[29] Jaffe was found guilty of serious medical misconduct, though surprisingly only received an admonishment. All this was happening at the same time as Godfrey's hypnosis sessions. It's clear that Jaffe is rather a scoundrel and his work should be treated with scepticism.

However, I have discovered an intriguing missing chapter in Alan Godfrey's adventures under hypnosis: the mystery of the Third Hypnotist. Why the third hypnotist has been ignored by ufologists and apparently airbrushed from Godfrey's autobiography will become clear.

The Third Hypnotist

The third hypnotist was Hamilton Bertie Gibson, a respected authority on hypnosis and one of the founders of the British Society of Experimental and Clinical Hypnosis (BSECH).[30] In 1982 he described his encounter with a UFO abduction case for the BSECH newsletter, and the account was reprinted in *The Skeptical Intelligencer* journal shortly after his death in 2001.[31] What we get is a rather different account of Godfrey being regressed.

Gibson describes how he was contacted by an anonymous solicitor from a northern town and asked if he would hypnotise a police officer. The officer had already been hypnotised by two different hypnotists and some strange facts had emerged. The solicitor, therefore wanted to confirm these by contacting a hypnotist who would have a 'more scientific' approach. Gibson, being the chairman of the eminent BSECH, seemed an ideal candidate. Gibson assumed the strange facts alluded to were some kind of political scandal and he was not very interested. The solicitor was clearly UFO researcher Harry Harris who had arranged Godfrey's previous sessions with Dr Blair and Dr Jaffe, and he was most persuasive. Dr Gibson described Harris as 'a man of high intelligence, engaging personality and expensive tastes.'[32] After being wined and dined, Dr Gibson's curiosity got the better of him and he agreed to do the regression.

The first thing of note in Gibson's account is that he suspected Godfrey (whom he refers to as PC Charlie) was faking his trance. Gibson performed some tests for hypnotic suggestibility on Alan and concluded that he was 'one of the least suggestible subjects I have ever encountered.'[33] The hypnotist felt Godfrey was resisting hypnosis, perhaps because he feared what it might reveal.

Despite his doubts, Dr Gibson continued with the session and hypnotically regressed Godfrey back to the night of his encounter. Alan described playing cards in the station while on night duty on that fateful night and how he went out to investigate the wandering cows. At this point, Alan exclaimed: 'Eee, what's that blocking road? It looks like a bloody great diamond! All lights, blocking whole road. Lights flickerin'. It's terrible.'[34] The hypnotist informs Godfrey that the UFO is illegally parked so it's his duty to investigate. Godfrey replies: 'Nay, I'm not going near there. I'm frightened! Tha's awful – tha's terrible. Nay, I can't move!' Godfrey now showed signs of hyperventilation.

Next, Alan describes what's inside the spaceship. There is, as we have seen, 'an 'orrible great dog – who isn't a dog' and, surprisingly, a 'giant spotted jellyfish that caresses him with its loathsome tentacles.' The jellyfish is a new development, though there is the return of a familiar face: Joseph (or Josef).

AG: There's someone I know.

Dr G: Who is he?

AG: It's Joseph.

Dr G: And is Joseph a local lad?

AG: Nay, 'e's from 'out there'. I've known 'im all me life.[35]

Godfrey says he first met Joseph when he was six years old, though when he told his mum about him, she said it was just a nightmare.

At the end of the session, Dr Gibson had a private talk with Alan and accused him of putting on an act. Godfrey denied this and described some other paranormal experiences he had had, including some with the ubiquitous Joseph. The doctor noted that Godfrey seemed genuinely concerned about his mental health. Finally, Dr Gibson suggested to Alan that he may be suffering from the sleep disorder narcolepsy, symptoms of which include the experience of waking nightmares and a feeling of paralysis, which seem to match Alan's experience somewhat. In summing up the session, Dr Gibson noted that Alan Godfrey 'certainly has histrionic talent and his vernacular account of his encounter with the flying saucer and the strange monsters therein was very racy.'[36]

Even if Dr Gibson was wrong about Godfrey's 'histrionic talent' and he was genuinely hypnotised, we are still left with the question of how reliable memories recalled under hypnosis are. This is an easy question to answer. Any 'memory' which is only recalled with the aid of hypnotic regression is unreliable and likely to reflect the subject's imagination. Indeed, psychologist and hypnosis expert Robert A. Baker calls the use of hypnosis to uncover cases of alien abduction 'one of the worst if not the worst misuse of so-called hypnosis.'[37]

Furthermore, if we examine the wider context in which alien abduction cases were investigated using hypnosis, a sorry state of affairs emerges. Alien abduction accounts (around 70-80% of which involve recovering lost memories through hypnotic regression)[38] proliferated in the 80s and 90s in parallel with another phenomenon: so-called false memory syndrome. During this time a number of self-help books were published aimed primarily at survivors of incest and sexual abuse, and many of these books relied on the highly dubious concept of repressed memories.[39] Through hypnosis and other controversial techniques, people who had no memory of ever being abused created false memories of childhood sexual trauma often involving satanic rituals, murder, orgies and cannibalism. Many families were needlessly torn apart and innocent people jailed as a consequence of this sordid but now almost forgotten hysteria.[40] It's important to view the role of hypnosis in the alien abduction experiences of this time with this point in mind: hypnosis was being unconscionably misused by practitioners who should have known better to unintentionally create life changing false memories, whether of Satanic ritual abuse or alien abduction.

What Happened to Alan Godfrey?

So, if we discount Alan's colourful pseudo-memories from the hypnotic regression sessions, how do we explain the missing time he experienced? The first thing to note is that 15 minutes is not much to explain. It would be quite easy to lose a quarter of an hour over the course of an evening that involved searching for escaped cows, seeing a UFO and then scrambling over park gates in the wee hours searching for witnesses. Even more telling is Godfrey's revelation that he hadn't actually noticed any time discrepancy. This was only 'discovered' by Detective Chief Inspector and UFO researcher Norman Collinson who, along with Harry Harris and Jenny Randles, was instrumental in investigating this case. Collinson went over Godfrey's experience minute by minute in order to squeeze in the missing quarter of an hour and this was several months after the encounter in the spring of the following year.[41]

Poster for Alan Godfrey's appearance at Todmorden UFO Meet 24 September 2019 (Colin Lyall)

A piece of supporting evidence that Godfrey seems to think important is the mysterious disappearance and reappearance of those wandering cows he'd been sent out to investigate. Alan thinks it unlikely that the cattle could walk from the housing estate across a road and river and into a locked park. However, a Todmorden cow farmer at Todmorden UFO Meet said that this is not at all unlikely. Being prey animals, cows are expert at moving noiselessly and are hard to spot in the dark where they may stand stock still and resemble the silhouette of a bush or rock. The farmer said he had often found his escaped cows roaming much greater distances without the aid of a UFO.[42] Also, I can't help feeling somewhat suspicious of Alan's fairly new revelation that an anonymous yet convenient old lady had seen the cows vanish after a flash of light as this is not mentioned in any of the earliest accounts.

Another mystery is the existence of multiple witnesses of the UFO on the night that Alan had his experience. It will be remembered that shortly after Alan had his encounter, his Inspector told him how four officers had seen a strange light that pulsed, changed size and zig zagged around the sky before zooming off towards Todmorden.[43] It later transpired, though, that this encounter took place a few *days* before, not a few minutes before, Alan's experience. Whatever this light was, the officers were convinced it wasn't an aircraft because aircraft don't pulse and it would break the laws of physics to zig zag at high speed. Surely, in that case, if the light was an alien craft, its occupants would have been thrust hither and thither across the spaceship like the crew of the Starship Enterprise in a meteor shower. One possibility, though, is that the light was from a car or motorcycle. With low cloud or heavy fog, headlights in the distance grow, move, distort and zig zag in strange ways as the vehicle turns sharply on the Calder Valley's windy hilltop roads. This frequently appears as a light in the sky if the road is towards the top of one of the many large hills in the area. Another possibility is the light was some kind of spotlight that some nightclubs have on their rooves; again, as these lights reflect off dark winter clouds, they can appear as a blob of light in the sky that darts around unpredictably. Whatever it was, the zig zag motion suggests its origin lay on the ground. And there's little reason to suppose it's the same object that Alan witnessed.

The other witness was school caretaker Leonard Smith who witnessed a strange light while seeing to the school boilers on the same day as Alan's sighting. It's not clear what time Smith's experience was though. The earliest account by Jenny Randles in her article for *Flying Saucer Review* in 1981 puts the sighting at 5.45 on the same morning as Godfrey's.[44] Randles' next account of the sighting is a couple of years later in her book *The Pennine UFO Mystery,* which puts the caretaker's sighting on the same day as Alan's but twelve hours afterwards.[45] Alan Godfrey's autobiography puts it at 5.15 the same morning.[46] The story of how Smith's sighting became known is also quite murky. Randles' first account says Smith came to Todmorden station to report his sighting and was actually doing so at the same time Alan was also discussing his own experience.[47] In her second account, Godfrey met Smith at the school (presumably some days later) when investigating a burglary that had taken place there.[48] Finally, in Godfrey's account, Godfrey heard about it from his brother Colin and later went to see Smith.[49]

The nature of this sighting also differs depending on which account one looks at. Randles' first account has a ball of white light with a tinge of blue streak into the sky and shoot off fast.[50] This sounds rather like a meteor, and the timing is certainly consistent with the November Orionids. Meteors may be tinged with blue. In Randles' second account, the caretaker sees a bright light in the valley below, which would be inconsistent with a meteor, though Ferny Lee school is not particularly high up.[51] Finally, Godfrey's account gives the caretaker a more dramatic sighting. This time the light is large and rises slowly rather than streaking, and then zig zags from one side of the valley to the other before shooting off like a bullet.[52] Because the exact timing of this sighting is murky and the earliest account is consistent with a meteor, it seems unlikely that this is the same object Godfrey saw, and that the account in his autobiography of Leonard Smith's strange light may have been embroidered over the decades.

So, just what did happen to Alan Godfrey in the early hours of 29 November 1980? Given that the third hypnotist, Dr Gibson, suspected Godfrey may suffer from narcolepsy, it's worth exploring this possibility. The symptoms of this sleep disorder include excessive daytime tiredness, falling asleep at inappropriate times (such as while driving), a feeling of paralysis and accompanying vivid hallucinations while transitioning into or out of sleep.[53] In Godfrey's case, we know he was working nights and this was taking a toll on his health as it does for everyone. At the end of a nightshift, he would no doubt be particularly exhausted and ready to sleep. We also know that when he suddenly came to and realised the UFO had gone, he was still driving down the road, though very slowly. Godfrey claims to have experienced a blinding light which he 'had always recalled,[54] though this is absent from the two earlier accounts by Jenny Randles, and the memory of the light seems to have been created under hypnosis.[55] I think it is highly unlikely that an experienced UFO researcher like Jenny Randles would have omitted to mention the blinding light had it been part of Godfrey's original, pre-hypnosis, memory.

My suggestion, then, is that an exhausted Godfrey fell asleep at the wheel for a few seconds, and possibly suffering from narcolepsy, experienced a vivid hallucination of a UFO in the road before him. A relaxing of the muscles often accompanies these attacks, which would explain why the panda car slowed down to a crawl. I suggest that he made the drawing of the UFO not when it was in front of him, but afterwards, from memory, on returning to wakefulness. The hallucinations that accompany narcolepsy are vivid and the sufferer often feels as though they are fully awake while they are happening. But if I'm correct, then one would expect Godfrey to have had other strange hallucinatory experiences in his life, and yet he mentions nothing in his autobiography. However, thanks to Jenny Randles and her book *The Pennine UFO Mystery*, we do have some knowledge of Alan's previous paranormal adventures.

Firstly, we have Alan's childhood encounter with a strange light in his bedroom. His mother remembers the young Alan's description of it as 'like the earth rushing towards me as if from space.'[56] The second encounter came when he was a young man in 1965.[57] He was driving a van full of equipment for his brother's rock band (not in the band himself as Randles mistakenly asserts) in the early hours of the morning near Todmorden, accompanied by his girlfriend. Suddenly Alan slammed on the brakes, convinced he'd seen a woman and her dog step out in front of the van. He was sure he'd run her over, but on getting out of the van, there was nobody to be seen. When they arrived home, two hours of time seemed to be missing. We have, of course, no way of assessing the accuracy of this recollection so long after it had taken place, nor can we be sure that there was a convenient witness (his unnamed girlfriend), but there is a similar pattern: driving in the early hours and a vivid hallucinatory experience.

The next weird event took place some five years later when Alan was walking his brother's dog in the park (all his episodes seem to feature dogs for some reason!). Suddenly, the dog seemed to go mad and ran off home, while Alan noticed a shape in the bushes that turned out to be a friend. Alan's brother later found him wandering about on his own. Alan said he'd been talking to a friend. The only problem was, the friend he had been talking to had died some months previously.[58] We have, then, what we might expect from someone suffering from narcolepsy: vivid hallucinatory experiences that seem real. As seen above, Godfrey also described some of his previous strange experiences to Dr Gibson. This explanation would, no doubt, be a difficult proposition for Godfrey to face, despite the fact that these hallucinations are relatively common and are in no way a sign of insanity. Indeed, it's been estimated that around 5% of people may experience a similar sleep related hallucination in their lifetime.[59] However, falling asleep while driving a panda car should be a serious concern, and it's understandable that Godfrey would want to avoid that conclusion. Randles notes that Godfrey was reluctant to talk about his childhood encounter, and I noticed that same reluctance when I asked him about his previous strange experiences in a talk he gave in 2003. This reluctance is understandable in that if he is prone to these hallucinatory encounters, this casts some doubt on his repeated assertion that he saw a nuts and bolts UFO.

Of course, there are several other possible explanations out there. Perhaps he really saw a nuts and bolts alien spacecraft. Some have suggested that Alan actually saw the Futuro house, a flying saucer shaped demonstration house that was well known in Todmorden in the 70s and 80s. Alan pours scorn on this idea. After all, he would no doubt have been very familiar with that landmark and unlikely to mistake it for a UFO. Others, such as Jenny Randles, have considered the possibility of him having encountered some kind of hallucination inducing atmospheric phenomenon,[60] which seems plausible in theory at least, though this phenomenon is disputed and little understood. In the light of the incomplete evidence we have, therefore, I think that a hallucination, to which Alan seems prone, is the most likely theory available.

Epilogue

Alan Godfrey received much media attention after his experience went public. Perhaps the most bizarre was his appearance on BBC Breakfast Time TV where he was interviewed by Frank Bough, with additional questions from former Dr Who Colin Baker and a pre-conspiracy theory David Icke![61] This media attention may be one reason for the alleged ill treatment Alan received from his superiors in the police. Alan claims they intimidated and threatened him, falsely accused him of arson and planted drugs in his locker.[62]

Finally, Alan had had enough. He was offered and accepted early retirement on the grounds of an earlier serious injury. Before he left the force, he was called in to speak to Assistant Chief Constable Keith Hellawell, later to become Britain's notorious 'Drugs Tsar'. Hellawell said, according to Alan, 'If only they had let sleeping dogs lie, none of this would have happened.' Alan was perplexed by this statement. Who did Hellawell mean by 'they'? In fact, this episode inspired the title of his autobiography, *Who or What Were They?* They must, he assumed, be more powerful than the police, but who could Hellawell have meant? Alan still strongly believes that it was his investigation into the Adamski Mystery and the publicity this case got and not his UFO report that led to him having to leave the force.[63]

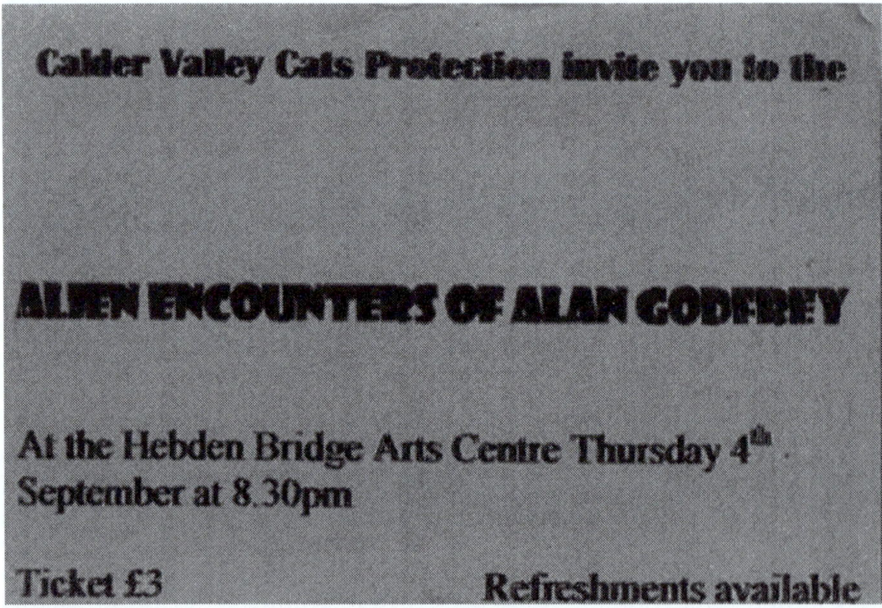

Invitation to an evening with an alien abductee courtesy of Calder Valley Cats Protection.

In any case, his talks were always entertaining and delivered with down to earth humour. Though he seems to have retired from the UFO circuit, several of his talks have been uploaded onto the internet. His strange story remains Britain's best-known case of alien abduction and cemented Todmorden's reputation as a UFO hotspot.

Tom Bell ~ The Exploding Outlaw of Hebden Bridge

Come, - since we love a pleasant walk,
Let's take our leisure while we talk;
And rambling slowly through the dell,
I'll tell a tale of old Tom Bell…

Tom Bell, the skulking villain, lay,
And in his cavern spent the day,
In pleasure base and glutting feast,
On stores by lawless force increas'd.

(William Broadbent, 1840)

Tom Bell, legendary outlaw, glutton and bogeyman, is said to have lived skulking in his cave in the wilds of Hardcastle Crags, the popular beauty spot near Hebden Bridge. Ballad poems were written about him and children were frightened by tales of his grim hideout and spectacularly gory death. At the end of the nineteenth century, a skull was found in Tom Bell's cave. Amidst much scepticism, the discoverer declared it to be the skull of Old Tom himself, but, as the town erupted in controversy, the cave proved to have even more secrets to reveal...

The Story of Old Tom Bell

What we know of Tom Bell comes mainly from two poems: *A Rural Walk on a Summer's Day in the Groves of Hebden (in Company with Mary and Martha)* by William Broadbent, published posthumously in 1840[1], and *The Vale of Caldene* by William Dearden, published in 1844.[2] Presumably both poets were referring to existing oral folklore that they were aware of. Broadbent's poem says the story of Tom Bell is:

A true, traditionary tale
Well known to dwellers in the vale.

However, there are no references to Tom Bell before these poems. A number of pamphlets and newspaper articles about the legend of Tom Bell seem to be based on the poems, though these also add some juicy elements to the tale. Compiled from the above sources, but mostly from *Stories from Hardcastle Crags and Heptonstall Number One*[3] which is the fullest account, this is the story of Old Tom Bell.

Many years ago, no one knows when, there was an outlaw called Tom Bell who lived in a network of caves that now bear his name in Hardcastle Crags. The caves ran deep underground and had other entrances near Mytholm Church and Hell Hole Rocks. At night Old Tom would leave the cave to plunder nearby farms and villages of their animals and valuables, always proving too clever to be caught. You see, he wore boots with the heels at the front and the toes at the back to confound anyone who tried to follow his footprints. About his appearance we are told he was unkempt and shaggy, to be expected from someone who lived in a cave, but also, unusual for a sneak thief, he dressed in clanking iron mail with brass adornments and carried with him a spear or a sword.

By day he skulked in his cave, gorging himself on his ill-gotten booty, with only rats, weasels and other vermin for company. He did have a friend, though, Willie the Woodcutter, who would sometimes visit him at night to share a stolen meal.

One particular night Willie was making his way to his friend's cave dragging along a stolen lamb when he was spotted by two little children. The children had seen Willie return to his house in the early morning on a number of occasions, so this time they resolved to follow him and see where he had been going. They saw him drag the reluctant lamb towards Tom Bell's cave and so they decided to return the next day to explore.

As Willie reached the entrance to the cave he was startled by two crows with bloody beaks still holding clumps of flesh as they shot past him. He ventured further into the cave and met with such a dreadful sight that he turned and ran for all he was worth, forgetting about the lamb which also bounded out of the cave...

The next day the two children enjoyed a pleasant walk through Hardcastle Crags until they reached the cave they had resolved to investigate. They ventured further and further into the labyrinthine den, only to be confronted with the same sight that had sent Willie screaming into the night. Tom Bell was lying dead, his eyeless sockets staring blankly at the dying embers of the charcoal fire. In his raised hand was his sword, the blade all black with clotted blood. Tom Bell had eaten so much that his belly had burst, and now the vermin that he had formerly kept company with were gorging on his spilt innards, the whole sight illuminated by the eerie green phosphorescence of a rotting root. The traumatised children crept away whispering: 'Willie's dead.'

Tom Bell's End

In the version of the story above the outlaw dies unknown. The children hadn't seen Willie leaving so they thought that the burst corpse was his. In fact, it's not quite clear how Tom died, but in his death we can trace some of the evolution of the legend. The Broadbent poem from 1840 only says that:

How long he liv'd, or where he died,
Lo! Nothing more is said beside.[4]

The Dearden poem, on the other hand, presents a very different take on the 'children find a corpse in a cave' scenario. In this long work, spanning six books, the author (referred to as the 'Pilgrim') makes a return to his childhood home and rails against the poverty and despair he finds. The part of the epic that concerns the Tom Bell legend is to be found in Book Six, though the outlaw is never mentioned by name. In fact, this part of the poem is concerned with Willie the Woodcutter. Willie is out of work and worried that he won't be able to support his wife Annie and his new born son. Willie searches in vain for work or charity, but his lack of success drives him to despair.

As Willie is walking home after being refused charity by the Guardians of the town, the final humiliation, he encounters:

a grim-visaged fiend, with deadly glare
And fleshless hand…[5]

This skeletal demon presents Willie with a horrifying vision of the fate of his wife and child:

He saw his wife,
Want-worn and ghastly, with her ebbing life
Striving to feed her famished child, that pressed,
With bony fingers, her cold milkless breast;
He heard its death-cry, and beheld it slide
A corpse, with thin pale face, down by its mother's side![6]

Here Dearden launches into full gothic horror mode. Willie wanders the hills and marshes of Hardcastle Crags as a 'raving maniac', gnashing his teeth, convinced of the death of his wife and child, telling his ghastly demonic skeleton companion that he will end his life somewhere where he won't be found so that a burial will not be needed:

So raved the maniac and with hasty stride,
Followed the footsteps of his demon-guide,
Until his form was lost to human ken,
In the thick gloom of HEBDEN's sullen den.[7]

Meanwhile, Annie, Willie's wife, waits at home having managed to obtain a supply of bread and cake, and their child sleeps contentedly. But they will never see Willie again.

But we do learn of Willie's fate. A starving man, referred to as a 'starveling', drags a stolen lamb towards a place known as the Robber's Cave. He sees two 'obscene' black birds fly out and assumes that they had been feeding on the remains of another starveling's stolen lamb. Instead he finds, glowing under the light of the familiar luminous root, a corpse with knife still in hand, its blade black with blood. Later, two innocent children make the same discovery and creep away, again whispering 'Willie's dead!' In this poem though, Willie *is* the dead man's name. In fact, the poem implies that rather than dying by overeating, Willie had cut his own throat, wracked with madness, starvation and despair, haunted by demonic visions. The downbeat tale ends with Willie being buried in unconsecrated ground 'like a dog', leaving behind his widow and son, while the poet hopes God will forgive the suicide and that the family will be reunited in heaven.

By the time the pamphlet *Stories from Hardcastle Crags and Heptonstall Number 1* was published in 1919 we are told that Tom had 'burnt himself and gone off with a quack'.[8] It's not clear what exactly this means. One possibility is that he fell asleep next to the fire after feasting, burned to death and then exploded. Or perhaps his rich, meaty diet led to a bad case of wind, which combined with an enclosed space and a naked flame had explosive results. A later pamphlet entitled *Stories and Folk-lore from the District Known as Hardcastle Crags* says that Tom had 'burst by overeating', now the best-known end to the legend.[9] One wonders, though, if 'burst' was misremembered from 'burnt' in the earlier pamphlet. In any case, it seems that the grim but romantic outlaw of Broadbent's poem was fused with the harrowing and tortured death of Willie the Woodcutter from Dearden's epic, except that Willie is now the discoverer of Tom Bell's corpse rather than the corpse itself. In the Dearden poem, it makes sense for the children who find the body to say 'Willie's dead!' because it's Willie's body that they find. In the 1919 retelling, it doesn't make sense that the children would say 'Willie's dead!' because it's *not* Willy that they find but Tom Bell. Furthermore, they knew Willie and so would realise that the ghastly corpse in the cave was not his. It seems to me that one or both authors of the two Hardcastle Crags pamphlets had read Broadbent's poem and the relevant section of Dearden's poem, but mistakenly assumed that Willie's death in the Robber's Cave and its aftermath was actually referring to Tom Bell himself. In Dearden's poem, a starving man ('starveling') finds Willie who had cut his own throat, though this is only implied in a rather subtle manner:

Round his lank throat the Starveling closer tied
His tattered kerchief, as if THERE *the gride [slash/cut]*
Of that black knife he felt already keen,
And life were ebbing from him![10]

The authors of the pamphlet perhaps missed the point or simply misremembered that the corpse with the bloody knife in hand in the Robber's Cave was Willie the Woodman who'd killed himself, and assumed the body was Tom Bell. The nameless starving man with the stolen lamb from Dearden's poem becomes Willie the Woodcutter, thus adding a new character, a sort of side-kick, to the story. To explain Tom's death, the authors of the pamphlet added a great little embellishment to the legend that makes sense of the horrible corpse: he was a glutton, so bursting his guts all over the cave would be a fitting end to the tale.

A Bone of Contention ~ Tom Bell's Skull

The strange story of Tom Bell does not end with his death. In 1894, the 'crumbling remains' of a wild boar's skull was found in the cave, perhaps the scraps from one of Tom's hearty meals.[11] However, controversy would not erupt until a more sensational discovery a few years later.

In 1899, Herbert Cooper, son-in-law of one Mr Thomas, the owner of the estate that included the cave, claimed to have made an amazing discovery while exploring the caverns looking for the lost treasure of Tom Bell. He told the *Hebden Bridge Times* what happened as he ventured deeper into the cave until eventually coming to a sudden drop which he had to scramble down. Herbert Cooper himself takes up the story:

> Well, there's a place a bit further in where, for a distance of seven yards, you have to crawl through like a snail. There's only just room for your body and I had to pull myself through by slow degrees, pushing my candle on in front of me a few inches at a time. At the end of the passage I one day found the skull... I was horrified.[12]

He couldn't bring himself to touch the skull, and he had to inch out of the tunnel backwards. He returned some weeks later and managed to reach the skull using some wire, and, with some difficulty, extricate it. On his way out of the cave he said he had got lost for two hours and so he vowed never to go into the cave again. The whole experience, he said, had left him with nightmares. As far as Cooper believed, though, he had found the skull of old Tom Bell.

The people of Hebden Bridge greeted this discovery with scepticism. The increase in tourist visits to the area that ensued from the find was rather advantageous to Herbert Cooper, as he and his wife ran a business providing refreshments to summer visitors to the Crags.

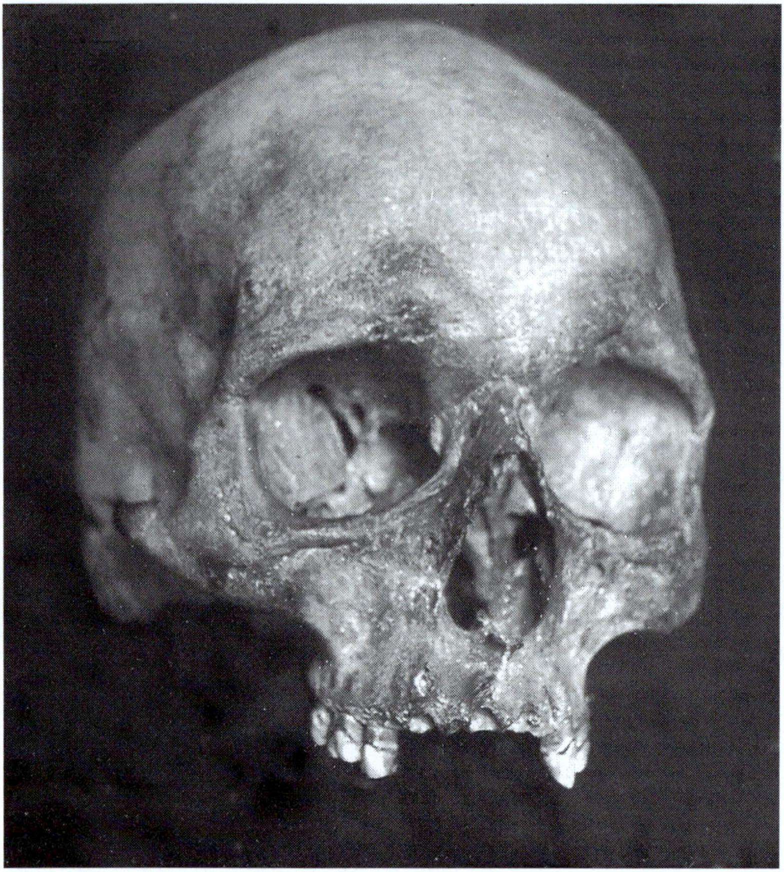

Skull from Tom Bell's Cave (courtesy of Hebden Bridge Local History Society)

However, Tom Bell's alleged skull set the whole town talking. For several weeks there were heated exchanges in the *Hebden Bridge Times* about the genuineness of the skull and the depth and extent of the cave. The people of Hebden were split in a light-hearted civil war between the 'cavists' who supported the contention that the skull was really Tom Bell's, or at least was not recently placed in the cave, and the 'anti-cavists' who suspected trickery. In a letter printed on the 27 October 1899 one John Clay said he had explored the cave thoroughly as a young boy determined to find the cave's second entrance at Eaves near Mytholm church but had found nothing, proving, he maintained, that the skull must have been placed in the cave recently.[13] John Clay was soon to play a key role in the growing controversy.

Another correspondent signing himself only 'Anti-cavist' described his own visit to the cave:

> If scrambling over and under huge boulders, covered with soft clay, and wriggling, writhing and twisting one's body all shapes, is the lot of the cave explorer, then I have done with it, and any tendency in this direction in the future I will smother... After traversing with the greatest difficulty for some distance there is a fair-sized place- Tom's reception room, I presume- and then comes about a five-yard drop into the bowels of the earth to his inner chamber. Of course you go down, and what do you get for your trouble? Oh, the pleasure of scrambling up again and adding more "paint" to your already much-bedaubed clothes.[14]

In October a party from the *Hebden Bridge Times* mounted an expedition to the cave. They found what they thought was the drop described by Cooper, but were too afraid to go any further: 'the place is somewhat eerie and begetful of ghostly thoughts' wrote the reporter. Their only discovery was 'J. Halliwell 1817' daubed on the cave's interior.[15]

After Cooper's find it wasn't long before the cave was besieged with armies of explorers in search of the rest of Tom Bell's skeleton, or even better, some of his booty.[16]

~

One possible candidate for Tom Bell's cave, Hardcastle Crags.

The Battle of Tom Bell's Skull ~ The Great Debate

Finally, at the end of January 1900 the education committee of Mytholmroyd Co-operative Society held a debate on the whole controversy. Representing the 'anti-cavists' was John Clay, author of a number of sceptical letters on the subject to the local press, while the 'cavists' were represented by Mr Abraham Foster Barrett, a hypnotist, magnetic healer and science teacher.[17]

The skull in question was produced. John Clay had already described it in one of his letters to the *Hebden Bridge Times* on 10 November 1899: 'The large bony protuberances over the eye sockets, the low, retreating forehead, and the prominence of the lower part of the face, indicate low development.' The skull had been taken to Dr Russell of Todmorden, and then shown to Professor William Boyd Dawkins of Manchester who believed the skull to be prehistoric, possibly Neolithic.

At the Mytholmroyd debate, Abraham Barrett argued that John Clay and the 'Anti-cavist' had actually been exploring the wrong caves. Indeed, there are a number of openings in the hillside, and it is anyone's guess which one, if any, was the original. The chairman of the debate, John Dewhurst, further confused the issue by pointing out that there were a number of places around the Calder Valley that carried Tom Bell's name, though I'm not aware of any or even if that was true at the time.

Barrett continued to maintain that the skull was Tom Bell's, but he admitted the possibility that it could have been placed in the cave in the last twenty years. Clay argued that a skull could not exist for more than fifty years in such a damp and porous environment.

Clay moved on to say that Herbert Cooper's own brother didn't believe the story of the skull being found in the cave. The audience greeted the revelation that mummified cats had been discovered in the cave with gales of laughter. More merriment followed the news that Cooper's brother had actually found the dead cats in an old malt tub in Cliviger.[18]

The debate didn't really settle anything, but by the time the pamphlet *Stories and Folk-lore from the District known as Hardcastle Crags* was published, the whole skull episode was put down as a hoax: 'A late proprietor of the holiday camp put a skull within, to attract visitors for refreshments, and hundreds came.' A further reason for suspicion may be that Herbert Cooper, the finder of the skull, worked with his father-in-law who was a former sexton and so may have had access to human bones.[19] In more recent times, Russell Dean, a local businessman, claimed that the skull was deliberately placed in the cave by his grandfather.[20]

Death of a Cavist

Abraham Foster Barrett, who led the cavists, came to a tragic end that strangely mirrors that of Willie the Woodsman in William Dearden's poem. In the summer of 1902, Barrett became 'unhinged' and came to believe that God wanted him not to eat, sleep or drink. He was suffering from hallucinations and was becoming violent and unpredictable. His mother said he went for sixteen days without sleep. He was confined to Clayton workhouse, but continued to be extremely violent: 'He assumed the strength of a madman, and there was not a single person in the workhouse who could keep him under control.'[21]

Barrett escaped from his confinement and hurled a huge boulder at the warden who tried to stop him. He was apprehended again but smashed every window in his room to tiny pieces. He was so out of control that the police had to be called to restrain him. He died the following day. The inquest ruled that the cause of death had been 'acute mania and cerebral apoplexy'. Barrett the Cavist's pitiful death, plagued by madness, hunger and hallucinations, is an uncanny reflection of that of Willie the Woodcutter, the forerunner of Tom Bell in Dearden's poem.

Return to Tom Bell's Cave

Whether the skull was a hoax or not, the story of Old Tom Bell resurfaced from time to time as more brave souls attempted to explore the Robber's Cave. Leading 'anti-cavist' John Clay led a band of explorers consisting of his son, and a few others later in 1900. They spent three and a half hours mapping every corner of the cave and made a plan of it. They found no evidence of human habitation, though they did come across the hook that Herbert Cooper had used to extricate the skull a year earlier. According to this party, 'The length of the cave is almost twenty yards, and it is composed of a number of intricate passages.'[22]

Sam Fielding led a walking party there in June, 1900.[23] They were prepared with candles, matches, lamps and ropes and some of the party had protective clothing. For this excursion, the party split in two and accessed the cave through two different entrances. Fielding's description gives us more of a feeling of what the cave is like:

> The entrance near the Crags was searched in all its bendings, the party sometimes creeping and worming themselves along narrow passages and then coming upon open chambers where several could stand erect.[24]

They could hear the party from the other entrance and catch glimpses of their lights, but couldn't find a passage that joined the two entrances together. Finally, a Mr W. Greenwood wriggled through a tiny cleft in the rock and joined the other party, but no one dared follow him as negotiating the cleft involved 'a fearful needle's eye ordeal'. The cave was also described as 'numbingly cold'. The party found a few animal bones and, oddly, some wires. They joked that the wires had been used to hold the skull in place by the hoaxer who had left it there! However, Fielding felt that the party had achieved something that all the other explorers like Cooper, Barratt and Clay had not: they had found the connection between the two entrances. Unfortunately, it's not clear from what Fielding writes where exactly the two entrances are, and this is a problem that will resurface.

Two unnamed Halifax youths tried their luck in the summer of 1958, and their adventure was related in the *Halifax Daily Courier and Guardian*, along with a rehash of Tom's legend.[25] With torches in hand and protective clothes, they went deeper and deeper into the cave until they were forced to turn back due to lack of air and failing torches. At one point they claimed to have encountered a 20-foot drop within the cave between two rock faces. The journey from the depths they achieved back to the surface apparently took them hours to complete, though this is quite possibly an exaggeration.

Tom Bell popped up again in an article by Max Tickner in the *Halifax Evening Courier and Guardian* 1967.[26] The article describes Old Tom as the Hebden Bridge equivalent to the Loch Ness Monster, cropping up at regular silly seasons when other news is thin on the ground. In any case, 'armed only with a rope, a lamp and a bottle of tranquilisers' Tickner valiantly set off to explore the cave hoping to find 'a lost treasure hoard'. He found the entrance easily enough and passed through four small chambers before a steep passage led him down 25 feet, through a small aperture and then to a large cavern. Here he found a small passage that was blocked by fallen rubble. The spooky atmosphere led to him imagining he could hear someone breathing noisily in another chamber of the cave. This was made worse by his torch flickering, even though the battery was new. But this was as far as he could go, in that direction at least.

Tickner did not give up easily. He then went in search of the second rumoured entrance near Mytholm church, at Choppy Knife Rock. Unable to find even the rock, he proceeded to Heptonstall quarry, (presumably Hell Hole Rocks) where he attempted to find a third supposed entrance. He did find a cave which had a passage that seemed to lead under Heptonstall and towards Hardcastle Crags, but again it petered out in a pile of rubble where a passage had apparently collapsed. At this point, he admitted defeat, as all explorers of the cave have done before him. Again, it's not always clear which entrance is the 'real' cave, and it may be that some of the intrepid adventurers are exploring another cave altogether,

In 2015 Mark Simmonds and some friends explored the cave and posted a video of their visit on YouTube.[27] They used ropes to help them clamber down through a narrow hole into a chamber. There appeared to be some small passages on the cave floor, and some were covered by unsafe looking fallen rocks (supposedly the cave was blocked off at some point due to someone nearly getting lost, though I'm not convinced that this is true as several of the previous explorers refer to being lost or venturing deep into the cave after the supposed blocking off). At one point in the video there was some excitement as a shiny material that looked like powdered gold was seen in some of the crevices. This turned out to be just water droplets glistening on the lichen. In the chamber of the cave they explored, they found an old bottle, an empty can of pop, a mushroom and a cave spider. The cave also, it seems, smells a bit 'pissy'.

Perhaps inevitably, one of the comments on the video by Tom Payton says that they too explored Tom Bell's Cave in 2019 and that Mark Simmonds had entered the wrong cave. The real cave, Tom says, has a narrow shaft that goes forty metres into the earth. It was, he claims, so deep that it felt as if they were descending into hell.

Will the real Tom Bell's Cave please stand up?

The Original Tom Bell Found?

The story of Tom Bell leads inevitably to the question of whether there is any historical truth to the legend. The skull that Cooper found in the cave was offered as proof of Tom Bell's historicity at the great debate in 1899, though as we have seen this is widely believed to have been a hoax. The present whereabouts of the skull is unknown, though in a 1993 article for *Hunter Archaeological Journal*, G.W. Gilks concluded that the skull was of a young woman from the Neolithic era.[28] Even if we assume the skull was genuinely found in the cave and not planted there, it's too old (and possibly too female) to be Old Tom. In any case, the skull has been lost, so it's impossible for a modern analysis of it to take place.

This raises the question of just when Tom Bell was supposed to have been carrying out his nefarious deeds. The article in the *Todmorden Advertiser and Hebden Bridge News* from 1894 which describes the finding of the wild boar's skull says Tom was active about 500 years ago, though gives no source for this.[29] An article from the *Halifax Courier*[30] in 1960 says Tom lived 'a century or so ago', which makes little sense as Broadbent's poem about him was published in 1841. Max Tickner's 1967 article plumps for the ninth century, again with no evidence.[31] From these disparate dates, we can only conclude that the legend of Tom Bell is not associated with any particular time.

There is, though, a plausible candidate for the 'real' Tom Bell. He was discovered by historian J.A. Heginbottom and reported in *Transactions of the Halifax Antiquarian Society 1989*.[32] This cave-dwelling thief was called Joseph Bailey, and this is his story as described in *The Annals of Yorkshire*:[33]

> About this time [i.e. 1779], a man passing by Hathershelf Scout [i.e. Scout Rocks, Mytholmroyd], observed his dog enter a narrow aperture: supposing him to have caught the scent of a fox, he pursued, and found the opening gradually expand into a small cave, where he found not a fox, but a savage who barred all further approach by a pistol. The astonished discoverer withdrew, but quickly returned with some assistants, one of whom boldly entered, and secured the inhabitant of the cave. The reason for his choice of this unknown retirement now appeared. It was a repository of stolen goods; among which were two surplices taken from the parish church of Rochdale, with the scarlet hood of a doctor in divinity. The plate stolen at the same time had been discovered at another place. The cave was not large enough for the reception of living oxen, but it was copiously stowed with slaughtered animal food, properly cured for a long concealment. The ruffian thus extricated from his lurking place, was transported for life.

Many of the elements that make up the Tom Bell story are to be found in this episode. We have a desperate, armed cave dweller surrounded by his booty and a large store of meat. We also have the surprise discovery of the villain in his lair, though of course Joseph Bailey was very much alive. Even the names Bailey and Bell have a similar ring to them, and it's easy to see how retellings of these events could evolve into the Tom Bell legend, with the location of the cave being misremembered or altered in the oral folklore of the area.

Epilogue

If you fancy your chances at discovering some of Tom's treasure, his cave is in Hardcastle Crags, near Hebden Hey Hostel, fifty yards up in the woods. The stone head on the wall of the present building was rescued from the original café that Cooper ran and is supposed to point towards the cave, though it's hard to say which of the openings is the right one. To further confuse matters, Hebden Hey's website says that the current cave entrance is different to the original which was walled up. The old stone head is actually described as being Tom Bell himself, keeping watch over his as yet undiscovered treasure.[34]

Tom Bell's stone head above the door to Hebden Hey (Photo: Larisa Moskaleva)

Magic on the Moors ~ The Hunt for the Mixenden Treasure

'...there was as much treasure in a place besides Halifax as would ransom a king; and that one Leventhorp now dead had seen the foot of the chest, and the devil sitting upon it, and Sir John said it could never be got but with loss of a Christian soul...'

(Henry Banke, 1510)

According to legend, somewhere north of Halifax there lies a hoard of lost treasure watched over by its demon guardian. Though some had seen the treasure with their own eyes, none had been able to defeat the demon and secure the gold. However, in 1510, an intrepid band of nine men, including priests, a former Lord Mayor of York and a sorcerer, armed themselves with a magic circle and other accoutrements, and set out on a carefully planned occult treasure hunt. It all went horribly wrong...

The Mixenden Treasure and its Hunters

There is a fortune to be found near Mixenden, Halifax, according to local legend. Upon this chest of gold is a 'sword of maintenance' (a ceremonial sword) and a mysterious black leather book.[1] Guarding the treasure is a demon or devil. Some said that only the sacrifice of a human soul could satisfy the guardian demon and allow the treasure to be taken.[2] This did not stop enterprising adventurers from hunting for the Mixenden Treasure. One Robert Leventhorp had successfully found the Treasure and seen for himself the devil sitting upon the chest. The bold treasure hunter attacked the demon with his sword, but the demon merely snapped his blade in half. So ended Leventhorp's attempt at the treasure, but several others followed also without success.[3] Perhaps what was missing from these attempts was the right mix of theological, magical and geographical expertise, something a daring but incompetent and disparate band of men tried to put right in 1510.

Most of what we know about the 1510 hunt for the Mixenden Treasure comes from the record of the trial of the treasure hunters.[4] Large parts of these depositions are in Latin and there is some confusion over dates as well as contradictory evidence given, which folklorist John Billinglsey has done much to untangle. However, we do know a little about this band of treasure hunters, three of whom were priests, one a former Lord Mayor and another a renowned sorcerer or 'cunning man'.

Two of the priests, Richard Greenwood and John Wilkinson, were from Bingley. The third priest, James Richardson, was from York. As well as being priests, these men, especially Wilkinson and Richardson, had a knowledge of the magical arts, with Richardson in particular being notorious for heresy and the use of divination.[5] Thomas Jameson was a merchant who had risen to high office, becoming the Lord Mayor of York in 1504. There was William

Otewell, also from Bingley, and his 21-year-old servant William Wilson, who may have been the originator of the plot. There were two other commoners, Thomas Wood (35) from Bingley and Laurence Knolles (58) from Harrogate. Perhaps the three priests thought that their magical knowledge would be insufficient to face the guardian demon, so they entreated the help of John Steward (48), a 'cunning man' from Knaresborough.

Steward, it seems, was well-known for his ability to find lost objects. It was rumoured that he kept three bumble bees hidden under a special stone and that when he called them, they would fly out one at a time to feed off blood from his finger.[6] The church suspected him of 'false and damnable conjurations, invocations and divinations', though Steward denied this saying he had never invoked demons or taken part in blasphemous rituals.[7] Like most cunning folk, it's likely Steward made use of Christian ritual, Biblical readings, folk magic and perhaps a dash of charlatanism to impress his clients. Surprisingly, in his trial he claimed that all he usually did was show his clients (who probably could not read) an astronomy book, and then do nothing, leaving his clients with the impression that all would be well, as it sometimes turned out to be.[8] However, he no doubt wanted to play down his magical activities during his trial.

These, then, were the adventurers who were preparing for an expedition onto the moors above Halifax to confront a demon and claim its treasure in the early days of 1510. They met in Otewell's house in Bingley to finalise their preparations. Two of the priests, Wilkinson and Richardson, along with the eminent former mayor, Jameson, went to a private room to prepare for the magic ritual that would be performed. Otewell's young servant, William Wilson accidentally (so he claimed at the trial) barged in on the meeting and was able to describe what he saw. The priests and

Jameson were copying Latin prayers to use in the invocation. There was a magic circle 21 feet in diameter made of virgin parchment (that is, from the hide of a cow's first calf), and bearing various names, symbols and 'superstitious signs'. He also saw religious robes, holy water sprinklers, frankincense and ritual books.[9] There was some 'singing bread' or 'singing loaves', which were the wafers used in Mass, and lamens (breast plates with magical symbols and charms inscribed upon them). On these magical breast plates were the names Storax and Oberion the demon. Perhaps, as John Billingsley notes, this private meeting was meant to hide aspects of the ritual from the others who may not have been comfortable with it.[10]

In any case, all was ready for the attempt on the treasure: the invocation, the religious and occult paraphernalia and the men themselves. The group would travel to the location of the treasure in three separate parties to avoid suspicion and meet up at a (now lost) cross on Soil Hill, near Ogden as the sun was setting. They would then head to the location of the treasure at a cairn (again, lost) known as 'Myxindale Hurde' and there the midnight ritual would take place.[11] The virgin parchment circle would be laid out and purified with holy water and the men would stand inside the circle for protection, with the exception of cunning man John Steward who would stand outside it, as he said he trusted in his own powers and was not afraid of any demon. Inside the circle, Wilkinson was to invoke the spirit Belphares (associated with finding treasure) and command the hoard be brought to them.[12] What could possibly go wrong?

The Treasure Hunt

Richard Greenwood and Thomas Wood went to Heptonstall for a chicken dinner with Greenwood's father and then headed for Soil

Hill where they successfully found the cross that was their meeting place.[13] The other seven treasure hunters met at Lee Farm, Wilsden, and then set off on their adventure. Unfortunately, a dense fog settled over the moors making the journey extremely difficult. Richardson somehow lost his holy water sprinkler. Worse than that, they all got utterly lost on the misty moor. It seems they roved blindly out of their way in the fog and ended up near Clayton before making another attempt to find Soil Hill and its cross. Eventually, they were no doubt relieved to see a cross looming out of the mist, but they soon realised it was the wrong one. They had arrived at 'Mickle Moss', west of Queensbury.[14] They were still hopelessly lost in dense fog on a marshy moor in winter.

Three of the party, Wilkinson, Otwell and Knoles, decided they would set off and locate the cross on Soil Hill and then return for the others when they were sure of the way. As luck would have it, they came across a local man who lived near Soil Hill and they paid him a couple of pence to act as their guide. However, the fog was so thick that even with this local expertise, they were unable to find their way and had to return to the rest of the adventurers at Mickle Moss. However, the others had become fed up and had gone to a nearby hamlet for supper, where Wilkinson, Otwell and Knoles joined them. Meanwhile, after waiting in vain at the meeting place for their comrades, Greenwood and Wood finally gave up on the adventure and headed back to Bingley. In fact, Wood had had enough of the whole affair and pulled out of the venture.[15] The rest of the band did not give up so easily and arranged to meet at Harden Wood the following day to try again. Wilkinson had said that they could perform the ceremony in the woods and command the spirit Belphares to bring them the treasure where they were, which would save tramping over boggy moorland in winter darkness. One wonders why he hadn't thought of this in the first place.

In any case, when the adventurers met the next day, Wilkinson failed to show up (or perhaps was not invited) and the others were in a bad mood. Greenwood, though, had brought two additional treasure hunters with him, his brother Edmund and his father from Heptonstall who actually knew people who had seen the treasure. As they discussed their plan, Edmund reportedly said to Jameson:

> Sir, you seem a gentleman, and I advise you not to proceed with this matter; there have already been wisemen and well learned after the treasure, and they could not get it, and you will just become the talk of the world.[16]

Edmund then offended Jameson and Richardson by suggesting they give him the magic parchment circle. Perhaps the Greenwoods were trying to get rid of some of the gang so that there would be more booty for themselves, but it did not work. The farce continued as the gang began to squabble about how to divide up the immense riches which they had not yet come anywhere near to finding. Jameson, a former Lord Mayor of York, argued that it would appear suspicious if all the commoners of modest means in the gang were to become suddenly wealthy, so he suggested that everyone be given £20 each while he himself would take the rest of the treasure. The rest of the band, of course, wanted equal shares of the spoils, though young Wilson was also keen to get his hands on the mythical sword of maintenance. Jameson was furious that the upstart commoners would not accept his magnanimous proposal of taking most of the wealth and threatened to report them all to the church authorities, a strange course of action as he was clearly guilty himself. However, the squabbles and threats had put paid to the venture and the unsuccessful treasure hunters went their separate ways.

It seems that the gentleman and three priestly scholars, Jameson, Richardson, Wilkinson and Richard Greenwood, at some point made another plan to find the treasure without John Steward and the other commoners, though it seems to have come to nothing.[17] But rumours of this strange band of men tramping over the moors with their magical paraphernalia had spread, and local gossip said that the terrible weather that had been plaguing Calderdale was a direct result of the nefarious mission. The Mixenden Treasure would return to haunt our band of adventurers.

Penance

The rumours and gossip reached the ears of the church authorities and the treasure hunters (except John Steward) found themselves on trial at York Minster on 11 June 1510. They faced charges of heresy and sorcery and were found guilty. The punishment of Otewell, Wilson, Jameson, Wood and Knowles was to be publicly whipped barefoot through the streets of York while carrying banners representing some of the paraphernalia they had used, in what must have been a shameful and painful parody of their misadventures on the moors. Their punishment was to be repeated in Bingley in August.[18] For a bigwig like former Lord Mayor of York Thomas Jameson, this must have been the ultimate humiliation. John Steward had a similar punishment but in August 1510 in York, Knaresborough, Ripon and Doncaster. It's not clear what happened to the three priests, but local historian T.W. Hanson suggests that their positions saved them from a public punishment and humiliation.[19]

The chest of gold above Mixenden and its ceremonial sword and black leather book remain undisturbed under the devil's watchful eye.

Epilogue

The story of the Mixenden treasure hunt from 1510 has passed into local folklore, probably, as John Billingsley suggests, as a consequence of the story making occasional reappearances in the local press.[20] Perhaps historian T.W. Hanson's paper on the treasure, published in 1926, played a role in giving the story new life among locals.[21] But the legend of the lost treasure made a surprising comeback in the 1940s, sparking another vain treasure hunt with occult trappings that again ended somewhat farcically.

It all started in the early 1940s when Jack Bolton of Odsal was working in Mixenden Old Hall and came across what appeared to be an ancient will hidden in a fireplace.[22] The document gave instructions for finding valuable deeds that were hidden in the grounds of the Hall, which were at the time owned by Mixenden Carbonising Company. In 1949, a group of interested parties obtained permission from the landowners to dig for the treasure in the overgrown gardens of the partly demolished Hall, though unfortunately the document with the instructions had been lost, so they had to do this from memory. One of the treasure hunters, Mr Ralph Higginbottom, told the *Courier*, 'If we find it, it will be the world's talk – not the town's talk.'[23] Mrs Higginbottom, who was responsible for obtaining permission to dig on the site, had also been contacted by a 'diviner' who knew where the treasure was.[24] Over Easter 1949 two six-foot holes were dug out in the grounds, though only some old pottery was found.

The whole episode soon descended into farce, as had the 1510 expedition. A letter dated 11 May 1949 and written by a science teacher in the Isle of Wight named Mr R.J. Macfarlane claimed the document in question was a hoax. Macfarlane was the son of a Pellon Lane newsagent and grew up in Mixenden. The mystery document was, he wrote, created by him when he was a schoolboy for a lark:

> I have always loved mysteries and stories of treasure trove, and I have made several sets of documents such as the one found in the ruined fireplace at Mixenden Hall… I used a very thick paper, Indian ink, and a mapping pen, and, because the family name was Murgatroyd, I believe I put that name in the 'will'… I said that all my savings had been buried in a spot so many paces from the termination of an old wall in the grounds.[25]

Mr R.J. Macfarlane (Yorkshire Observer)

The trickster's father added that his son could reproduce excellent gothic style script and had used a medal and red wax to create an authentic looking seal. Macfarlane wrote a letter to those concerned in the treasure hunt apologising and hoping that they would see the funny side. They didn't. In fact, one of the lead searchers, Mrs Higginbottom, refused to believe that a young lad was capable of such an elaborate and clever piece of hoaxing. Indeed, she had received advice from three 'diviners' and had other documents to support her claim. Unfortunately, though, the accounts of lost treasure on the land made the local press and no doubt attracted other unofficial bounty hunters, and so permission to continue digging in the grounds was refused by the owners.[26]

Prophet of Doom ~ The Halifax Astrologer

'On December 25, 1935, there will be an eclipse of the sun in the first decanate of Capricorn. This signifies the passing of a king and danger to great men.'

(Charles Everard Mitchell, the Halifax Astrologer)

Charles Everard Mitchell, also known as The Halifax Astrologer, had a string of successful predictions printed in the newspapers of West Yorkshire in the 20s and 30s. His macabre speciality was predicting air disasters and royal deaths, and many of his predictions were widely published before the events themselves unfolded. But the greatest challenge facing an astrologer in the early 1940s was predicting the outcome of World War Two. This was a mammoth task involving the calculation of astrological charts for all the nations affected as well as for all the leaders involved. Mitchell's reputation as a prophet rested on him being correct…

The Halifax Astrologer

Charles Everard Mitchell lived happily unmarried and with his mother in the build up to the Second World War. In his book *Foretold by the Stars,* he writes:

> The opposition of the Moon to Saturn and Neptune has delayed marriage through home responsibilities. My father died when my Sun reached the conjunction of Saturn in the 8th house, and on the day of his death he asked me to stay with mother as long as she lived, and I have carried out this promise for 30 years and remained unmarried in order to do what I considered a duty and have not regretted the sacrifice.[1]

Charles Everard Mitchell, The Halifax Astrologer (from Foretold by the Stars)

His mother was winner of the 'Grand Old Lady' competition as part of Halifax Shopping Festival in October 1936.[2] Mitchell himself had an unsuccessful stint as an electrician before turning to advertising, cinema management and military service.[3] However, he had long been a keen student of astrology and it was this field that led to his fame as The Halifax Astrologer. He was invited to write an article about astrology for the *Halifax Evening Courier and Guardian* in 1921 in which he predicted that in July 1926 'extremists' would attempt to overthrow Britain's constitution. Mitchell would claim that he had thus successfully predicted the General Strike of 1926 (though it happened in May not July as he had foretold), and his reputation as a prophet took off.[4]

His next major prediction was the result of the Halifax by-election of 1928. This was sent to the *Courier* before the vote but only published after the results had been announced to be fair to the candidates. Mitchell said that Alderman Longbottom, the Labour candidate, had 'the Sun par Jupiter, which signifies Honours, and will be elected.'[5] The Conservative candidate, Major Crossley's moon had 'many adverse aspects in force.' How much of this successful prediction was due to knowledge of the local politics of Halifax and how much was written in the stars is not easy to say, but Mitchell felt his abilities had been vindicated and his astrological star continued to rise.

In 1932 he stood as an Independent candidate for the council elections in South Ward, Halifax. He did this because 'I came under the aspect of Ascendant Trine Sun at birth and this brought about a desire for public service.'[6] South Ward was a Conservative area, but Mitchell's stars looked promising so he decided he could contest the council seat without having to hold any meetings or do any campaigning: 'I relied entirely on the Planetary Influences operating at the time.' He lost. His friends, though, assured him that if he'd consented to put in a little effort to assist the planetary rays, he would have won. His lack of electoral success was not foreseen, he maintained, because he did not receive the birth details of his Tory opponent in time to create a chart for him.[7]

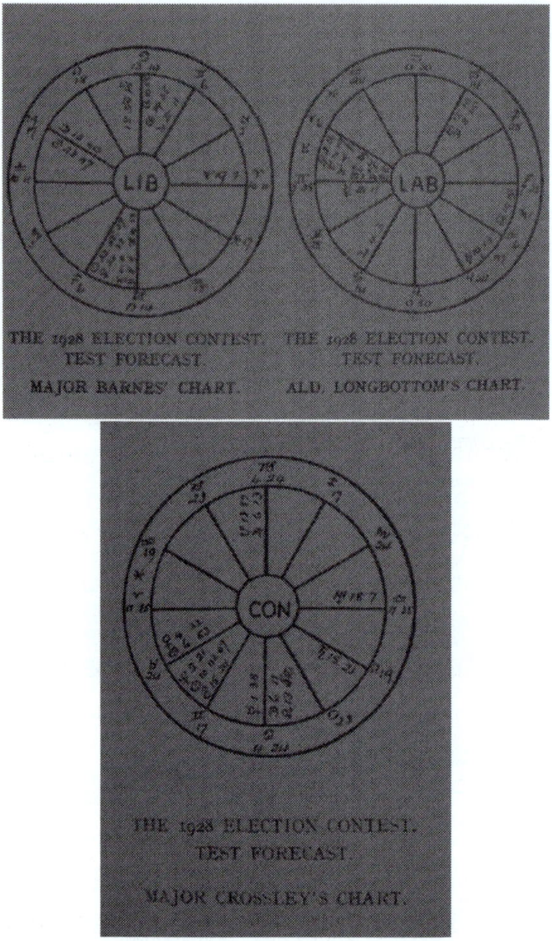

Mitchell's charts for the Halifax candidates in the 1928 general election

Prophet of Doom

However, his next major success was to be one of his most spectacular. Mitchell had a theory that certain astrological influences made some days dangerous to embark on powered flight. He predicted that in 1933, the danger days for flights in July were the eighth, fourteenth and twenty-second. On the 22 July aviation pioneer Amy Johnson along with her husband Jim

Mollison were planning a transatlantic flight, and so Mitchell wrote to *News Chronicle* which published his warning that if the flight went ahead on that date, it would end in disaster.[8] Johnson and her husband Mollison ignored the warning and although they successfully crossed the Atlantic from England to the USA, they crash landed near an unlit airport. The couple were not seriously injured, though Mollison needed stitches to the head and Johnson broke a finger while both had various cuts and bruises.[9] Again, Mitchell felt he had been vindicated. No doubt it would be churlish to point out that both Mollison and Johnson had a string of other near misses behind them: aviation was a dicey business at the time. Mollison himself thought that had they landed at Boston during daylight, the crash would not have happened. Was it the stars or fatigue and judgement error that led to the accident? Whatever the case, the Halifax Astrologer now had a wider fame and he kindly offered to inform the government about his predictions of bad days for flying for the common good, though it seems his offer was not taken up.[10]

Another theory Mitchell had concerned the deaths of royalty. Mitchell had learned from a Master Astrologer from India that when five planets are found in the same sign, it heralds a royal demise or at least the death of a great man.[11] This knowledge allowed him to predict that on 3 February 1934 there would be such a royal or high-profile death. Sure enough, on that day King Albert I of Belgium was killed in a mountaineering accident. The next time this republican configuration of planets would occur was 29 August 1935, so Mitchell sent this prediction to the editor of the *Halifax Courier and Guardian* and it was printed a week before the fateful day. Sure enough, on 29 August the confusingly named Astrid of Sweden Queen of Belgium was killed in a car crash. Mitchell wrote to the *Courier* pointing out that his prediction had proved true and calling for a thorough investigation of astrology by 'men of science'.[12]

Mitchell was now on a roll. He announced more danger days for royalty, one of them being Christmas Day 1935. 'On December 25, 1935, there will be an eclipse of the sun in the first decanate of Capricorn. This signifies the passing of a king and danger to great men.'[13] When King George V passed away on January 20th 1936, it led to rumours spreading throughout Halifax that the King's death had been predicted by Mitchell, despite the prediction being nearly a month out. In any case, Mitchell felt the need to inform his public through the *Courier* that he predicted the death of a king but did not name King George, though by January he knew that it would be George who would die.[14] It's not quite clear here what Mitchell's purpose was in that he seems to be simultaneously claiming he did and did not predict the King's demise, while at the same time completely ignoring the obvious fact that his prediction of a royal death was for Christmas Day 1935, not 20 January 1936.

More danger days for royalty were announced. The Princess Royal was taken seriously ill and the King of Egypt died (though it should be noted these events happened the day after the date predicted by Mitchell).[15] His next date was 17 July 1936, though it's not clear if he actually published this date in advance. However, although there were no royal deaths on that day, there was an apparent assassination attempt on Edward VIII though the gunman was subdued and no shots were fired.[16] Cynics may note that Mitchell's definition as to what counts as a successful prediction becomes more elastic, starting out as a royal death on a specific day and then extending to include illnesses, near misses and events happening the day before or the day (or month) after the chosen day. Indeed, one anonymous sceptic with atheistic tendencies wrote to the *Courier* to express his doubts as to the Astrologer's abilities:

> He seems to take great credit for his prophecies coming true, but really, what does he prophesy but generalities and nothing definite? Anyone can say that within the next three months death will claim a member of Royalty or great men and be fairly on the mark, because they, along with us all, have to succumb. If Mr. Mitchell had definitely prophesised that the Queen of Belgium would be killed in a motor accident, one would be compelled to sit up and take notice. Does he claim that this painful and distressing accident, ending so tragically, was predestined? If so, it seems to me to be a terrible indictment on the predestinator. I prefer to believe in cause and effect as the true explanation of all happenings. I submit that Mr. Mitchell has failed badly as a presager. — Yours. etc., E.H.[17]

Indeed, the Halifax Astrologer provoked many letters to the local press in the 30s and 40s from both supporters as well as 'Doubting Thomases' (as he often referred to them) who often signed off with punning names like 'Stella' or 'Astra'. And Mitchell would invariably reply, often furiously, to any letter doubting his abilities and would frequently announce his retirement from public predictions.[18] His fuming reply to E.H.'s letter above is a typical example:

> Sir,- I am sorry my successful forecasts seem to have annoyed 'E.H.,' as the tone of his letter implies, but

> as he has not the courage to sign his name, I don't consider he is entitled to any explanation… Really 'Doubting Thomas' would have been a better nom de plume for him to use… He says anyone can say that a member of Royalty will die in three months. If this is so, why doesn't he say it publicly in your paper and sign his name to the forecast… To be candid, 'E.H.' is afraid of the subject, and really does not want to be convinced, and, if ignorance is bliss to 'E.H.' then I can assure him I will do nothing to upset his contented state of mind. I think I shall have to cease sending any further forecasts in case 'E.H' and those of his type commence to suffer from sleepless nights, frightened of those things which shall come to pass on earth…[19]

He was, though, never out of the papers for long.

As the 1930s progressed and World War Two loomed, Mitchell made a return to public prophesy. He predicted the outbreak of the war some months in advance, setting the date as July 1939.[20] In fact, it was September of the same year when Britain declared war on Germany, but the astrologer was happy to accept that as a hit. Mitchell took great pains to make it clear to his public that all the Spiritualist journals had printed messages from 'the other side' saying there would be no war, and the same thing had been said by virtually all the world's astrologers. All the worlds astrologers had been wrong and the collected prescience of the afterlife had not foreseen the outbreak of war. But Mitchell, the Halifax Astrologer had. In his piece for the *Courier*, though, he forgot to mention that he had also predicted the war would start in 1935 and end in 1936.[21]

Prophet of Peace

The important test for Mitchell's skills in 1939 was to predict the outcome of the war, and his predictions appeared in the local papers as well as in his book, *Foretold by the Stars.* Plotting complex astrological charts for all the countries and leaders involved and analysing how they would interact was a formidable task. Mitchell wrote that 'Hitler means well, he is a Libra man' but he will 'overstep himself'. Hitler would fall from power sometime in 1940, betrayed by a friend, and that the war would end in the same year with no victory.[22] 'All computations', he wrote, 'point to a sudden termination in 1940.'[23]

Perhaps the Halifax Astrologer's predictions were less in demand after this spectacular and very public miss, or perhaps he went into retirement from astrological science as he had been threatening to since the early 1930s. Whatever the case, his public star seemed to wane. He did, though, get married in 1941 to Ethel Rosina Conway from the Isle of Wight. She was also an astrologer and had written the first ever astrological song to be published.[24] He married again in 1948 to Mary Spiers.[25]

Epilogue

The last prediction I can find from Mitchell comes from 1952, and this is one he can thankfully claim as a hit. It was widely reported that a famed Indian astrologer called Pandit Ram Swarup Sharma predicted World War Three would begin in Korea at the end of 1952 and would lead to the end of the world.[26] Charles Everard Mitchell, the Halifax Astrologer, however, quite correctly predicted that it would not.[27]

Bewitched ~ Witches, Wizards, and Cunning Folk

'Let their children be made orphans. Cursed be the thief, be they in the field, in the grove, in the woods, in their houses, barns, chambers, and beds… And cursed be their flesh, and their bones, and the marrow that is within their bones. And cursed be they – by the milk of the Virgin Mary. I conjure thee Lucifer, with all thy soldiers, by the Father, Son, and Holy Ghost- that the thief rest not day nor night….'

(Curse on a Halifax thief, 1807)

Calderdale has an eccentric collection of witches, wizards and cunning folk. These were often outsiders, frowned upon by the establishment, but still sought out by ordinary people. Some were figures from folklore, like Auld Betty the Witch of Halifax who could change into a huge black cat. Others were all too real, at least in the eyes of their accusers. And then there were the 'cunning folk' who specialised in lifting witches' curses, finding lost or stolen property and creating charms with some fortune telling and nefarious other services offered on the side. There are stories of charms and curses, prophecies and strange powers. But there also true tales of love, death, madness and betrayal and of what happens when these cunning folk fall foul of the powers that be…

Auld Betty the Witch of Halifax

Auld Betty was a mischievous witch who had the power to turn herself into a cat. This allowed her easy access to and quick escape from whichever places she went to do her witchery. When a child sickened or a loved one died, the people of Halifax might mutter about 'having hurt done them', a euphemism for being under a curse from a witch. And this was the kind of wickedness Auld Betty would cause.

If you suspected that Auld Betty had bewitched you, there was a remedy: attract the witch, draw some of her blood and break the curse. To do this, first make a cake. Set the cake baking on the fire until it starts to burn, and arm yourself with a three-pronged fork to draw her blood when she appears. Auld Betty, it seems, like many a witch, could not resist the smell of cake. All you had to do was be patient and on no account utter any blasphemous oaths.

At least one man succeeded in defeating Betty this way. As he sat with his three-pronged fork watching his aromatic cake smoke and turn black round the edges, he suddenly became aware of a large black cat sitting by the hearth casually washing its face. The man could not understand how the cat came to be there.

As the smoke from the burning cake started to fill the room, the cat cried: 'Cake burns!'

The man replied, 'Well, turn it then.'

'Cake burns!' repeated the cat ever more desperately.

'Well, turn it then.'

'Cake burns!'

The constant crying of the cat got so vexatious to the man that he forgot the no swearing stricture and let rip with a thoroughly blasphemous oath. The cat suddenly pounced onto the man's face and sunk its claws into his chin, scratching him dreadfully before making its escape up the chimney. But not before the bloodied man had managed to stab the cat with his three-pronged fork.

Auld Betty (Larisa Moskaleva)

Auld Betty was laid up sick for several days after that, proving she and the cat were one and the same. She never bothered that household again.

This version of the story is taken from William Henderson's 1879 work *Folklore of the Northern Counties.*[1] However, although the tale may be folklore, many of its themes can be seen in the rumours, tall tales and real events described below. The fear of bewitchment is a recurring theme, as is the ritual to break the witch's spell by drawing blood, as well as the ways in which a ritual can go wrong.

As for Auld Betty, according to naturalist W. Moore of Greetland in a talk to the Calder Valley Poetry Society in March

1935, she resided in Sowerby Bridge and ended up being hanged for witchcraft.[2]

Old Sally Walton, the Widdop Witch

Old Sally Walton, the Widdop Witch, was supposed to live in a cottage overshadowed by stunted trees somewhere between the Ridge and Clough Foot bridge.[3] The story told of her is similar to that of Auld Betty the Halifax Witch, but without the cake.

An old farmer who lived near Sally Walton's house was having trouble with his cattle being ill and was lying awake one night when he suddenly became aware that a strange black cat had appeared at the foot of his bed and was staring at him. The farmer picked up a handy knife and hurled it at the creature, hitting it on its front paw. The cat immediately vanished and the farmer could find no trace of how it had got in or where it had gone.

The next day, he told some neighbours about his nocturnal experiences. His neighbours then informed him that Old Sally had been seen that morning with her arm in a sling and with a handkerchief wrapped round it. This was all the proof that was needed to convince these neighbours that Old Sally Walton was indeed a shape-shifting witch and to be avoided.

The Horsehold Witch

At the top of the steep climb of Horsehold road in Hebden Bridge, a little gate on the right leads off to a popular bench with commanding views over the valley. In times gone by, however, the picturesque settlement of Horsehold was troubled by a notorious witch. Cattle would die unexpectedly, and after the death of a much-loved horse, some of the farmers decided to consult a cunning man. These cunning folk were specialists in removing witches' curses, finding lost or stolen goods with some healing and fortune telling thrown in for good measure. They certainly existed in the Calderdale area well into the nineteenth century as will be seen in several of the stories below.

The cunning man the people of Horsehold consulted was widely-respected and he confirmed what the farmers had suspected: a witch was responsible for all their hard luck. The wise man said that he could show the witch to the farmers by magical means, but the ritual required absolute silence. If anyone spoke, the spell would be broken.

The cunning man and the farmers congregated in Horsehold barn and a fire was lit in the centre of the floor. The wise man proceeded to recite incantations and to perform various magical gestures, the details of which are unknown. Suddenly an old woman hobbled into the barn to warm herself by the fire: the witch had been trapped. It's not recorded who spoke or what was said, but speak someone did and the magic failed. The old woman was gone. We don't know what happened to the witch, if witch she was, nor do we know if the spell cast to attract her led to her ceasing her mischief.[4]

A Tale of Two 'Witches'

Two Heptonstall women, Elizabeth Crossley and Mary Midgley, were accused of witchcraft in 1649, as recorded in the *Depositions from the Castle of York Relating to Offences in the Northern Counties in the Seventeenth Century*.[5] The earliest accusation seems to be against Elizabeth Crossley: Daniel Briggs of Wadsworth claimed that seven years previously his mother on her death bed had expressed the fear that she had 'had hurt done' by Elizabeth Crossley and that was the cause of her decline.

Daniel Briggs also described how two years ago a two-year-old infant called John Shackleton had started having convulsions and was in pain for months. The minister of Cross Stone Chapel visited the child and advised Briggs and the maid who were taking care of the infant that if they should meet anyone on their way home, they should 'mawle them in the head'.[6] This refers to the belief that drawing blood from the bewitcher would allow the bewitched to recover.[7] However, it's certainly surprising advice to be given by a man of God.

Briggs and the maid did indeed meet somebody on their way home: Elizabeth Crossley. The maid, who was carrying the ailing child, shied away, but Crossley asked after the child's health. The maid did not want to give Crossley the satisfaction of knowing how bad the child was, so instead lied about his health saying he was 'indifferent well'. This news seemed to make Crossley very angry. Neither Briggs nor the maid attempted to maul Crossley in the head at that time, but later the maid came across Crossley and bashed her over the head with a candle stick. The next day the child got better, though the day after that the fits returned and the boy died several weeks later. On the morning of the child's burial, Briggs met Elizabeth Crossley who asked him 'Have you brought this witched childe to towne?' Briggs replied that he did not think the child had been bewitched, though this seemed to anger Crossley and she swore that it had been.[8]

Another witness, Henry Cockcroft, a clothier from Heptonstall, also claimed to have suffered from the alleged malignant witchcraft of Elizabeth Crossley. A few months previously Crossley had come begging for alms at Cockcroft's house and was not happy with what she received. Two days later Cockcroft's infant son William became ill and was 'sicke by fitts, bendinge backward, changinge his coulor and scrichinge,' despite being previously in good health.[9] He recovered somewhat the next day but was still 'dull and stupid', and the fits returned a few weeks later. He seemed to recover again, but relapsed and died in December.

Cockcroft suspected that his child had been bewitched and went to see Mary Midgley who he believed to be a confederate of Crossley's. Cockcroft confronted Mary Midgley and blamed her for his son's death, and Mary did admit that she could 'witch a little', though it seems this confession was beaten out of her by Cockcroft as another witness (Samuel Midgley of Heptonstall) said Cockcroft 'did both threaten and strike her'.[10] However, Mary denied being responsible for the child's death, instead blaming Elizabeth Crossley and her daughter Sarah, along with Mary Kitchinge.

Mary Midgley faced another accuser, though. Richard Wood of Heptonstall claimed that the previous summer Midgley had come begging wool from his house. Richard's wife, Martha Woods, refused to give Midgley any wool as she had given her some a few weeks ago and instead gave her some milk. This made Midgley very angry. The next day, several of the Briggs's cows sickened and the obvious conclusion for Richard and Martha Woods was that they had been bewitched by Mary Midgley. Martha went to see Mary and asked her to cure the cows and eventually she agreed for the price of sixpence. Mary told Martha to put a handful of salt and some old iron underneath the sick cows and that would cure them. Later Richard met Mary who confessed that she had 'done hurt' to him several times and gave him an apple, promising not to do so any more.[11]

This rather convoluted story certainly suggests that both Elizabeth Crossley and Mary Midgley had a certain reputation in Heptonstall in the mid-seventeenth century. The fact that both women resorted to begging for alms implies they were on the edges of society. It seems unlikely that both accused were malicious witches casting death spells on local children and cattle, but Mary's admission that she did a little witching might mean that one or both of them were cunning women, specialising in charms, finding lost or stolen items and lifting curses. Both women denied the accusations.

The Wise Man of Widdop

In the wild moors on the Yorkshire-Lancashire border near Widdop there lived a wise man who was often consulted for his arcane knowledge. His name is lost, and the period in which he lived is also unknown except that it was in 'olden times'. The two vignettes below are both taken from a lecture delivered by Mr Tattersall Wilkinson and reported in the *Todmorden and District News* at the end of the nineteenth century.[12]

An elderly couple who lived over at Bouldsworth End at the head of the Thursden Valley were having difficulty churning their cream into butter. It was a cold winter's day, and the poor husband and wife were exhausted from continuously churning the cream to no avail. Eventually, they despaired of ever getting the cream to turn to butter. The only possible explanation was that a witch must have placed a curse on their churn.

The next day the old man set off over the moors to see the wise man of Widdop who had a great reputation for the breaking of witches' spells. The wise man told him to take his churn full of cream to the bridge at the foot of Stoney Bank and at exactly midnight to tip the contents of the churn into the running water. However, the wise man warned, this was to be done in complete silence for if a word was spoken, the power would be broken.

Whether this process worked or not is unknown, but we might assume it was successful. This is because when the old man and woman looked into the churn after casting its contents away, they were surprised to see the distinct image of a cross burnt into the curds at the bottom of the churn.

The second story featuring the wise man of Widdop (assuming it's the same wise man) is also a story of bewitchment. The farmer at Red Lees farm near Burnley began to suspect that the illness that was inflicting his cattle was caused by witchcraft. On this occasion, the wise man gave the farmer some mysterious ingredients and told him to boil them in a pot and to stir continuously for an hour. Again, this was to be done in absolute silence or the spell would not work.

The farmer's wife took the first shift at stirring the pot until she became tired. She beckoned to her husband to take over, but as he took the spoon he accidentally splashed his hand with some of the boiling hot contents. He let out a loud curse: 'Damn it!' and put his scalded fingers into his mouth. But the magic had been broken. Suddenly, the whole mass of pot and ingredients exploded in a huge blue flame. The explosion was so violent that it blew a piece out of the oak beams near the fire and the damage is still visible to this day.

Witchcraft at Blackshaw Head.

An old weaver of Blackshaw Head called Robert Sutcliffe came to believe his house was haunted by evil spirits. This happened in 1804, according to the *Todmorden and District News* in 1913.[13] To rid himself of these spirits he enlisted the help of a Bradford exorcist called John Hepworth who had a reputation for banishing such evil forces. The wizard went to Sutcliffe's house and instructed him to heat a large pot containing human blood and human hair. This was done but for some reason the pot exploded with great violence killing old Robert Sutcliffe before the very eyes of the wizard.

The Iniquity of Witchcraft ~ Two Sermons Delivered at Warley, 1807

The Reverend Thomas Hawkins was so dismayed by the good people of Calderdale's penchant for witchcraft, folk magic and superstition that he delivered two thundering sermons against these practices in the summer of 1807. Not only that, he felt the issue was important enough to publish his thoughts the following year under the catchy title of *The Iniquity of Witchcraft, Censured and Exposed: Being the Substance of Two Sermons, Delivered at Warley, Near Halifax, Yorkshire.*[14] Hidden mostly in the footnotes to the preface of this work, though, are some fascinating insights into folk beliefs in Yorkshire in the very early nineteenth century.

One of the examples of iniquitous witchcraft that Hawkins gives concerns a gentleman whom he refers to as J.C. who had had his watch stolen. He went to see a 'wizard or necromancer' who gave J.C. a piece of paper sealed and folded into a triangular shape. The charge was two shillings and sixpence. When an acquaintance of Hawkins gained possession of the paper and opened it, it was discovered to contain a long and 'blasphemous' incantation. It contained entreaties to God, Jesus, Mary and John the Baptist as well as a call for a spirit known as Sagrigg, who is commanded to 'torment the thief both day and night' until the watch is returned. There then follows a lengthy, detailed and impressive curse on the dastardly watch thief, a short extract of which is below:

> Let their children be made orphans. Cursed be the thief, be they in the field, in the grove, in the woods, in their houses, barns, chambers, and beds... And cursed be they in the church, the church-yard- in eating, in waking, in sleeping, in drinking, in sitting, kneeling, standing, lying, in all their works, in their

> body and soul, and in their five wits. And cursed be the heart, back, liver, bowels, and spleen… And cursed be their flesh, and their bones, and the marrow that is within their bones. And cursed be they – by the milk of the Virgin Mary. I conjure thee Lucifer, with all thy soldiers, by the Father, Son, and Holy Ghost- that the thief rest not day nor night….

What seems strange about this curse is the curious mixture of elements of Christianity with solicitations to Lucifer as well as the mysterious Sagrigg. No doubt it was this blasphemous eclecticism that offended Rev. Hawkins so much. Unfortunately, Hawkins does not tell us if J.C. ever got his watch back.

Hawkins also describes a man who set himself up in the 'diabolical profession' of wizardry in L________n, which perhaps refers to Luddenden. He was so popular that he would have crowds of thirty or more waiting for his wisdom. A young mother whose child was ill was convinced by a friend that her child had 'hurt done' her, the phrase often used to denote being bewitched. The friend obtained a paper charm, perhaps similar to the one J.C. was given and presented it to the mother and told her to place it about her sick child. However, as Hawkins notes approvingly, she instead threw it in the fire.

There are a couple more examples that Hawkins gives to prove the inefficacy of magic charms like these. In one case a woman whose husband was very ill became convinced that he had been cursed and so spent eleven shillings on a wizard's charm, but it failed to save him and he died shortly after. However, this didn't convince his wife that the charms were useless; quite the opposite, it seems. She returned to the wizard and purchased three more of these charms: one to place on her door, one to put in her cap and the other to hide in her corsets.

Another woman (perhaps in Warley) became convinced that she 'had hurt done' her and sought out a wizard for assistance. He visited her five times to try and lift the curse but to no avail. The wizard therefore instructed the woman to come and live in his house with him so that he could lift the curse, no doubt at some expense. It didn't work and she died shortly after.

In several of the cases Hawkins describes, there seems to be a thin line between what Hawkins calls a wizard and what we might call a healer, or less charitably, a quack. But it's not really the inefficacy of the charms and spells that Hawkins is concerned with; it's the affront to God and the way folk magic happily took aspects of Christianity and demonology and stirred them together with traditional spells. Not shy of using exclamation marks, Hawkins thundered at his flock:

> Perhaps there is no greater proof that a man is actually bewitched from the circumference of his body to the centre of his heart, than his wearing a wizard's charm for his preservation!!! This is attempting to form a coalition which will never stand, it is an attempt to unite Christ and Belial – holy prophets and vile sorcerers![15]

The Witch Bottle

In February 1844 a woman called Nancy Houldsworth and an unnamed friend burst into the newspaper office of the *Halifax Guardian*. Nancy proceeded to tell the astonished journalists a true 'tale of mystery'.[16] A tale of love, death, curses and witchcraft.

The story begins in 1841 with two sweethearts, Mary Wilson and Samuel Bottomley, both of Old Bank, Halifax. The young couple were in love and were planning their future together. Unfortunately, poor Mary sickened and died and a witch's curse was suspected. Samuel was distraught and mourned his lost love. Sometime later, though, as he recovered from his loss, he began to develop feelings for another young woman. This time the object of his affections was Nancy Houldsworth's niece, Sarah. Things seemed to be going well for the couple and Samuel once more started to look forward to a happy future with his beloved. Unfortunately, it seems the curse, whatever it was, had not been lifted and poor Sarah also sickened and died earlier in 1844 leaving Samuel bereft again.

Even before Sarah died, though, Samuel's eye had been caught by a young lady who went by the name of Mary Baxendale and he whispered many 'sweet nothings' into her ear. But the same curse struck again. Mary number two developed a sudden illness and seemed to be at death's door. Neither Samuel nor the people in the neighbourhood could understand the poor lad's misfortune in love.

Now, Nancy, the narrator of this sad tale, was contacted by a mysterious unnamed person. This mystery person offered to tell her the truth about the curse on the condition that she would promise to keep it a secret. Nancy was told that beneath a flag in the cellar of Betty Wilson's old house there was buried a witch's bottle that would bring bad luck to whoever walked out with Samuel Bottomley. However, Nancy didn't keep her promise and immediately told everyone she knew around Old Bank about the cursed bottle.

A man called John Lister was employed to dig up the cellar and he did indeed uncover a buried bottle, bottom up under the flag. The bottle was made of stone with flat sides and had a cork in the top. Unfortunately, Lister damaged the bottle when he was digging and a 'bottle imp' flew out and disappeared leaving a noxious smell behind it.

Nancy produced the broken bottle (sadly without the imp) for the inspection of the gathered journalists and assured them that now the charm was broken and that young Mary Baxendale was on the road to recovery.

But that's not the end of the story. The newspaper did some digging of its own and found that the bottle was actually buried by one Mrs Sutcliffe, the sister of Mary Wilson, Samuel's first lost love. At the time Mary (number one) was suffering from Tuberculosis and her sister suspected that she had been bewitched. To try and cure Mary, Mrs Sutcliffe had contacted 'an old hag of a fortune teller' named Jenny Jardine for help. The fortune teller said that Mary must fill the witch's bottle with a liquid (the report is coy, but we may assume that she was told to urinate in the bottle). Then the bottle must be buried bottom up and parts of the Bible recited with one foot touching the bottle.

'So much for the age we live in,' was the reporter's conclusion to this strange tale.

'Melancholy Results of Pretended Witchcraft at Halifax'

One night in late January 1858, two young Halifax women went to see their neighbourhood fortune teller. Fortune tellers, though, were seen as rather disreputable at this time, and polite society viewed them with suspicion. Their visit would have dramatic repercussions for one of the women and for the man who told her fortune.

The two women were Ellen Amber and Elizabeth Bunney of Haley Hill, Halifax. The man they went to see was John Hodgson of Coach Fold, Haley Hill, a fortune teller of some local repute, especially among young women, we are told.[17] The two women were invited into Hodgson's house where the thin, cadaverous-looking fortune teller was sitting by the fire. He invited the women upstairs and they followed, no doubt feeling a frisson as they broke Victorian taboos by entering a strange man's private rooms. The price was three pence each.

The consultation started with palm reading. Hodgson said that Elizabeth would have two chances to marry this year. But for Ellen, the message was very different. Hodgson told her she had a 'very unsettled mind' and that she had to return to see him again in two weeks. He told her to read the first chapter of the Book of Ruth from the Old Testament while also reciting her sweetheart's name.

The second part of the consultation utilised the crystal ball. Hodgson told Elizabeth that he could see two young men, one with light hair and one with dark hair. He then made some mysterious marks on some paper and kept it to himself.

Finally, Hodgson produced a pack of playing cards. Elizabeth's cards were good, but the cards for Ellen were bad. Ellen must, he repeated, read Ruth and return two weeks later, though Ellen was much afraid and said that she daren't. It's hard to say whether Hodgson was genuinely concerned about Ellen, wanted to get more money out of her or was hoping to take advantage of her.

Some days after the consultation, Ellen's parents noticed something had changed about her and that she was continuously in low spirits. Then she suddenly deteriorated and became 'raving mad'. At one point it took four people to restrain her, but even they could not hold her long. She fought free and ran into the streets nearly naked. On another occasion she sunk her nails into her mother's flesh so deeply that it was hard to pull her away. The situation was so bad that her mother had to leave home. By now she had been 'out of her mind' for some days. She was refusing to see anyone or to allow anyone to speak to her. She was convinced everyone was trying to take her to the devil.

The family called in Reverend J.C. McMichael. The fact that they turned to a man of the cloth is interesting because it suggests they feared their daughter was possessed and in need of exorcism. In any case, Rev. McMichael brought police support in the form of Superintendent Pearson. They were shocked at the condition Ellen was in.

A 'medical man' was consulted and it was his expert opinion that this was a case of 'hopeless lunacy' and that Ellen would probably have to be committed to the workhouse asylum. What's more, he was certain that her madness was caused by the advice given to her by the fortune teller she had consulted several days before.

The case was heard by the magistrates at Halifax Town Hall on 23 February 1858. The sad condition of Ellen had led to a great deal of local interest in the story, and the hearing was filled with respectable people. Elizabeth related her story, and the crystal ball and the paper with mysterious markings that Hodgson had produced during the consultation were brought forward as evidence. Hodgson denied ever seeing the women before. His housekeeper, Ann Wilson, gave evidence in his defence, saying that she was rarely ever out and she had not seen the two women. Elizabeth, though, testified that the housekeeper was by the hearth when they entered the house and Wilson was ordered to stand down.

In his defence, Hodgson, who we are told spoke 'very correctly', argued that anything he said was unlikely to have caused lunacy several days later. He did, though, still deny ever seeing the women. The Chairman of the Magistrates Court, John Crossley, treated Hodgson with extreme indignation. He found John Hodgson guilty of extorting money by the practice of palmistry and sentenced the fortune teller to three months' hard labour.

As Hodgson was taken into custody, his belt was removed. The belt proved to be hollow and was cut open and all kinds of strange objects tumbled out. There were many old pieces of paper with 'grotesque marks' on them that were rotten with age. There were medals, a compass, a mirror, quicksilver in a needle case, magnets, crucifixes, and parchments. This may have surprised the officials searching Hodgson, but this was not out of the ordinary for cunning folk. Cunning folk tended to be craftsmen, traders or farmers and so had a higher rate of literacy than the general population and this was a source of their power. Literacy allowed them to consult magical manuscripts and books of spells as well as to write the kind of written charms that spilled out of Hodgson's belt. These were frequently written on expensive virgin parchment (from the hides of animals that had not reached sexual maturity) or even unborn parchment (from the hides of aborted animals). The charms would contain spells, verses from the Bible, magic words and occult or astrological symbols.[18] Unfortunately, these charms did not offer much protection to Hodgson.

Whatever Hodgson's intentions, it does seem like a miscarriage of justice that he was blamed for an unfortunate woman's insanity. But this sad tale does give us an insight into the superstitions, rituals and religious ideas of these people. It's clear that Hodgson was not, or not just, a cynical charlatan in that his belt stuffed with old magic and religious paraphernalia suggested he had an eclectic range of beliefs. I'm also sure that Ellen Amber's unfortunate story would have been told as a warning to curious youth as to the dangers of dabbling in the unknown.

Witching on a Black Cat's Back

In 1862, one Mrs Greenwood of Mankinholes was taunted for being a witch by her opposite neighbours Susannah Uttley and Wright Feather (or Foster). Her neighbours accused her of bewitching a woman who was bed-ridden and of using witchcraft to kill her own grandchildren. They even went so far as to charge her with riding on the back of a black cat. Mrs Greenwood had indeed had four grandchildren who had died, and was no doubt much vexed by the name calling and so took Uttley and Feather to court for slander, and the accused became the accuser. Times had changed, though, and the revelations about riding on the back of a black cat were greeted with much laughter in court. This was clearly a feud between neighbours with a bit of superstitious gossip thrown in for good measure. The case was dismissed.[19]

Marian Wood the Fortune Teller

One autumn night in 1879, a young woman named Martha Westwood turned up at the house of cunning woman and fortune teller Marian Wood (32) in Haley Hill, Halifax. She had come to ask Marian what the future had in store for her. At this time, fortune tellers were often prosecuted under the vagrancy act, so the profession carried some risk. In this instance, neither woman was all that she seemed and both had secrets to hide.

When Martha arrived at Marian Wood's house, the fortune teller was not at home. In the meantime, more clients arrived and joined the queue. After half an hour, Marian Wood returned home and invited Martha into a separate room for the consultation. Here Marian carried out some 'mysterious performances', though there is no record of what these were.[20] Then she shuffled some cards and made the pronouncement: 'You had two husbands, but they are both dead.' Martha replied that she had only one and he was still living. On hearing this, Marian offered a charm that would kill her husband. Martha refused this offer.

The consultation was obviously not going well. Marian reshuffled the cards and this time pronounced that Martha's husband was a tailor and was seeing other women, but that she could offer her a charm to fix this. Martha said she already had the charm she needed and paid the fortune teller a shilling. As this was Marian's first shilling of the day, she invited her client to have a drink with her and they went for beer and whisky at a nearby pub. However, Marian's fortune telling skills let her down catastrophically: she had failed to see that her client had been sent by the police to entrap her and that the shilling she had taken as fee had been marked. While the women were drinking in the pub, Inspector Newburn and Sergeant Harland had entered Marian's house and found evidence of fortune telling in the form of cards and a glass. They also found a woman from Queen's Road waiting to see Marian who was unhappy with her services: Marian had apparently used her powers to identify the name of a ship which the woman's sweet heart had joined as a sailor. The information had proved incorrect. Sergeant Harland went to the pub and the marked shilling was identified. When Marian arrived home again to find Inspector Newburn, she was reported to cry: 'O my God, what is the matter; tell me the worst; is it anything worse than fortune-telling? I tell fortunes and keep my husband by it. Do tell me the worst!' Marian's husband, Samuel, was said to do nothing but drink.[21]

From what Marian said it seems she had something greater to fear than arrest for fortune telling, though it is strange that she would draw attention to it in this way. In any case, Marian received one month's hard labour. Another Halifax fortune teller, Hannah Horsfall, was also entrapped by Inspector Newburn in the same way using Martha Westwood and a marked coin and she was given two months hard labour, taking a previous conviction into account. During the trial, the Chief Constable summed up the police's attitude to the practice: 'Fortune-telling was becoming a too common practice in this town and they were determined to put a stop to it if possible.'[22]

The prison sentence did not deter Marian Wood from her occult activities. In the summer of the following year a woman called Maggie Wallace sought Marian's services. She told the fortune teller that her husband was ill and that she wanted to know what would become of him and her own future. After a 'magical stare', Marian pronounced that the woman had been bewitched by a grey-haired old man and that she lived in a house that was haunted and unhealthy and she would never have any luck so long as she continued to live there.[23] Marian then said that if the client would return, she would give her some 'stuff' that would either kill or cure her husband. It's unlikely that Marian was proffering poison here, but rather that she was offering create a magical charm. Maggie replied that she did not want her husband killed. There was some more fortune telling with cards and a glass and then the client left after paying a florin for Wood's services.

Once again, Marian's powers had failed her. She had not foreseen that the client Maggie Wallace had been sent by the police and that the coin she had taken was marked. Inspector Newburn had struck again and Marian had walked into his trap a second time. Apparently, there had been several complaints about Wood's activities, leading to this second operation.[24] During the trial, Wood understandably complained about the police sending people under cover to entrap her. She also made the point that her clients came voluntarily to her and asked if it were customary for people to pay for a crime to be committed? It seems that press coverage of her previous conviction had actually been rather good publicity for her and she was now 'tormented' with potential customers waiting for her services.[25]

This was certainly not to be Wood's last brush with the law. In February 1883, now living in Southowram Street, she was visited by Elizabeth Jackson Boyes, a domestic working at the Plummet Line Inn, Halifax. She said to Marian: 'I don't exactly want my fortune telling; I am pregnant, and I am told you can give me something to help me.' Wood said that she usually charged three sovereigns for this service, but would only charge one on this occasion.[26] Wood then performed an operation on her client and gave her some medicine. Elizabeth was told to return for two further treatments. However, on the third visit, Marian Wood's nemesis was waiting: Inspector Newburn. Newburn sent Elizabeth for medical examination where it was determined that 'violence had been used' upon her. Elizabeth was removed to a workhouse where she soon after miscarried and her life was described as being in 'grave danger'.[27] The Inspector searched Wood's house and discovered implements likely to be used to cause an abortion and fortune-telling cards hidden up the chimney.[28] In her trial, Wood pleaded guilty to fortune telling but said: 'If it is for the other, I am not guilty.' The jury did not believe her and she received seven years penal servitude.[29] This was the worst that she had feared when she had been entrapped by Inspector Newburn in his first sting four years earlier.

On her release from prison, life did not get much better for Marian. She was again found guilty of performing an illegal abortion in 1891, this time on a Burnley woman named Harriet Grant. Halifax police arrested her for drunkenness on 1 December and removed her to Burnley to await trial.[30] This time her sentence was to be even harsher: twelve years of penal servitude.[31]

Marian Wood and Hannah Horsfall were not the only Halifax cunning folk to be snared by the police using marked coins or fake clients. In 1886 Mary Ann Hall fell victim after receiving a marked coin in payment for fortune telling from police informants posing as clients. The Chairman of the hearing at Halifax Borough Court, James Bairstow, told Hall:

> You know that this is a thing that cannot be permitted. You know that you have been getting a livelihood by imposing upon silly girls. You have carried this business on for some time, and the Bench think they ought to mark their disapprobation of your conduct, that it may be a warning to others. You will have to go to prison for two months with hard labour.[32]

The last account of a similar police sting in Halifax that I could find occurred as late as 1932 and involved Leslie Crowther, 62, of Stannary Lane. In her trial, Crowther maintained that she only gave advice on health and business matters, but it was clear from the evidence that she was actually making predictions involving her young female clients and the dark- or fair-haired youths that would be their future husbands. It seems that Crowther had been telling fortunes for over a decade, but that the police had been struggling to obtain enough evidence against her. However, compared to the fortune tellers of the previous century, she got off rather lightly with a fine of £12 and 8 shillings.[33]

By this time belief in witchcraft had declined. This was a blow for cunning folk as their main trade was in protection against witches. The fact that many more people were literate than in previous centuries also helped bring about their decline and cunning folk became extinct in the UK in the 1940s, according to expert on popular magic Owen Davies.[34] This was the end of the cunning trade and its strange mixture of curse-lifting, folk magic, fortune telling and quackery.

Close Encounters of the Tod Kind ~ Disco Lights in the Sky

'It showed different coloured lights which seemed to split the thing up. And it rotated slowly...it had lights like disco lights.'

(Lora McArthur, 1982)

It seems that UFOs just can't keep away from Todmorden. In 1982 over 100 people witnessed a 'disco light' in the sky over the town on three consecutive evenings. Then, just as suddenly as it had started, it all ended with a bang. A very BIG bang...

Disco Lights in the Sky

The headline in both the *Hebden Bridge Times* and the *Todmorden News* on 23 April 1982 read: DISCO IN THE SKY PUZZLES 100. 'Have the space invaders returned to the Calder Valley?' asked the papers as over 100 people claimed to have seen a UFO over Todmorden on three consecutive evenings, the 'biggest mass UFO report ever known in the district.'[1]

On Saturday 17 April father and son Les and Gary Barber were driving over the tops above Todmorden when they saw a 'dark pylon shaped silhouette on the moors towards Walsden' at around 10 p.m. The car's lights stopped working, possibly, they speculated, from a power surge causing a thermal overload in the car's circuits.

It later turned out that Gary Barber's wife Gladys had also seen a UFO from the Ashenhurst area of Todmorden on the same evening. Gary concluded that the two incidents might be connected. He said: 'For all we know, what they saw might have passed right over us. It never occurred to me at the time but you hear all these things about people in cars.' Alan Godfrey, you may remember, was driving his police car in Todmorden when he had his close encounter with a UFO in 1980 (see chapter 4).

On the same night as the Barbers' sightings Lora McArthur, also of Ashenhurst, Todmorden, heard a call on her CB radio about a UFO in the area. At first, she thought it was a joke, but on looking for herself she saw, along with seven other people, a cigar shaped object in the sky. Lora said: 'It showed different coloured lights which seemed to split the thing up. And it rotated slowly… it had lights like disco lights.' The lights were described as red, blue, green, white and turquoise.[2]

The next night the UFO was seen again. The Barbers also witnessed the second showing and they too described it as a disco light which seemed to be rotating. Lora McArthur, however, said the second object was different to the one seen on the previous night as this one had no definite shape.[3]

On Monday more CB radio enthusiasts along with the occupants of three police cars and a police motorcyclist saw the light again. The object apparently jumped from side to side before dropping over the hills. An unnamed man said that through a telescope the object appeared grey and round with a black cross and rotated while its lights changed colours. All in all, it is estimated that over 100 people witnessed the mysterious object.[4]

It's interesting to consider the role that CB radio played in the unfolding of this UFO flap. Citizen's Band radios are short-wave radio communication systems typically associated with truck drivers, but in the late 70s and early 80s they became hugely popular in the home (or teenage bedroom) in the UK despite being illegal until 1981. Shortly before they were legalised, there were estimated to be 300,000 illegal users in the UK.[5] In a world before email, texts and ubiquitous mobile phones, CB radios provided direct and instant contact between strangers and friends. By the end of 1981, CB radios were legal, easily available and had been one of the most popular Christmas gifts for the year.[6] Calderdale was no exception, and by the time of the 1982 flap we can see how CBs were used to spread news of the sightings further and faster than word of mouth or the press could ever do. It allowed news of a sighting to be reported to multiple users in real time, and it's certainly plausible that this flap was influenced to some degree at least by the popularity of CB radio.

Sometime on that Monday evening an unnamed UFO researcher from Rawtenstall near Bacup arrived in time to witness the phenomenon and offer his expert opinion. His verdict: a star! Photographs taken of the object showed nothing of interest and the police too suspected it was a star or planet twinkling colourfully because of atmospheric conditions.[7] But could over 100 people have been fooled by a twinkling star? The fact that photos showed no 'disco lights' and a UFO researcher dismissed it as a star when one would have expected him to have been very open to the possibility of a non-mundane explanation suggests they might. Certainly, while staring at a single bright star it often appears to jerk or zigzag from side to side due to the slight unconscious swaying of the body. As has been noted, Todmorden is also on flight paths to Manchester airport so some of the lights witnessed may have been from aircraft. Another strong possibility is that some of the witnesses were observing the annual Lyrid meteor shower, made up from the remains of comet Thatcher. This peaks every year around 22 April, and the displays in 1982 were much more active than usual.[8]

As well as the lack of photographic evidence, another problem with this case is the wide disparity in descriptions of the UFO. It was, apparently, cigar shaped, pylon shaped and a light in the sky. During UFO flaps people can often misinterpret mundane phenomena such as aircraft lights or stars or planets under unusual atmospheric conditions, seen at night when visibility is less than perfect, in the light of their expectations. By 1982 Todmorden already had a reputation as a UFO hotspot and the media frenzy over the Adamski-Godfrey affair would still have been fresh in people's minds.

The UFOs on Saturday, Sunday and Monday night were witnessed by over 100 people, but the strange events of the following day must have been witnessed by many thousands…

Boom-Boom! The Big Bang

I was walking home from school on Tuesday 20 April 1982 at around 4.30 in the afternoon, when just 30 yards from my parents' house behind Hebden Bridge station I stopped in my tracks as the whole valley erupted in a colossal boom, just about the loudest noise I had ever heard. This was at the height of the cold war, and I remembered a Campaign for Nuclear Disarmament pamphlet distributed at the time claiming that the USSR had a nuclear missile aimed at nearby Huddersfield. I looked around dreading to see a mushroom cloud appear on the horizon…

Meanwhile, at Sowerby Bridge fire station the fire fighters also feared nuclear armageddon had arrived and dived for cover under the fire engines.[9] Local police units were dispatched to Todmorden and Heptonstall as reports flooded in of crashed aircraft, earthquakes and explosions.

The shock waves from the boom caused buildings to shudder across the Calder Valley and hundreds of people ran out into the streets to see what had happened. The terrifying thought that nuclear war had begun must have crossed many of their minds, if only for a split second. This is understandable. The early 1980s were a paranoid time and the possibility of a nuclear catastrophe, whether by accident or design, seemed depressingly plausible. These concerns can even be seen in a local newspaper like the *Hebden Bridge Times*. Headlines like these from the early 1980s would be unthinkable today, and these are just a few of many:

NO REAL DEFENCE AGAINST THE END OF THE WORLD (08/01/82)

DRIFT TOWARDS NUCLEAR WAR? (07/05/82)

DON'T BOMB US TOWN COUNCIL TELLS THE REDS (07/05/82)

So, what could this mysterious explosion have been? A number of theories quickly emerged. The first was that it was a sonic boom from one of the many military jets flying over the valley at the time. The second possibility was that it was an earthquake as the Craven Fault line runs through the valley. Another theory (suggested by a schoolboy in a letter to the *Hebden Bridge Times*) was that the boom was the UFO seen on the previous three nights taking off at high speed. Indeed, the UFO, whatever it was, was not seen on subsequent nights. The *Hebden Bridge Times* reported: 'Another theory, widely circulating in local pubs is that in true "close encounters" style the Government is having a secret endevous [sic] with intergalactic visitors at a local quarry.'[10]

~

What Caused the Big Bang?

Notwithstanding the speculation in local drinking establishments about craft from other planets, the most likely contenders for an explanation of the mysterious bang are an earthquake or a sonic boom. Let's look at each of these in turn.

In her book *The Pennine UFO Mystery,* Jenny Randles plumps for the earthquake theory. This has the advantage of also explaining the preceding nights' UFO sightings. Randles suggests that both the boom and the mysterious lights are related to what are sometimes called Unidentified Atmospheric Phenomena (UAPs, pronounced 'whaps'). These UAPs may be seen as floating lights in the vicinity of fault lines like the Craven Fault running through Todmorden.[11]

Unfortunately for this theory the Institute of Geological Sciences in Edinburgh said that no earthquake was recorded at the time of the boom, so either the tremor was very small or we have to find another explanation.[12]

The *Hebden Bridge Times* of 23 April 1982 reported the mystery explosion with the headline: BOOM BOOM! The paper joked that 'Hebden Bridge became a "boom" town on Tuesday afternoon, but only for a split second.' The fact the explosion was heard as a *double* boom suggests that a supersonic aircraft was responsible. When planes break the sound barrier they give off what is known as an 'N-signature' – in effect, a boom-boom. The time lapse between the two explosions depends on the speed of the plane and the position of the witness in relation to the jet.[13]

RAF Finningley near Doncaster confirmed that military planes were in the Calder Valley area at the time, but they would not confirm responsibility. The *Hebden Bridge Times* reported that the RAF would launch a 'Boom probe',[14] but the conclusions, if any, were never announced. If a pilot had been responsible he would have incurred serious penalties as it is strictly forbidden to break the sound barrier over land, especially populated areas.

At the time low flying military jets were causing controversy in the Calder Valley. This is reflected in headlines from the *Hebden Bridge Times*:

SUPER SWOOPERS SHOULD NOT FLY OVER TOWN (25/09/81)
SUPER SWOOPERS HIT VALLEY (26/03/82)

There were fears that the jets on training missions were causing farm animals to stampede on the hill tops and there was widespread opposition to the training exercises. At the height of the cold war it was such a sensitive issue that there would have been every reason for the RAF or an embarrassed pilot to cover their tracks and deny everything.

However, a further contender for the cause of the Boom was to emerge. Astronomer Sir Patrick Moore suspected that the explosion was caused by a meteorite crashing through the atmosphere above the Calder Valley before coming to ground somewhere in Northern Ireland. I wrote to him and asked him about his investigations and he replied that in the end he had failed to uncover any evidence for the meteorite, and he feels 99% sure that, despite the denials of the RAF, the culprit was indeed a sonic boom caused by a low flying military jet.

It's worth noting that mystery booms occurred throughout southern England in 1976 and in some cases strange lights were seen in the sky around the same time.[15] These big bangs were reported widely and speculation again centred on aircraft, though this time a team from Bristol University put the blame on passenger jet Concorde. The planes, they said, were creating a sonic boom over the channel and certain temperature and atmospheric conditions meant the boom was heard at a much greater distance than usual.[16] This may certainly explain some of the strange booms of 1976, but the fact that some have been heard before the era of supersonic travel means there is still some mystery remaining. Certainly, the reports in the *Fortean Times* in 1976 and 1977 suggest the booms are associated with strange lights in the sky just as was the case in the Calder Valley in 1982.[17]

Sir Patrick Moore in 2009 (South Downs Planetarium)

Epilogue

In the summer of 2008 the skies over the Calder Valley were once again invaded by mysterious lights, seen by witnesses from Mytholmroyd to Todmorden. MYSTERY LIGHTS FUEL UFO SPECULATION was the headline in the *Hebden Bridge Times* of 21 August 2008. Unlike the very varied descriptions of the strange lights of 1982, these sightings were remarkably similar.

In Todmorden on 26 July, Gemma Kipping's guests had just left her house when they phoned her to say that 'aliens' were hovering above her roof. These 'aliens' were yellow glowing balls that moved slowly and silently through the night sky. Many others contacted local newspapers to say that they had seen similar objects. According to Chris Granger, an ex-RAF technician, the lights could not have been aircraft:

> They moved in a very erratic manner and did not display the flight characteristics of a conventional aircraft. Nor did they display the normal lighting array of a conventional aircraft – flashing white strobe and red and green navigation lights.[18]

Local press reports the 2008 UFO flap

The mystery seems to have been solved by two girls out walking their dogs. Amy Cheetham and Louise Neil found the spent remains of Chinese lanterns on their walk and suggested that these might have been behind the sightings.[19] This is certainly plausible: Chinese lanterns glow orange or yellow, appear as eerie lights in the sky and change direction unpredictably as they are buffeted by air currents.

In fact, the *Sun* newspaper told its readers of an 'alien invasion' several times in June 2008, many of the descriptions and photos being very similar to the ones described in the Calder Valley. It appears that the trend for letting off Chinese lanterns at wedding receptions and birthday parties triggered a nationwide UFO flap. The significance of these lanterns should not be underestimated: UFO authority Jenny Randles, who fielded reports of UFOs for Jodrell Bank Science Centre, gave the following breakdown. In 2007, 15% of UFO sightings she investigated were likely to have been Chinese lanterns. By 2008, this had risen to 50% of sightings. By November of 2009 it was a phenomenal 90% of UFO sightings that were suspected of being caused by lanterns.[20]

Snow Booth ~ The Farm That Dripped Blood

'I think it is the most brutal case of murder you are ever likely to hear. The story is at once sordid, tragic and pitiful.'

(Mr Morley, KC, 1933)

Snow Booth, a lonely farm above Hebden Bridge, was the isolated setting for a violent and gruesome murder that shocked the Calder Valley in 1933. The murder and the sensationalist press coverage sparked a national debate about the execution of women as well as generating a fanciful local myth about a headless piano player…

The Legend of Snow Booth

Snow Booth is a lonely farm house in Wadsworth overlooking the hills and valleys of Hebden Bridge. During the harsh winter and great freeze of 1947, the farm was completely snowbound for months. An old couple lived there, and to pass the long hours while snowed in, the husband spent his time playing on his piano. His wife, though, was going stir crazy, stuck in the dilapidated farm listening to her husband's incessant piano playing. One day she snapped. Picking up an axe, while her husband was playing his beloved piano, she came up behind him, swung the axe and sent his severed head tumbling over the keys. As the years passed, the children of the area would dare each other to walk past the farm after dark. And if they were brave enough to do so, they might hear the headless ghost of the piano player picking out a melancholy melody.[1]

The legend, though, bears little resemblance to the reality. The time period is wrong. The murder weapon was different, though the actual crime was even more grisly than the legend.

I Have Killed My Husband

Police Constable Constance Irving was patrolling his Hebden Bridge beat just after midnight on 30 June 1933. Where Station Road meets Burnley Road he came across a stumbling woman with dripping wet clothes. He shone his light at the bedraggled figure and asked: 'Now, what is the matter?' She replied: 'I have tried to commit suicide, but I couldn't. I have killed my husband.' PC Irving cautioned her and led her to Hebden Bridge police station. On the way, she added: 'I wish that I could undo all that I have done.'[2]

The woman's name was Elizabeth Agnes Rhodes, a 41-year-old Irish woman who lived with her husband at Snow Booth farm. As she sat in the police station, a pool of water from her sodden clothes gathered under her chair and a strong smell of smoke filled the room. She was obviously in a state of great distress. Sergeant Weatherhead was on duty at the station and he asked his wife to find Mrs Rhodes some dry clothes and bring her a cup of tea. She was again cautioned, but went on to tell Sergeant Weatherhead and PC Irving: 'I know he is dead, I killed him with a hammer. He was always on at me.'[3]

Mrs Rhodes was charged with murder. 'I didn't mean to kill him,' she told the police. 'My husband always threatened to take my life. He said he would drag me by the skull down the road.'[4] Although seemingly too distressed to make a written statement, she agreed to tell the police everything. Meanwhile, other officers took her key and headed up the hill to Snow Booth farm. They would face a very grim discovery indeed.

Snow Booth Farm in 1933 (Larissa Moskaleva)

The Scene of the Crime

The police arrived at Snow Booth farm and let themselves in with the key supplied by Mrs Rhodes. The first thing the officers noticed were two crimson patches of blood on the ceiling. As they mounted the stairs to the bedroom, the room was so full of smoke that they were unable to enter. Going back outside, they found a ladder, climbed up and opened one of the windows. As they peered in through the smoke, they could see flames on the bed so the fire brigade was called for. By around 3.30am the full horror of the room became evident.[5]

Inside the bedroom were two beds at right angles to each other. On one of these was the smouldering form of a man burnt beyond recognition. He was lying with his arms peacefully crossed over his chest in death. One of his feet was completely burnt away and one of his hands subsequently fell off when the body was later moved. He had a catastrophic head injury. His right cheek was fractured, as was his upper jaw and pieces of loose bone were visible. His lower jaw had been severed.[6] His right eye had ruptured. It was later found that his lungs were empty of smoke, confirming he had died before the fire. However, his stomach was full of blood indicating that he must have gulped it down immediately after his injury. Teeth and parts of the jaw were also found in his stomach.[7] This was what was left of Samuel Redmayne Rhodes, Elizabeth's husband.

Next to the bed with the ghastly remains was a heavily blood-stained sledgehammer. Blood had splashed onto the walls and the ceiling of the room. The second bed had brown stains and vomit on it. There was a tin of paraffin. The dressing table had a bloody razor and a glass containing a reddish-brown liquid which later turned out to be sheep dip. Later, a crime scene photo was taken by George Snidall, police sergeant of the photographic department of West Riding constabulary and Leeds surveyor George Calverley carefully made a plan of where the blood splashes were.[8] These were to play an important role in the subsequent trial. Meanwhile, back at the station, Elizabeth Agnes Rhodes had dictated her statement.

Then I Killed Him

Samuel Redmayne Rhodes was brought up in Samlesbury, near Preston in Lancashire with his twin brother George. In his youth he was a bell-ringer in the local church as well as being a member of the choir. During the Great War he was gassed in France and also received injury to his toe, meaning he couldn't walk far. He was invalided out of the army and moved to Dublin as part of the Royal Medical Corps where he met his future wife, Elizabeth.[9] The couple then joined Samuel's father George Rhodes at Egypt Farm, Colden, until George moved back to Preston and the couple took over Old Chamber before finally moving to Snow Booth above Hebden Bridge. The farm was a poor one. They had some poultry and cattle and Samuel made ends meet by also working as a weaver in CWS Works, Nutclough. The couple had a child that sadly died in its first year.[10]

Their marriage, it seems, was not a happy one and they quarrelled frequently. They often fought about money. Elizabeth wanted to know where all their money went and complained her husband could never earn enough for her. According to Samuel's father, George: 'She was the most impudent and could get into the worst temper of any man or woman I know… She had such a violent temper that she had often to remain in bed for two days.'[11] For her part, Elizabeth claimed her husband was violent and abusive. He had, she said, choked her on several occasions and neighbours testified that he had dragged her through the street by her hair, thrown stones at her, beat her and generally treated her 'like a dog'. Sometimes she had to escape the farm and take refuge from her husband on the moors.[12] Indeed, the situation had become so bad that Elizabeth had consulted a solicitor to complain about her cruel treatment, but it seems her Catholic beliefs prevented her from leaving her husband.[13]

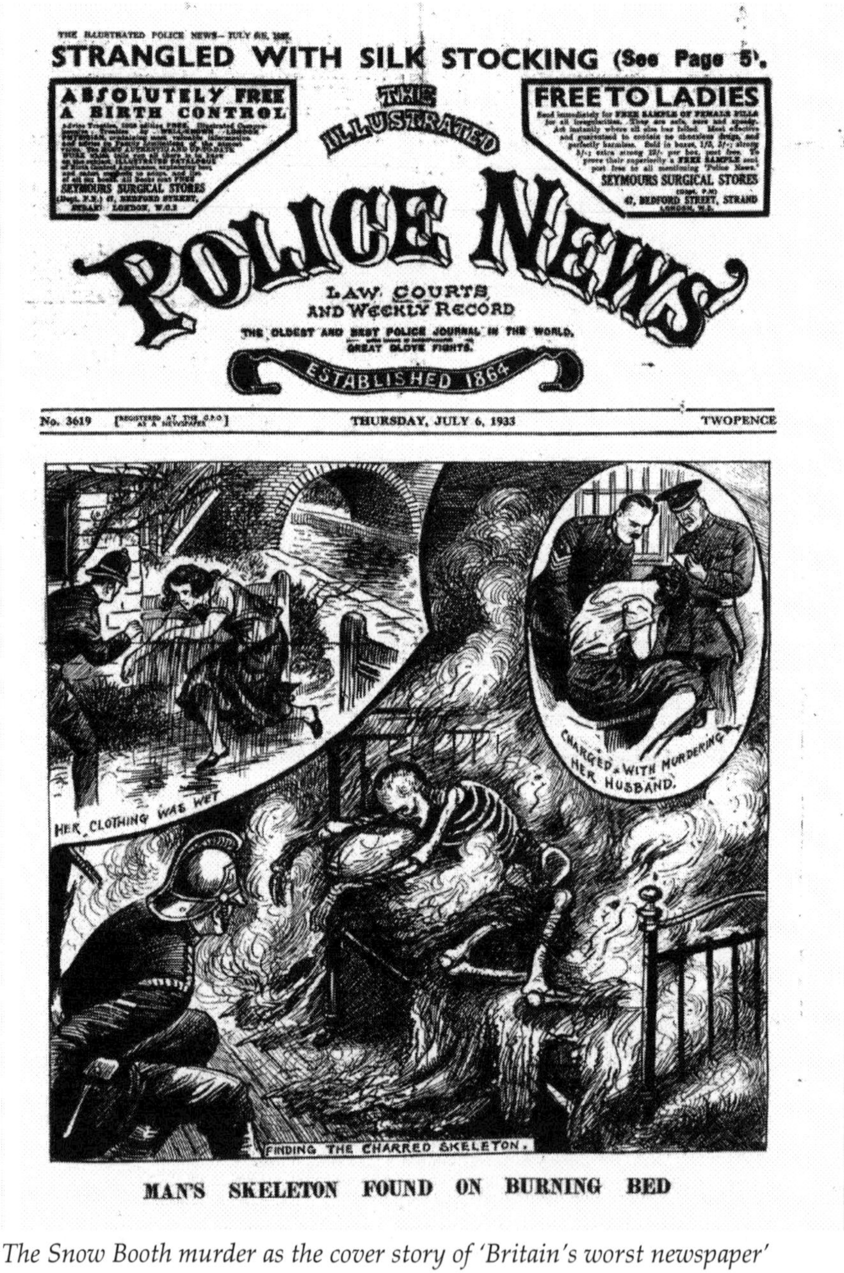

THE ILLUSTRATED POLICE NEWS—JULY 6th, 1933.

STRANGLED WITH SILK STOCKING (See Page 5).

ABSOLUTELY FREE
A BIRTH CONTROL
SEYMOURS SURGICAL STORES

THE ILLUSTRATED
POLICE NEWS
LAW COURTS,
AND WEEKLY RECORD
THE OLDEST AND BEST POLICE JOURNAL IN THE WORLD.
GREAT GLOVE FIGHTS.
ESTABLISHED 1864

FREE TO LADIES
SEYMOURS SURGICAL STORES
47, BEDFORD STREET, STRAND
LONDON, W.C.

No. 3619 [REGISTERED AT THE G.P.O. AS A NEWSPAPER] THURSDAY, JULY 6, 1933 TWOPENCE

MAN'S SKELETON FOUND ON BURNING BED

The Snow Booth murder as the cover story of 'Britain's worst newspaper' (6 July, 1933)

Despite the ill treatment, Elizabeth was a jealous woman and was furious that Samuel had 'introduced a woman' to the farm.[14] This led to conflict, as did any other associations Samuel had with other women. It's not clear if Samuel was unfaithful to her or not, but it led to Elizabeth refusing to sleep with him. The spare bedroom was too damp to sleep in, so Elizabeth dragged the extra bed into the main bedroom and used a large hammer to set the bed up. The hammer was left in the bedroom.[15]

On the last day of his life, Samuel Rhodes returned to Snow Booth after helping out at a nearby farm at around 7pm. He quarrelled with his wife and then deliberately turned off the wireless when she was listening to the Irish national anthem.[16] He threatened that he was going to 'finish her' and then he went to bed.[17] This is Elizabeth's statement made to the police:

> My husband came home about 7 o'clock on Saturday night, June 24th. We quarrelled about money. He was always on to me. He has beaten me and pulled the hair out of my head and kicked me. I waited till he was in bed, then I killed him, I did it with a hammer. I put some paraffin on the bed and tried to burn myself. I laid on the bed but the smoke got in my throat and nose. I know he is dead because he stopped making a noise. Last night I drank some disinfectant. It was sheep dip, like soft soap. I was sick all night. I tried to cut my throat with a razor. I stayed in the hay loft all day. I think I slept. I came down to Hebden Bridge tonight. I think it was about 11 o'clock. My throat was bad and burning. I walked down and jumped into the water, but I could not sink. I floated all the time. I turned over once and got

> my mouth full of water. I thought I was going to sink. I floated all the time. I could not kill myself. I must have nine lives like a cat.[18]

The murder was a sensation and no doubt shocked the residents of the Calder Valley. The case had numerous elements that were soon seized upon by the national press. There was the dramatic, windswept location, the brutality of the murder, the horror of the burning skeleton and the fact that the murderer had tried to kill herself by fire, suffocation, poison, razor and drowning and miraculously survived each attempt. It also featured in the national press, including 'the worst paper in Britain' *The Illustrated Police News,* which featured the murder as the cover story with a typically lurid illustration.[19]

Sordid, Tragic and Pitiful

The trial of Mrs Rhodes began in Leeds on the 24 July. Mr Morley KC delivered his opening address for the prosecution with the words: 'I think it is the most brutal case of murder you are ever likely to hear. The story is at once sordid, tragic and pitiful.'[20] Elizabeth appeared anxious and agitated and wept throughout.

The defence was handled by Mr Paley Scott, KC. His approach was to prove that Elizabeth had acted in self-defence. In order to do this, he first had to cast doubt on the statement given to Sergeant Weatherhead which contained the incriminating words: 'I waited till he was in bed, then I killed him'.[21] The implication is that Samuel was killed in cold blood and the crime was pre-meditated. First Scott outlined the abuse Elizabeth had suffered and several neighbours confirmed this. Then he turned to Elizabeth's incriminating statement. It was pointed out that it took 15 minutes for the statement to be dictated, though it only takes less than a couple of minutes to read out. Therefore, he argued, there must have been substantial pauses while Elizabeth dictated it, proving that she was in a distressed condition and not able to make a properly coherent statement. This was vital, because when Elizabeth took the stand, she added a new element to her story. She now testified that when she went to get into her bed, Samuel commanded her to join him in his. She refused. She then claimed Samuel said 'I'll get you' and went to get into her bed. 'I thought he was going to take my life,' she said. 'I swung the hammer up and struck him. He fell back on the bed with his head away from me. He moaned. I cried to him to come back. Then the moaning stopped. I knew he was dead.'[22] She then crossed her husband's arms over his chest as she had seen done to the deceased in Ireland. Asked why she had not mentioned this in her statement to the police, she answered that she was 'dazed'.[23]

Elizabeth Rhodes (Larisa Moskaleva)

In support of her claim of self-defence, Scott referred to the pools of blood on the bedroom floor that had dripped through to the room below. If she had killed her husband when he was asleep in bed as the prosecution claimed, then these pools of blood would not be in the position they were in. This demonstrated that Samuel was out of bed when Elizabeth struck him.[24] Mr Morley for the prosecution countered that even if her story were true, it was still murder. He also questioned the evidence of the blood stain. He argued that there was a full beam of wood between the bedroom and the room below, so the ceiling stains must have been something else as the blood could not soak through a thick beam of wood.[25]

The judge, Mr Justice Charles, summed up. The statement Elizabeth made to the police was an admission of murder and had been made under caution. There was no mention of self-defence. The judge emphasised the words 'I waited until he was in bed. Then I killed him.' Furthermore, he also pointed out that if Samuel had been getting out of bed and approaching her, his fatal wound would have been on the left cheek not the right. After 97 minutes, the jury returned a guilty verdict but with a strong recommendation of mercy. The judge agreed, and placing his black cap on his head, pronounced the death penalty though also said that a recommendation of mercy would be posted to the appropriate authorities. On hearing her sentence of death, Elizabeth cried out bitterly: 'Let me join my husband!'[26]

Crowds had gathered outside the Leeds court where the trial was held, so after the verdict 'extraordinary measures' were taken to avoid them. Elizabeth was taken to Strangeways prison, Manchester, by train in a special compartment with police guards and female wardens. Due to her distress, she was admitted to the prison hospital.[27]

A Monster Petition

The appeal against the death sentence took place on the 18 October 1933. Again, a frail and ill-looking Mrs Rhodes sobbed with her head bowed between two female wardens. Mr Scott for the defence argued that the judge had incorrectly directed the jury on twelve occasions and furthermore the judge had been wrong not to direct the jury to consider the position of the pool of blood. He further argued that Elizabeth had not mentioned self-defence in her original statement as she was sorry to be alive (as seen in her repeated suicide attempts) and was not thinking of defending herself.[28] The appeal was heard by Mr Justice Swift, Mr Justice Branson and Mr Justice Mackinnon. They ruled that the judge in the trial had properly directed the jury, the confession Elizabeth made to the police was the true version of events and therefore there was no need to interfere. The appeal was dismissed and the execution of Elizabeth Agnes Rhodes for the murder of Samuel Redmayne Rhodes was now due to take place in early September. A distraught Mrs Rhodes was again taken sobbing back to Strangeways to await her fate.[29]

Elizabeth spent the next few weeks in the prison hospital knitting, sewing and talking quietly with those around her. She spoke about her aged mother in Dublin who was unaware her daughter was a condemned murderess and instead believed she was still happy on her Yorkshire farm with her cattle and chickens. She begged her solicitors not to inform her mother about her situation as 'it might kill her'.[30]

However, there was a great deal of national disquiet about the sentence. The British public were beginning to get squeamish about the execution of women and it had been a decade since a woman was last hanged. In fact, only sixteen women were hanged in the twentieth century up until the abolition of the death penalty in 1964.[31] During this period, 90 per cent of women sentenced to death were reprieved, and yet here was Elizabeth cruelly awaiting her fate. As the editorial of the *Daily Herald* asked, 'Why this agony?'

The editorial continued: 'If it is not intended to carry out the sentence upon her, why in the name of humanity and common sense is she not reprieved and freed form the agony of anticipation?'[32]

This feeling was shared by many throughout the Calder Valley. The MP for Sowerby Bridge, Mr McCorquodale vowed to use his influence with the Home Office.[33] A petition was created by Mr Hirst, a Halifax solicitor, and signed by Bishop Frodisham, the vicar of Halifax. The 'monster petition', as the *Todmorden Advertiser* referred to it, was distributed in shops, clubs and churches and rooms were made available in Todmorden specifically for people to sign the petition. And sign it they did by the thousand.[34] The monster petition, however, would not be completed. Bishop Frodisham had sent a personal appeal to the Home Secretary and received a reply from the Permanent Under Secretary to the Home Secretary: 'I am directed by the Secretary of State to inform you that he has felt warranted, in all the circumstances, in advising his majesty to respite the capital sentence with a view to commutation to penal servitude for life.'[35] After several agonising weeks, the threat of the death sentence was finally lifted from Elizabeth's head.

Epilogue

In fact, Elizabeth Agnes Rhodes only served two years, one month and eight days of her sentence. She was released on 2 September 1935.[36] On release, she returned to her native Ireland.[37] And within forty years this shocking but dimly remembered murder would evolve in people's folk memory into a tale of insanity, decapitation and a headless pianist.

Merlinus Rusticus ~ Todmorden's Wizard Priest

'In the second year of his Reign, he saw in his dream a dreadful Image, whose head was of God [sic], the Breast and Arms of Silver, the Belly and Thighs of Brass, the legs of Iron, and the feet part Iron and part Clay. When awaked, he had forgot what he had dreamed; but with it he was mightily astonished, and calling together his Magicians, Astrologers and Soothsayers, he commanded them under pain of death, and the interpretation thereof; neither of which they were able to perform...'

(Book of Daniel, quoted in Merlinus Rusticus, 1685)

When Henry Krabtree became curate of Saint Mary's church in Todmorden in 1665, his reputation began to grow. Not just as a priest, but also as a healer, astrologer and some say as a necromancer. He produced a strange almanac under the pseudonym 'Merlinus Rusticus' that mixed geopolitical prophecy with a down to earth and very messy guide to monthly health. He also found the time to persecute Quakers and deal with the odd troublesome spirit, but his final challenge was a bizarre case of supposed demonic possession from Lancashire know as 'The Surey Demoniack'...

The Wizard Priest

Henry Krabtree was born in 1640 in Sowerby and grew up against a background of the English Civil War. He attended Heath Grammar School and studied at Christ Church, Cambridge, though he did not complete a degree. In 1665 he took over the curacy of Saint Mary's church in Todmorden, which at the time was a village of scattered houses and farms.[1] Nothing very weird in that, but it would soon become clear that Krabtree was no ordinary priest.

One indication of this is the fact that Krabtree was not above inserting various arch or sarcastic comments in the church register. The best-known (and longest) concerned the burial of John Bairstow in 1667, where Krabtree described Bairstow's life as a battle between Bacchus, the god of drunkenness, and Apollo, the god of healing: an odd approach for a Christian priest. After the death of Bairstow's wife and daughter, Krabtree wrote, the widower 'presently began to offer sacrifice unto Bacchus for joy'. This overindulgence in drink led to illness, but Bairstow was eventually treated and cured. Unfortunately, Krabtree tells us Bairstow then returned to his old profligate ways and began again to 'worship Bacchus ye god of drunnesse' and drank 'an Ocean of old ale':

> But Apollo seing his ingratitude, caused ye Sun with hot scorching beams to dry up all ye rivers, fountains, springs and streams of strong drinke, and then was all ye Liquor-ladys, Ale-nymphs and Beer Brats lamentably left upon dry ground… [Bairstow's] heart burst for very griefe, and he dyed in a rage for want of ale and came to Todmurden to be buryed – May 1.[2]

Of the death of Edmund Kershaw in 1669 he wrote he was buried 'with all men's consent'. Other register entries are critical of the deceaseds' godlessness or drunkenness, though Krabtree himself was no prohibitionist and he was perfectly happy to countenance strong drink if the stars were right, as we shall see presently.

To supplement the meagre income Krabtree earned from his religious duties, he resorted to treating the physical ailments of his flock, a practice that wasn't unusual at the time. The treatments on offer would no doubt include bleeding, application of leeches, prescription of laxatives and vomiting as well as various herbal remedies.[3] We might also suppose that Krabtree incorporated local superstitions into his medical armoury. These might have included treating flu by eating a spider and its web inserted in an apple. Warts may have been treated by allowing snails to crawl over the patient's hands before hanging the poor critters in the chimney. There were several local treatments for whooping cough reported around Krabtree's time. You could roast a mouse and then eat it. Or you could give a ferret a bowl of milk and then drink the leftovers. Hare's blood applied to the face was thought to get rid of freckles and if you had warts, you could rub them with stolen bacon.[4]

By the 1860s, Krabtree was branching out into astrology. This can be seen in the fact that in the church register he started to record birth dates rather than baptisms and added various astrological symbols to the records. It's certainly possible that he offered the parents of new born babies private consultations as an extra income stream.[5] There were rumours that as well as astrology, Krabtree also dabbled in the black arts.

By this time, he had married a wealthy widow and was living in Stansfield Hall, Todmorden. Servants reported hearing strange noises at all times of the day and night, and assumed it was Krabtree indulging in his occult practices.[6] On one occasion, the story goes, Krabtree was in his church delivering a sermon when an amateur necromancer broke into his study and tried to make use of the magic circles and occult books he found there. Not really knowing what he was doing, he raised a spirit which proceeded to wreak havoc in the room, causing this inept 'sorcerer's apprentice' to flee. Meanwhile at Saint Mary's church, Krabtree was interrupted mid sermon by a black mouse scuttling across the prayer book in front of him. Taking this as a sign, Krabtree pretended to be taken suddenly ill and dashed home to Stansfield Hall to see his study in chaos with his precious books scattered about and the whole room ransacked by the mischievous spirit. Immediately, Krabtree emptied a sack of salt over the floor and commanded the spirit to count the grains. With the spirit thus distracted, he was able to gain control of it and banish it back to whence it came.[7]

Another story (or perhaps a variant on the same tall tale) features the Boggart of Stansfield Hall. Normally, 'boggart' means a mischievous little imp, though it was also used for other supernatural phenomena such as poltergeists or ghosts.[8] The 'boggart' in this case was the ghost of a priest who had died around 50 years previously and had been seen in the vicinity of Stansfield Hall. One Thomas Sutcliffe, ill and unable to sleep one night, was walking in the Hall's gardens when he saw the spectre with its jet-black face and holy cassock flying past him. However, Krabtree used his magical knowledge to ensnare the spirit under a yew tree, though he kindly gave the ghost permission to leave its resting place to wander around and have a look at the moon in the neighbourhood until the water in the local river flowed backwards.[9]

~

Merlinus Rusticus

In 1685, Krabtree published his almanac: *Merlinus Rusticus* (the Country Merlin). To give it its full title:

Merlinus Rusticus 1685
Or, a Country
ALMANACK
YET
Treating of Courtly Matters, and the most Sublime Affairs now in Agitation Throughout the whole World

This strange and now rare little book comprises the astronomical and astrological information one would expect, as well as month by month health guidance followed by some geopolitical predictions based on Biblical prophecies.

Should you wish follow Krabtree's monthly astrological health plan, the details are reproduced below in his own words, with original spelling and punctuation. The guidance (which for some reason omits January) is based on Krabtree's magical, astrological and herbal studies, though it also involves quantities of various bodily fluids:

> February: If occasion be, you may Vomit, Purge, and Bleed. 'Tis exceeding good to take a little quantity of Honey and Roses, every morning, 3 hours before Dinner; it will comfort the Stomack and cleanse the whole Body.
>
> March: This Month fat Mutton's good, old Sack [fortified white wine] no less, Always provided you avoid excess.

April: Physick is now very profitable; Purge, Vomit, and let blood; but abstain from Wine and Strong drink, for it more defiles the Blood in this Month, then in any other.

May: Now every Garden and Hedge, affords thee Food and Physick. Rise early, walk in the Fields, by running streams of Water, and feast they Lungs with the fresh Air. Sage and sweet Butter is an excellent Break-fast, claryfied Whey, with Sage, Scurvy-grass Ale, and Wormwood-beer, are now very wholesome.

June: Beware of lying on the Ground this Month and of drinking too hastily, or much when you are hot. Let honest labour, and moderate exercise, procure your Sweat. To lie too much or long upon the lower Sheer, is very hurtful for the Body this Month. A sparing and a thin diet is best.

July: Beware of Purging, Vomiting, or Bleeding, whilst the influence of the Dogstar rule it. Though it pleased *Cardan* to say, *cants non mordet in Anglia*; yet if he spoke Absolutely and not Camparatively, I must needs say *Cardanus non amnia videt.* This Month eat no strong Meats, nor drink over much strong Dring, beware of violent Heats and sudden Colds.

August: Beware of Purging, Vomiting, and Blood-letting especially when the Air is hot, for then the Dogstar will, bite both by his Manifest and Occult quality --- To eat Sage is wholesome --- All Meats and

Herbs that are moderately cold of quality are wholesome. A glass of brisk Wine moderately taken is good.

September: This Month is good for Physick, Blood-*letting; now take Diet drinks several Morn*ings together, to prevent Diseases in Winter and to preserve your Bodies in health till the next Spring.

October: The time now requires that you consult with your Taylor as well as with your Physitian: Therefore a good Suit or warm Cloath, is worthy two Purges and one Vomit. Keep warm betime, for cold creeps upon Men insensibly, and Fogs oft beget a whole Winters distemper.

November: The best Physick this Month is warm Cloaths, good Diet, and strong Drink; the best exercise is Hunting, or Tracing Hares; but be sure that the Park or Lordship be your own, and then you need not fear an Indictment, nor a Fine at the next Sessions.

December: The best Physick this Month is good meat and the strongest Drink you can get, warm Cloaths and moderate exercise, Hunting or Tracing Hares.[10]

In the last section of *Merlinus Rusticus* Krabtree examines the Biblical visions experienced by Daniel and Nebuchadnezzar and applies them to the geopolitical events of his day. Based on these visions, Krabtree predicts that the Turkish Empire is past its peak and about to fall and that the Holy Roman Empire (actually a group of central and western European countries which developed in the middle ages and not to be confused with the Roman Empire) would last until the end of the world. His predictions were wrong. The Turkish Empire lasted into the 1920s, whereas the Holy Roman Empire came to an end in the Napoleonic Wars in 1806.[11]

However, Krabtree would require all his medical and perhaps magical expertise for the next great challenge he faced: the strange case of apparent demonic possession in Lancashire known as the 'Surey Demoniack'.

The Surey Demoniack

Richard Dugdale was a 19-year-old gardener living near Whalley, Lancashire. One night in the summer of 1688 he was drinking at the Whalley rushbearing festival when he saw a young woman he wanted to dance with, though he was not much of a dancer. He went as far as to say he would give himself to Satan if only he could be a great dancer.[12] And that's when his troubles began.

Soon after, Dugdale experienced a sudden burning in his side as if he was being stung by nettles or pricked with needles. He began to hear voices and see visions, one of which was a disembodied head, and he felt an irresistible inclination to dance. He started to have frequent and violent fits, and people suspected he was possessed by the Devil.[13] The Reverend Thomas Jolly collected many witness statements and published them in his 1697 pamphlet *The Surey Demoniack.* People claimed to have seen Dugdale float up out of his chair such that he had to be held down. He was said to have vomited stones and curtain rings, and to have spoken in a voice that was not his own, as well as in Greek and Latin, languages which he did not know. Others said Dugdale produced horrible noises like those made by a pig or a bear, or that he would describe in awful and graphic detail the torments awaiting in Hell. It was said that a lump as big as a cat or dog appeared on his leg and then migrated along his body to his chest. A knife suddenly appeared in his mouth lengthways. Witnesses also said that during his fits Dugdale would be as light as a feather and then become as heavy as a horse.[14]

Dugdale was taken to a barn known as the 'Surey'. There his father exhibited him in what must have been a grotesque Satanic freakshow, and many came to see Richard Dugdale, 'the Surey Demoniack' as he danced, leapt and performed his possessed repertoire before a drunken crowd of onlookers. This is how the Reverend Jolly described his dancing:

> [Dugdale's dancing] … excelled all that the Spectators had seen or heard of, or probably all that meer Mortals could perform; for he oft, for 6 or 7 times together, leapt up so, as that part of his Legs might be seen shaking and quavering above the Heads of the people; from which Heights he oft fell down on his Knees, which he long shiver'd and travers'd on the Ground, at least as nimbly as other Men can twinkle or sparkle their Fingers; then springing up into his high Leaps again and then falling on his Feet, which seemed to reach the Earth but with the gentlest, and scarce perceivable Touches, when he made his highest leaps.[15]

Sometimes a thousand would come to see the spectacle and to witness Reverend Jolly converse with the Devil himself through the medium of the Demoniack.[16]

Richard Dugdale, the Surey Demoniack, from a 1697 pamphlet

Thomas Jolly

In the spring of 1689 Richard Dugdale and his father Thomas travelled to Todmorden to seek the help of Henry Krabtree. They stayed for two weeks while Krabtree bled young Dugdale. The first time this happened, his blood was as black as ink and only drawn with great difficulty. At a later time, Krabtree gave Richard 'physick at once enough for six men'.[17] Krabtree was said to have been amazed at Dugdale's ability to predict the weather, something an almanac writer would certainly be interested in.[18] It's not known which, if any, other treatments Krabtree employed, though perhaps he followed some of the advice he gave in his almanac, and possibly administered herbs or even performed magical rites. Although Dugdale's fits abated while staying at Stansfield Hall under Krabtree's care, they returned more violent than ever when father and son returned home. Krabtree said he could cure Dugdale if they had the money to pay for more treatment, and at another time that if the lad was possessed by a water spirit, then there was no hope of cure.[19] But by that time the patient had had enough, and furthermore, the treatment was proving too costly. The Reverend Jolly's pamphlet claimed that Krabtree said 'there was no hope for him except from the Ministers'.

After Krabtree's unsuccessful treatment of him, the Surey Demoniack's fame continued to spread. But while Dugdale was capering, blaspheming and gibbering, Krabtree fell ill. He died on 13th July 1689.[20] However, the strange story of this curious character from Todmorden's past, his peculiar almanac and his odd supernatural adventures deserve to be more widely known.

Epilogue

On the day Krabtree died, Richard Dugdale the Surey Demoniack was visiting the Reverend Jolly and over the next year Jolly and several other prominent dissenting ministers attempted to exorcise him.[21] One year later, Dugdale's strange fits ceased. The reverend Jolly claimed to have successfully exorcised him, though doubters said Dugdale had also been treated by two different doctors.[22]

A war of pamphlets rolled on between 1697 and 1699. Reverend Jolly's pamphlet claimed the Demoniack was a genuine case of possession and argued that even Henry Krabtree, a Church of England curate, said that only these dissenting ministers could save him, which, they claim, they did.[23] A rival pamphlet written by the Reverend Zachery Taylor was shocked at the suggestion that Krabtree, a representative of the Church of England, would ever say such a thing.[24] Taylor pointed out that Dugdale's fits stopped while Krabtree was treating him and that he said he could affect a cure if there was 'money enough'.[25] It turned out that Jolly's witness statements concerning Dugdale's amazing feats while possessed were signed by illiterate witnesses who did not know what they were signing.

However, there is a certain irony in the way that the gullible dissenting ministers weaponised Krabtree's memory to boost their exorcism narrative. This is because Krabtree was not without his dark side and enthusiastically persecuted local dissenting Quakers during his time in Todmorden. In the Reverend Taylor's rather backhanded defence of Krabtree, he writes that he was:

> …no great Scholar, a blunt, but an honest Man, and served at a poor Place for about Twelve pounds a Year, which he augmented by venturing to give Physick to the Country People.[26]

But Krabtree was much more than that, and Taylor, shocked that some thought Krabtree a conjurer or wise man, would have been even more shocked had he discovered that Merlinus Rusticus was indeed a priest, healer, astrologer and magician.[27]

Haunted Streets ~
The 'Rippers' That Time Forgot

'Dear Old Boss, I shall be over soon. Thursday is a day alright. Redd stuff. I am ready for work. Now for it. Yours etc – Jack the Ripper.'

(Letter to a Todmorden Magistrate, 1888)

The Whitechapel Murders of 1888 attributed to Jack the Ripper cast a long shadow. In the years after the London murders there were rumours, letters and suspicions that Calderdale may have had its own 'Jack the Rippers'. There were reports of a mysterious 'Man Woman' haunting Greetland, a Phantom Dog Poisoner roaming Halifax, and even a gang of 'Rippers' who had set their evil sights on 'the fine plump girls of Todmorden'....

Dear Old Boss

In 1888, three weeks after Jack the Ripper had claimed his fourth victim, a Todmorden magistrate was surprised to receive the following letter scrawled in red ink:

> Dear Old Boss, I shall be over soon. Thursday is a day alright. Redd stuff. I am ready for work. Now for it. Yours etc – Jack the Ripper.[1]

The paper looked as if it were splattered in blood because of the red ink blots that made it hard to read. The letter would have had some resonance as the London Ripper murders were a media sensation, and moreover, just three weeks prior to the Todmorden letter, the Central News Agency in London had received the famous 'Dear Boss' letter signed by Jack the Ripper. It's widely thought that the London letter was a hoax perpetuated by journalists, though it was this letter that gave the Whitechapel murderer his infamous nickname.[2] Of course, Todmorden police suspected that the 'Dear Old Boss' letter was a hoax, too. This may be because the envelope was unstamped, having instead a crude attempt at a drawing of a stamp. And it had been posted in Todmorden.[3]

The following year in Halifax, Jack the Ripper actually (albeit indirectly) caused some actual harm. The victim was Police Constable Emmet who was on duty at Halifax train station. He noticed a lady struggling to get her gloves out from the boxes she was carrying, so he offered a hand. He noticed that the box, as well as the gloves, also contained a revolver. He asked the lady why she was carrying it and she replied that it was to protect herself from Jack the Ripper. Why she expected him to attack in Halifax, miles from his usual hunting grounds, is unclear. The officer took the gun out and, assuming it was unloaded, pulled the trigger and shot himself in the finger.[4]

Jack the Ripper's Catched at Last!

Two inebriated 'Jack the Rippers' turned up at different times in Cragg Vale but in remarkably similar circumstances, though unlike their Whitechapel counterpart, managed to embarrass the police without the bloodshed. In November 1892 a navvy working at Withins water works named John McLaughlin was walking through the village drunk and uttering 'utterly profane oaths'.[5] PC Morrison accosted him and sent him home, only to discover him some time later still drunkenly staggering around and swearing. McLaughlin was promptly arrested for being drunk and disorderly but was not a cooperative prisoner and kept throwing himself on the ground and refusing to move. Every time people walked past the arresting officer and his prisoner, he would embarrass the officer by shouting: 'Jack the Ripper's catched at last!'

A few months later in March 1893 another worker from Withins water works was also discovered drunk and disorderly in Cragg Vale on a Sunday afternoon. This time the arresting officer heard shouting and bad language coming from a field and upon investigating saw three girls running away from James Facey who was lying drunk in the middle of the road 'cursing, swearing and making use of disgusting language'.[6] The officer arrested the drunk man who refused to give his name and frogmarched him to the police station with the prisoner again shouting that he was Jack the Ripper at passers-by and detailing what he would do to them to the embarrassment of the hapless policeman.

~

The Greetland Man Woman

This odd little panic occurred in early 1892 in the neighbourhoods around Greetland. The Man Woman was a little man with a large white face and a peaked cap, and the young people of the village were terrified of him. He was seen to have stopped young girls on their way to and from work, though did not harm them in any way. In fact, it's not at all obvious what he did. The *Halifax Evening Courier* wrote that it's not clear if the Man Woman is a ghost, a robber, a joker or 'a Jack the Ripper'. It's also unknown why he was even called the Man Woman. Whatever he was, we are told that many young women were scared to leave the house for fear of meeting this nebulous creature.[7]

Interestingly, the *Courier* report of the Man Woman makes a brief reference to another panic that happened in Greetland sixty years prior, so presumably around the 1830s. Rumours spread that a flying 'Wild Woman' had appeared in the town and landed in a field below Moorbottom Road. The arrival of the flying Wild Woman coincided with children coming out of school so word got round fast and led to 'the liveliest excitement among youngsters'. The 'Wild Woman' turned out to be an ostrich that had escaped from a menagerie.

The Phantom Dog Poisoner

When prize pooches started mysteriously dying in Halifax at the end of the nineteenth century, many believed that a cruel fiend was deliberately and maliciously poisoning pets with a slow and subtle toxin. As more and more dogs fell victim to a 'Phantom Dog Poisoner', it became clear that something had to be done.

The suspicion that a Phantom Dog Poisoner was at work in Halifax began to grow in early January, 1899. Mr R.M. Stansfield of Exley House, Salterhebble, claimed that two of his valuable prize-winning chows had been 'intentionally poisoned' in a 'dastardly outrage', as the local press described it.[8] At first Stansfield thought his dogs were suffering from distemper, but a post mortem carried out by veterinary surgeon P.M. Walker found that a 'slow and subtle poison' had been ingested by the unfortunate animals. Mr Walker was to play a key role in spreading awareness of the phantom dog poisoner.

A few days later, a collie named Laddie, belonging to Mrs Broadhead of Milton Place, died after a 'brief and painful illness'. At the same place and around the same time, Heywood Kitty, a pedigree Irish Setter and sire of many prize-winners belonging to Thomas Wadsworth, died in similar circumstances.[9] Several other similar reports followed. With so many valuable pedigree dogs dying with similar symptoms at around the same time and all in the same region of Halifax, foul play was suspected. The *Halifax Courier* speculated that some disturbed individual was deliberately spreading poison around the locality, targeting expensive prize-winning dogs.[10] The *Courier* interviewed a nameless 'dog expert' who opined:

> Nay, it is altogether beyond me. I should not like to say poison has been administered to all the dogs you speak of, but it certainly is very, very curious… One of the cases you have named came under my observation, and in it there was a twitching of the body and legs suggestive of strychnine poisoning, but I cannot bring myself to believe that strychnine had been swallowed because the dogs lingered, some for days, and strychnine would assuredly kill them off in double quick time.[11]

Some wondered if carelessly discarded rat poison could have been ingested by the dogs, and perhaps this theory is more palatable than the alternative: a doggy serial killer.

At the end of the nineteenth century, 'dog-fancying' emerged as a hobby activity and 'the fancy' as it was termed led to an established circuit of prize dog shows. As middle-class dog lovers began to seek out exotic breeds, pedigrees soon began to be seen as an investment.[12] The Fancy was particularly popular in the textile towns of Lancashire and West Yorkshire, and Halifax was no exception. But if someone in Halifax was deliberately poisoning pedigree dogs, what could the motive be? 'And the question is therefore still shrouded in deep mystery' concluded the *Courier*.[13]

More poisonings were reported as January progressed. Several occurred in the Pellon Lane area, quite a distance from the first cluster of deaths. These were reported to the *Courier* in a letter from Mr E. Stead telling how his valuable collie had fallen victim, suffering from 'nausea, purging, alteration of the pupils of the eyes, paralysis of the limbs etc.' Fortunately, the collie recovered, though Stead's neighbour had three dogs die in suspicious circumstances. The letter continued:

> My opinion is that it is not by accident, but by design, and that there is some fanatical and ill-disposed individual with a mania for wholesale destruction in the canine world, roaming through the town.[14]

Mr Stead concludes by calling for a thorough and public investigation into the string of dog deaths. However, as yet, there were no leads in this strange case.

'The poisoning of Halifax dogs still continues,' reported the *Courier* on 21 January 1899, 'and the lovers of the canine tribe would dearly like to catch the miscreant at his deadly work.'[15] An unnamed gentleman of New Road took his pet fox terrier with him to the post office, but the dog ran off. Two hours later, it returned showing signs of 'being handled' and fell ill the next day. P.M. Walker, the vet who first alerted the town to the poisoning of dogs, examined the fox terrier and immediately announced that it had been poisoned. It died two days later. The dog of Mr C.T. Rhodes also fell ill and poisoning was assumed to be the cause, though this dog was strong and healthy and made a full recovery.

The *Courier* interviewed Walker about the poisonings. Walker pointed out that the symptoms displayed by the stricken dogs had been 'precisely' the same in all cases, and though he could not say which poison had been used, it was a very 'subtle' one. 'I have a theory,' he told the paper, 'but I cannot divulge it at present.' What that theory was, we never find out, but Walker did share some of his ideas. The *Courier* asked Walker the question on everybody's lips: 'What can be a man's object in poisoning dogs in this way?' Walker replied, 'What was Jack the Ripper's object? Simply a morbid craving to take life.'[16] It was, indeed, just over a decade since the Whitechapel murders attributed to the serial killer Jack the Ripper had taken place. With these senseless murders still fresh in people's minds, perhaps it's understandable that their thoughts would turn to a canine serial killer when faced with these strange deaths.

By the end of January, the situation in Halifax was such that the Royal Society for the Prevention of Cruelty to Animals became involved. The RSPCA's secretary Mr John Colan arranged for a large placard to be displayed prominently in the town centre. It read:

> Whereas it is alleged that persons in this neighbourhood have cruelly and maliciously

> poisoned sundry dogs, this is to give notice that the Act of Parliament relating to such criminal offences will be put into operation by the undersigned upon the production of evidence against the persons.[17]

The placard, though, did not result in any prosecution. But as dogs were also dying mysteriously in other parts of the country, the theory of a doggy serial killer began to lose traction.

Poisonings were also reported in Southsea where the belief that an 'anonymous scoundrel' laying poison down indiscriminately led to the suggestion of dog fanciers forming a band of vigilantes. Similar events occurred at Bristol, though in that city Mr A.J. Sewel, a vet and dog specialist, denied the deaths were related to poison.[18]

But if the deaths weren't the result of deliberate poisoning, what could be the cause? One possibility could be accidental poisoning resulting from careless disposal of pesticides. Another was an infection such as one that affected horses some years previously known as 'pink eye'. Some Halifax vets suggested canine flu was to blame, though others did not accept this. The wide area in which the deaths occurred suggested poison was not solely to blame, so an epidemic was certainly a possibility.

However, the belief in a Phantom Dog Poisoner persisted. A letter to the *Courier* signed by 'A Lover of Dogs' dated 4 February 1899 said that two of his dogs and two of his cats had been poisoned in the King Cross area. The vet, he claimed, examined the second dog and confirmed poison was found in the animal's liver. This must be the work, wrote the correspondent, of a 'fiend who is bent on the destruction of our canine pets.'[19] Could the fiend now be extending his repertoire to include cats, too? In any case, the letter writer urged all his neighbours to take care with their animals.

Three shepherd's dogs died of suspected poisonings near Widdop Reservoir in the hills above Hebden Bridge, though by this time the *Courier* was rowing back on the Poisoner theory and suggesting instead a 'mysterious disease'.[20] However, an unnamed lady's dog was reputedly poisoned with strychnine wrapped in silver paper and then inserted in a piece of liver.[21] In the summer, several dogs and cats were poisoned, supposedly with strychnine, in Fairfield, Hebden Bridge.[22] And then, thankfully, either the poisonings stopped or the local press stopped reporting them.

The idea of a person or persons deliberately poisoning dogs is not wholly implausible. The 'Dog Question' was much debated in the nineteenth century: what should be done about the various stray dogs roaming the streets and how should the spread of rabies be prevented? Compulsory muzzling of dogs was frequently tried by local authorities, but was considered cruel by animal charities and unpopular with voters.[23] It is certainly conceivable that one or more people might have decided to use easily available poisons to reduce the canine population and thereby solve the Dog Question. But if that were the case, surely the poisoner would target the mangy strays rather than pampered prize-winners. It is notable that at the start of the year, names and details were given about the owners whose dogs had died, but as concern about the poisoner spread, the local press began reporting rumours with no names and few other details, so there may be an element of hearsay involved in some of these stories. It also seems to me that Mr Walker's confident assertion that the first doggy victim was poisoned may well have led other owners to attribute their dogs' deaths from other causes or from accidental ingestion of toxic substances to a Phantom Dog Poisoner.

We will never know if these strange deaths of beloved pets were caused by mystery illnesses, accidental poisonings or a malicious fiend out to punish man's best friend, but it's also plausible that all three of these possibilities could be true at the same time. And cases of mysterious dog poisonings continue to be reported to this day. A doggy serial killer was believed to have been bumping off the contestants at Crufts in 2015.[24] Dogs were mysteriously dying around Holmfirth in 2019.[25] But at least the hounds of Halifax and surrounds have remained largely untouched.

The Fine Plump Girls of Todmorden

In 1908 the Ripper appeared again in Calderdale, this time in Todmorden, where he caused a great deal of alarm. REIGN OF TERROR AT TODMORDEN read the local headlines.[26] It began when the parents of a 16-year-old girl received a four-page letter from 'Jack the Ripper of Manchester'. The letter was described as having being written by someone who was 'more or less illiterate'.[27] The letter claimed that gangs, presumably led by the aforementioned Jack the Ripper of Manchester, had heard that Todmorden offered 'some fine plump girls' and that the Ripper's gang planned to kidnap them and worse. After they had finished with the plump girls, the letter went on, they would turn their attention to the town's schoolchildren and their teachers.

Around the same time the unnamed girl whose parents had received the threatening letter described an attempted abduction. She was, she said, coming home from visiting a neighbour at night when a strange man grabbed her violently, though fortunately she managed to get away. This all led to an atmosphere of considerable fear. Anxious parents waited outside school gates every evening to escort their children home. Children, it was reported, were too afraid to play outside and extra police had to be put on patrol to allay the fears. The local newspaper said, rather ominously, that 'strangers about the place will just now experience a warm time if any suspicious action is attributable to them.'[28]

The police suspected it was a hoax. After all, the Jack the Ripper of Manchester letter had been posted in Todmorden. One wonders if the girl who described the attempted abduction and whose parents received the letter was the guilty party. In any case, the panic soon passed. All the same it did foreshadow the much bigger Halifax Slasher scare of 1938, but thankfully didn't take off to the same extent. The fine plump girls of Todmorden could rest easy in their beds.

Robin Hood's Grave and The Kirklees Vampire

'Like a bat she hung there for what seemed like an eternity, her black nun's robe flapping eerily while her eyes flashed red and venomous and her teeth bared sharp and white between snarling blood red lips…'

(Barbara Green)

According to legend, folk hero Robin Hood was slain by his cousin the evil Prioress of Kirklees and her lover Red Roger of Doncaster. The outlaw's blood-drained body was buried in unconsecrated ground close to the priory's gatehouse, near Clifton. In medieval times Kirklees Priory was well known for the riotous exploits and easy virtue of its Cistercian nuns, and in more recent times Robin Hood's grave and its surrounds were said to be haunted by a variety of colourful ghosts. But in the 1980s, there were sensational stories splashed over the tabloids claiming that the wicked Prioress who had murdered Robin was now a vampire haunting the grave. Stake-wielding vampire hunters and psychic investigators also haunted the grave, and they were all caught up in the whirlwind of a ferocious occult feud that stretched back decades. Robin Hood, naughty nuns, blood, murder, ghosts, vampires and black magic: no wonder the tabloids loved it. This is the story of how Robin Hood's grave became the home to Britain's second most famous bloodsucker, The Kirklees Vampire…

The Death of Robin Hood

Deep in the forests of Yorkshire, Robin Hood, infamous outlaw and hero, is about to make the last journey of his life. He announces to his band of Merry Men that he is going to travel to Kirklees Priory, near Brighouse, where his cousin is Prioress. There he intends to be bled, a standard medieval medical treatment. Will Scarlet, however, warns Robin against this dangerous journey, especially as he wants to travel with only his trusty friend Little John as his bodyguard.

Robin takes no heed, and he and John set off through the forest. On the journey they come to some 'black water' with a plank laid over it, and kneeling there is an old woman. The old woman is 'banning' Robin, though it's not clear if this means she is cursing him or lamenting him.[1] Whatever it is, it can't be good, but we don't know why the old woman was 'banning' Robin as here the original manuscript telling the story is damaged. When the narrative resumes Robin assures us that the Prioress of Kirklees is his cousin and so he has no reason to fear anything.

Little does Robin know that his treacherous cousin and her lover, Red Roger of Doncaster, are plotting his demise, though why they want to murder him is unclear. The two travellers arrive at the Priory and soon the bleeding operation begins:

Shee laid the blood-irons to Robin Hoods vaine,
Alack, the more the pitye!
And pearct [pierced] the vaine, and let out the bloode
That full red was to see.
That full red was to see.
And first it bled, the thicke, thicke bloode,
And afterwards the thinne,
And well then wist [knew] good Robin Hoode
Treason there was within.[2]

Here the manuscript breaks off again leaving Robin bleeding to death. The story resumes with the weakened Robin in a desperate battle with Red Roger, who succeeds is thrusting his sword into Robin's side. Even so, Robin manages to deal Roger a mortal blow between his head and shoulders, 'a wound full wide'. The dying hero tells John of the treachery and forbids him from taking revenge on the Prioress or any other inhabitants of the Priory. Before he expires Robin has enough strength to ask his faithful friend to carry him to his grave:

And sett my bright sword at my head,
Mine arrows at my feete.
And lay my yew bow by my side,
My met-yard [measuring rod] wi...[3]

And again, the manuscript breaks off, leaving Robin's last words forever hanging.

However, near the gatehouse of the old priory, almost hidden in dense vegetation, lies an old tomb surrounded by iron railings. The epitaph reads:

HERE UNDERNEAD THIS LAITL STEAN
LAIZ ROBERT EARL OF HUNTINGTON
NEA ARCIR VER AS HEI SA GEUD
AN PIPL KAULD IM ROBIN HEUD
SICK UTLAWZ AS HI AN IZ MEN
WILL ENGLAND NIVR SI AGEN

In modern English:

Here underneath this little stone
Lies Robert Earl of Huntington
No archer was as him so good
And people called him Robin Hood
Such outlaws as he and his men
Will England never see again

Could England's best-known legendary hero really be buried in a crumbling grave on unconsecrated ground by the ruins of an ancient priory's gatehouse in West Yorkshire?

Kirklees Priory gatehouse where Robin Hood is said to have been murdered.

Robin of Yorkshire?

The earliest reference to Robin Hood is generally accepted to be in William Langland's poem *Piers Plowman* which mentions rhymes about the outlaw.[4] This suggests that these ballads were widely known in the early fifteenth century. Indeed, the account of Robin's death and the quotations in the previous section were taken from the fifteenth century poem *A Geste of Robyn Hode* and the later *Robin Hode His Death.* But was the Robin Hood of these ballad poems based on a real historical character?

The evidence is tantalizing, sparse and inconclusive. There are a number of candidates for the 'real' Robin with the right name and in roughly the right place at roughly the right time, including a few from Wakefield and even some from Sowerby, near Halifax.[5]

The problem is that the earliest Robin Hood stories seem to have been contaminated by other legendary outlaw heroes such as Eustace the Monk and Fulk Fitz Warin.[6]

The issue is further complicated by the fact that Robin Hood was quite a common name and became a frequently used criminal alias. This means that if any of the stories are based on fact, they might well be about a number of different outlaws using the same name.[7] Although there are many conflicting theories about the identity of the 'real' Robin, one point is clear: the ballads are often set in Yorkshire rather than Nottinghamshire. This suggests that there is a strong argument that the original Robin Hood, whether man or myth, was quite probably a Yorkshire man.

Robin Hood's Grave (Photograph: Anon)

Robin Hood's Grave

According to legend our hero was murdered and buried in the grounds of Kirklees Priory. In some versions of the story the dying Robin fires one last arrow from the window of the Priory gatehouse and asks Little John to bury him where the arrow falls.[8] Historian Richard Rutherford-Moore staged a reconstruction of this final arrow shot using a replica of the type of bow and arrow that would have been in use at the time. The grave lies some 600 yards uphill from the gatehouse, and Rutherford-Moore's experiment suggests that to be an impossible distance for a healthy archer, never mind one who has just been fatally wounded.[9] This may be so, but if we see the legendary Robin as a kind of proto-superhero with superhuman abilities, then this final feat is what we might expect. But how much is really known about Robin Hood's grave, and who or what lies beneath it?

The Grave's inscription (Photograph: Anon)

A number of antiquarians refer to the grave slab. Most famously Nathanial Johnston (a doctor and historian from Pontefract) made a sketch of it in 1665. The drawing shows the grave slab with a large cross and around the edges is the inscription: 'Here lie Roberd Hude, William Goldburgh, Thomas'[10]. The two latter names do not appear in Robin's legend and it is anyone's guess who they were, though one could speculate that William Goldburgh could refer to Will Scarlett. The inscription itself was no longer legible by the 18th century, and furthermore, the published version of Johnston's sketch may well be a copy of a copy of the original picture leaving us in some doubt as to how reliable the drawing is.[11]

The sketch of Robin's grave attributed to Nathanial Johnston

In the 18th century the slab was surrounded by iron railings and the epitaph quoted in the previous section was added. This epitaph was based on one that Thomas Gale, Dean of York from 1697 to 1702, claimed to have a record of. Unfortunately, the epitaph is spurious, not least because it puts Robin's death on 24 kalends of December 1247, a date that does not exist in the Roman calendar. The fake antiquity of the language also arouses suspicion. Moreover, the Robin Hood of the earliest ballads was a yeoman, not the earl of the epitaph. Towards the end of the sixteenth century, however, the character of Robin Hood was elevated to nobility. This process was helped by two plays written by Anthony Munday in 1598 where Robin is portrayed as Robert Earl of Huntington. Robert Earl of Huntington, though, is widely regarded as a work of fiction; if Robin Hood existed as a single historical figure, the evidence points to him being a yeoman.[12]

The Passing of Robin Hood by N. C. Wyeth, 1917

In the early 18th century Sir Samuel Armytage, the owner of the estate, was said to have excavated the site of the grave. He found that the earth had not been disturbed. As Kai Roberts points out in his history of the Kirklees site *Grave Concerns,* it's not clear how extensive or careful this excavation was, and there may also be doubts as to the sobriety of the excavators.[13]

In the nineteenth century labourers building the Yorkshire-Lancashire railway would chip chunks off the grave. If a fragment was placed under one's pillow, they believed, it would cure toothache.[14] In the 20th century, however, the grave would attract very different pilgrims. Before we meet them, though, it's worth looking at what records tell us about Kirklees Priory itself, the nuns who inhabited it and Robin Hood's murderer, the evil Prioress.

Drawing of Robin Hood's Grave (Batley Reporter 26 July 1901)

The Wicked Prioress and Naughty Kirklees Nuns

Kirklees Priory was founded in the twelfth century under the reign of Henry II and was occupied by Cistercian nuns for over 400 years before finally being dissolved by Henry VIII in 1539. The Priory was demolished some decades later and some of the original stones from the Priory were used to build Kirklees Hall nearby.[15]

Although the Cistercian Order was renowned for being strict, the nuns of Kirklees had an altogether different reputation. Many of the women and girls were the unwanted daughters of the rich, and so must have felt little calling for the austere life on offer in a priory. Indeed, the nuns were admonished (or pardoned) for all kinds of rebelliousness including meeting men in private, altering their habits and apostacy.[16]

As for the wicked Prioress who is said to have murdered Robin Hood, no one knows for sure who she was. It's been assumed that the Prioress in question was Elizabeth de Staynton, who attained that position in the mid-fourteenth century and whose grave still exists on the Kirklees estate.[17] However, as Kai Roberts notes, the only flimsy evidence to support this identification is the presence of her grave on the estate.[18]

Haunted Kirklees

Although one might expect Kirklees to have a long history of hauntings, the ghosts are rather conspicuous by their absence, at least until the twentieth century. However, as that century progressed, spooky stories began to proliferate, and by the 1980s and 1990s the supernatural took a turn for the weird. Perhaps surprisingly, though, the earliest spooky experiences were rather light-hearted.

Take the recollections of Edith Ellis, told to Barbara Green of the Yorkshire Robin Hood Society in the late 1980s. Edith's cousin Alice lived near the church in Hartshead in the early twentieth century and told Edith that while tending to her window box she heard the ghost of Robin calling for Maid Marian. Edith continued:

> I once stayed for the weekend and I looked out of the window. It was a clear moonlit night. Suddenly, over by Kirklees Hall, a light flashed in the fields. Next day Alice and I walked over and we found an arrow embedded in the wall.[19]

Another early ghostly experience from the grave was told to me by Steven Hill, and concerns his father John Hill. Steven suspects it's one of his 'one too many' stories, but his father swore that it was true. In late 1924 John Hill was working as a tenant farmer on the Kirklees estate and actually living in the gatehouse where Robin Hood is supposed to have met his death. Steve wrote:

> John my father had been to the Three Nuns Inn and he decided to walk home. It was half an hour's walk from the Nuns. He walked through the woods a little worse from drink and on approaching the gatehouse from the woods he was knocked to the ground by something falling out of the tree. When he regained his sensibility, he saw a figure in the gatehouse window: a man with a bow. He ran to the kitchen door of the farm and got his mother to go to the gatehouse with him and when they entered the room there was no one there. Even when he was in his seventies he always said it was Robin Hood's ghost.[20]

In her book *The Mystery of Robin Hood's Grave* Barbara Green quotes another experience of the same hapless farmer. This time he was sitting on Robin Hood's grave shooting rabbits when he felt a tap on his shoulder. This caused his gun to go off accidentally knocking two of his front teeth out on its recoil.[21] We are not informed of his sobriety or lack of it, but he was sure that nobody was around at the time. However, the romantic and mischievous spirits encountered in these early accounts are very different in tone to the darker reports that followed in the second half of the twentieth century.

Guitarist Roger Williams also claimed that he had ghostly encounters at Kirklees. The first was in 1963 when, walking through the forest after visiting the grave with an anonymous companion, he saw what he first thought was a gamekeeper, but later realized was the form of a woman:

> ...she seemed to kind of glide towards us and there wasn't any noise of feet walking over the dry fallen leaves, twigs and dry bracken on the ground. As she came to within five yards of us we saw her very clearly. Her eyes seemed very dark and she looked mad, annoyed at us. Then she moved on past us; didn't look back, then she was gone.

What is unusual about this account is that it happened in broad daylight on a sunny afternoon.

The second of Roger's encounters was in 1972 with his bass guitarist Phil Marsden. They were returning from the grave on a Saturday afternoon when they saw what Williams said was the same woman with the same mad staring eyes. In Roger's own words:

> I'll never ever forget the experience. She wore a long off-white dress kind of squarish round the neck with long sleeves. The dress had some sort of pattern to it. But again it was her eyes I remember most: dark, mad, set in her pale face. She looked at me and then at Phil so close I could have touched the hem of her dress as I was still crouched down messing with my shoelace. Then she moved on right past us and she was gone. Well, I thought Phil was gonna drop right there, cos he'd gone really white. We got out of the wood very fast.

The encounters were followed, according to the musician, by poltergeist activity in his home.[22] It should be noted that Williams' accounts were written several decades after they occurred.

In 1995 Judith Broadbent, a journalist for the *Dewsbury Reporter*, and photographer Sue Ellis visited the grave while researching an article for *Yorkshire Life* magazine. Judith claimed that she heard heavy footsteps and felt herself being pulled to the ground. She shouted 'Get away!' and the tugging stopped. Sue's camera jammed and a week later she found herself paralysed for two weeks.[23]

Ghosts, though, are not the only supernatural entity said to infest the grave and its surroundings. It has been said that the evil Prioress who drained Robin Hood of his life blood is now the infamous Kirklees Vampire...

The Kirklees Vampire

It's not easy to get to the bottom of the Kirklees Vampire story. The accounts have changed over time. Several of the people involved are rather fractious, forming alliances followed by tempestuous fall outs, insults and recriminations. It's certain that Robin Hood's Grave sucked fissiparous eccentrics into a maelstrom where they swirled round bouncing off each other while dragging a host of other people into the vortex.

Three figures are central to the story. The first is Barbara Green of Brighouse, founder of the Yorkshire Robin Hood Society, a group that campaigned to protect the Kirklees grave and raise awareness of Robin's Yorkshire connections. Barbara was instrumental in collecting and recording the ghostly accounts described above. Another central figure is Bishop Sean Manchester, Britain's foremost vampirologist. Manchester (ordained as a Bishop of the Old Catholic Church) claims to have destroyed two vampires by staking them through the heart. First there was the infamous Highgate Vampire of Highgate Cemetery, London and secondly his former partner Lusia who was unfortunate enough to have been infected by the undead and proceeded to turn into a giant spider.[24] Barbara Green met Manchester (then calling himself 'Lord' Manchester) at a carnival in Barnet in the late 1980s and asked him to become the patron of the Yorkshire Robin Hood Society, which he did. The third figure was occultist and rival vampire hunter, David Farrant. Farrant had been caught in Highgate Cemetery, London, in possession of a crucifix and a wooden stake on more than one occasion while hunting the Highgate Vampire, even finding time to take some naked photos of his girlfriend among the vaults. This was at a time when there was concern over Highgate graves being vandalised and corpses being removed and defiled. Bizarrely, 60s pop star Long John Baldry accused Farrant of ritually sacrificing his cat in the cemetery. Farrant retaliated by sending Baldry some miniature coffins which freaked the singer out so much that he asked his friend and fellow 60s musician Graham Bond to perform a ritual to protect him, which he did. Bond was killed by a tube train in mysterious circumstances the following year, with Long John Baldry believing Farrant's curse contributed to his death.[25] In 1974, Farrant was given a surprisingly harsh four-year prison sentence for damaging memorials in the cemetery.[26] David Farrant's and Bishop Manchester's rival accounts of the Highgate Vampire escalated into a vindictive feud which would spill out into Calderdale and consume the Yorkshire Robin Hood Society.

It seems the Kirklees Vampire was born from correspondence between Barbara Green and Bishop Manchester. Barbara had read of the Bishop's Van Helsing-style exploits in Highgate Cemetery, and it occurred to her that there may be a vampire connection with Robin's demise. After all, the Prioress had drained Robin of his blood, and that is what vampires do.[27] And if Robin Hood's Grave was indeed infested with the vampiric presence of an evil prioress, then what is required is the assistance of Bishop Sean Manchester, Britain's leading Vampire Slayer. Manchester fired off a letter to Lady Armytage, the estate owner, asking for permission to 'examine the contents' of the grave and also to hold vigil beside it for several nights.[28] On receiving this request from Manchester's organisation (which was called 'The International Society for the Advancement of Irrefutable Vampiriological and Lycanthropic Research'), she tersely declined to consider it.

The next step the vampire hunters took was to send copies of the request and Lady Armytage's reply to the press. Predictably, the media had a field day. Who could resist a story that included Robin Hood, naughty nuns, murder, blood, vampires and vampire hunters? The story hit the tabloids and local press around the country and beyond. A typical headline ran:

> DID A VAMPIRE KILL ROBIN HOOD? BAT MEN WANT TO DIG UP ROBIN HOOD[29]

With the sensational story all over the news, it was clear that Lady Armytage would not change her mind about allowing Robin to be exhumed (if indeed he's there at all) or any vampirological investigation of the grave. If our vampire hunters were to investigate the grave, they would have to do it illicitly.

However, before we look at what happened during Manchester's nocturnal jaunt, we should take his advice on how to protect ourselves from vampires and the best ways of slaying them, taken from his book *The Vampire Hunter's Handbook*.

Vampires have many, if not all, of the properties ascribed to them in any Hammer Horror film. They don't like crosses, crucifixes, garlic or holy water. They sleep in their coffins by day and rise at night to gorge themselves on blood before returning to their graves before sun up. The victims of the undead will eventually die, perhaps in turn becoming vampires.[30]

There are a number of ways to exterminate a vampire. According to the Bishop, the best method to destroy the undead is to incinerate the body. However, if any cockroaches, snakes or other loathsome creatures try to escape from the flames be sure to force them back into the fire; they may be the vampire trying to escape.

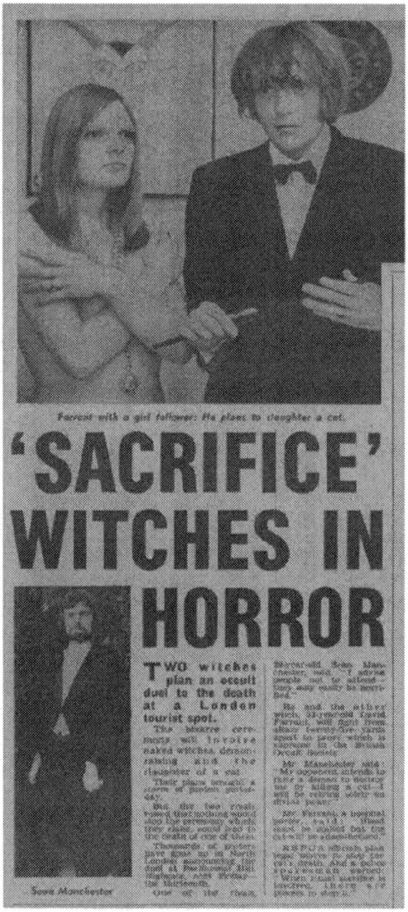

Farrant with a girl follower: He plans to slaughter a cat.

'SACRIFICE' WITCHES IN HORROR

TWO witches plan an occult duel to the death at a London tourist spot.

Cutting from Sunday Mirror 8 April 1973 with Farrant (above) and Manchester (below)

If cremation is impractical, the next best remedy is a wooden stake driven through the vampire's heart in one sure blow. Be aware that blood is likely to spurt and gush; to avoid contamination you need to have some holy water ready to wash off any splashes. Once the stake is in place, while the vampire is screaming in agony, his or her head must be hacked off, preferably with a gravedigger's spade, and the mouth stuffed with garlic. The vampire may be hundreds of years old, and after death his or her body will return to its true age at once so the corpse will blacken and crumble, just like in the films.

Armed with this information we are ready to join Bishop Manchester and his fellow researchers on a vampire hunt. They visited the grave on 22 April 1990 and experienced at first hand the tangle of brambles that have to be fought through to get to the site.[31] This is how the Bishop describes the scene: 'The place was infused with a lingering atmosphere of malevolence that had seemingly set into action powerful forces that were not leaving the dead in their tombs undisturbed.'

They found occult symbols scrawled on the gatehouse where Robin Hood is said to have died. They found a dismembered goat drained of its blood and blown with black flies. Also, around the grave were little finger-sized holes, where, they believe a vampire could enter and leave his resting place.

Armed with crucifixes, holy water, stakes and other accoutrements, they hid and waited. Again, the Bishop takes up the story:

> Eyeless sockets of impenetrable darkness watched the watchers as bats squeaked overhead. Almost three hours passed. Then we heard it. Wafting faintly on the night air came a discordant sound. Could it have been the wind howling in the trees? It grew louder still - and closer! A dreadful wailing noise. It was approaching…[32]

Manchester stepped bravely out from behind the tree where he was hiding, crucifix aloft, intoning: 'Behold the Light!' He was confronted by one of his own terrified researchers: he said he had seen a 'darkly clad woman' that was at first serene but then had suddenly transformed into a horrible red-eyed wraith.[33]

The team placed holy water in the holes around Robin Hood's Grave and planted some garlic. The vampire, if it exists, may be restrained by these measures, but only temporarily.

There has been some doubt cast on Manchester's account. For one thing, finding the grave in the dark of night is not easy. It's hidden in woodland and surrounded by brambles, nettles and thick undergrowth. Even Barbara Green with her local knowledge and experience of clandestine grave visits could find herself lost in the scary wood. It would be much harder for novices. Furthermore, as Kai Roberts notes, Manchester also claimed to have visited the grave of the Prioress Elizabeth de Staynton, which is not hidden away in woods but in the back garden of Lady Armytage.[34] There is also the strange coincidence that after Manchester's visit, Barbara Green had her own rather spectacular experience on an illicit nocturnal visit to the grave.

One frosty winter night in 1992 Green and three young men decided to pay a visit to the grave.[35] Two of her friends, Damian and 'Spaceman' were intoxicated with sherry and marijuana, whilst the third companion, an unemployed nuclear physics graduate called Mervyn, was seeing 'molecules dancing' under the influence of lighter fluid. Barbara herself had not taken anything but also felt high with the exhilaration at the thought that this merry band was cocking a snook at the aristocracy by trespassing on their land under cover of darkness, something that Robin himself might have approved of. They scaled the wall on Wakefield Road then climbed through the woods until they eventually came across the grave. Barbara had brought a curtain with her, and told Mervyn to climb through the railings, drape the curtain over his head and make like a ghost while she took some photos. Mervyn obliged and photographic evidence for a ghost at Robin Hood's Grave was obtained. Unfortunately, the photos were too dark to be identified as of the grave and the befuddled 'ghost' was clutching a tin of extra strong lager.

After this larking around, Damian, Spaceman and Mervyn went to smoke and Barbara was left alone at the grave on which she placed some palm crosses. Suddenly she was consumed with panic. Her hair stood on end and she was rooted to the spot fearing she was about to die. In Barbara's own words from *Secrets of the Grave*:

> ...from the surrounding trees I saw, and felt, streams of evil pouring forth and washing over me. I felt, in that instant, that I was going to die on the spot. Then, even more terrifying, I saw, materialising before me, a person I knew well. Hideous, sneering and hateful, surrounded by tongues of flaming red hair, I was looking into the freezing grey eyes of my ex-lover, yet as I recognised that foul and malevolent visage, I was at the same time aware that I was seeing the spectre of the wicked prioress' paramour, Red Roger of Doncaster.[36]

Her companions laughed off Barbara's story when they returned, and Barbara herself recovered enough from the shock of her experience for a few more larks on the estate before battling their way back through the woods.

Barbara certainly tells an exciting story of how a terrifying visage of a cruel ex-boyfriend morphed into Red Roger of Doncaster, the lover and accomplice of the murderous Prioress. However, Green herself wonders if the experience may have been a result of coming off prescription drugs prescribed by a psychiatrist after being on sick leave from her work as a district nurse.[37] It's also clear that different versions of this story have appeared. In an earlier version of Barbara's experience (published in *International Vampire*) she describes seeing both Red Roger and a vampiric vision of the evil Prioress herself in this oft-quoted passage:

> Like a bat she hung there for what seemed like an eternity, her black nun's robe flapping eerily while

> her eyes flashed red and venomous and her teeth bared sharp and white between snarling blood red lips.[38]

It's obvious how this description would play a part in establishing the legend of a vampire haunting Robin Hood's Grave. However, Green now maintains the beautifully lurid description of the Prioress was actually a semi-fictionalised account of her experiences. When I asked her about this she told me that she had seen the vision of Red Roger, but also saw a black shape that she thought could have been the Prioress.[39] It's fair to say this account, like many others associated with this spooky site, is rather fluid.

Return to the Grave

In the late 1990s, Barbara Green was introduced to Bishop Manchester's nemesis and Highgate Vampire rival, David Farrant.[40] Green and Farrant corresponded about the supernatural aspects of Robin Hood's Grave for some time, but when Manchester heard about this it led to a long-standing rift between Green and Manchester, such was the Bishop's vitriolic hatred of Farrant. Indeed, when researching the previous edition of this book, Manchester (or at least someone from his organisation, The Vampire Research Society) was happy to send me unsolicited newspaper articles about Farrant's 1970s antics and his criminal record.[41] Manchester withdrew his patronage from the Yorkshire Robin Hood Society, and in what must have seemed to him an act of extreme provocation, Green offered the post to Farrant. Farrant and the secretary of the YRHS Catherine Fearnley became lovers, and the focus of the society moved away from vampires. This may have been the end of the Kirklees Vampire, but it was by no means the end of the intrigue surrounding the grave, in this strange supernatural soap opera.

I interviewed Farrant in 2004 and asked him about his thoughts on the Kirklees 'mystery'. He dismissed the idea of a vampire roaming the Kirklees estate and said that genuine paranormal phenomena had been effectively hijacked by Bishop Manchester and given a vampiric spin. Farrant also doubted that Manchester had ever visited the grave and had simply made up his adventure at the graveside.[42] Bishop Manchester, for his part, claims that Barbara Green is unbalanced and he also curates a number of blogs and message boards reminding the world in great detail of Farrant's ghoulish misdeeds in Highgate Cemetery.[43] Manchester is keen to make clear that he never said the Kirklees phenomenon was definitely vampiric in nature, though he claims to have evidence from over forty witnesses that is at least consistent with this theory.[44] However, as Kai Roberts noted in his definitive history of Robin's grave, Manchester supposedly armed himself with vampire repellents like garlic and holy water when visiting the site, and wrote about it in a chapter called 'The Kirklees Vampire' in a book called *The Vampire Hunter's Handbook*![45]

Nonetheless, in April 2005 the grave would receive another clandestine visit. This time the intrepid band of trespassers consisted of David Farrant, Christine Fearnley and Barbara Green. Also along for the trip was Gareth J. Medway, an occultist who was to perform a ritual at the graveside to dispel the powers of evil. Furthermore, they were accompanied by a two-man film crew from an independent production company called Red Monkey Films who wanted to make a documentary about the site, including the paranormal investigation and blessing that the band were to perform.[46]

As they reached the grave, Farrant noted that it was unusually quiet; there was no birdsong except for the alarm call of a solitary blackbird. Farrant also measured a coldness surrounding the grave and noted that the compass seemed to misbehave in the vicinity. Medway performed a two-hour ceremonial blessing which included the invocation of Greek deities: Athena was called on to disperse the evil, Hecate was called on to guide any lingering spirits of the dead to the next world and Themis was asked to bring harmony to the site. Medway conducted the ceremony with a wand crafted in the Himalayas and specially flown over to Yorkshire for the purpose of this ritual.[47] Unfortunately, though, the formerly ubiquitous ghosts and vampires were camera shy and did not make an appearance for the film crew.

Catherine Fearnley believed that the blessing had been a success. She told the *Huddersfield Examiner* of May 2 2005 that the ritual 'was completely successful in that the powers of darkness at the grave have now been fully dispersed.'[48] The evidence for the success of the ritual in ridding the grave of its evil presence (if indeed it ever had one) seems to be the psychic sensibilities of some of the participants. How reliable these are we are unable to tell, but Bishop Manchester is completely unconvinced. Farrant and co are called amateur occultists and publicity seekers in the emails sent out by Manchester's Vampire Research Foundation.

Are the reputed hauntings and vampire infestation the effects of a gloomy atmosphere surrounding a place rich in folkloric history on the overactive imaginations of impressionable people jumping at their own shadows, or is there something more sinister at play? Whatever your opinion, the place, is undeniably spooky and it takes a brave soul indeed to fight through razor sharp thorns and clutching trees after the sun has gone down…

Epilogue

Many of the characters involved with the escapades at Robin Hood's Grave have filled the internet with unedifying insults and counter insults. There were acrimonious fall-outs, brief reconciliations and more fall-outs too complex to go into here. The claims and counter claims continue. David Farrant died aged 73 in April 2019. He was the first person in English legal history to be prosecuted for activities related to vampire hunting.[49] Farrant's long-term nemesis, Bishop Manchester penned a thoughtful, if somewhat tart obituary, keeping it brief, he said, to avoid speaking ill of the dead.[50] The Bishop himself has a large internet presence and still vigorously defends his own account of events in Highgate Cemetery.

Barbara Green is no longer active in relation to Robin Hood's Grave, though she is still surprised that the monument remains hidden away from the public. She believes that the site may be being used for witchcraft.[51] But this seems an apt place to leave the story and let Old Robin have some peace.

Season of the Witch ~ The Lion, the Witch and Cliff Richard

'There is no need for anybody to be afraid of a witch. We are not evil and we do not practise black magic: There is no need for anyone to be scared of what we will be doing in the old chapel. I have cast a spell on my proposed purchase of the chapel. The deal will go through and everything will be well and public reaction will be favourable. The tarot cards say that things will work out to my liking...'

(Barbara Brandolani, 1984)

It began as a silly season story in the summer of 1984: a notorious witch called Barbara Brandolani wanted to move her coven to a deconsecrated chapel near Heptonstall. Local clergy objected and very soon a worldwide media circus began as even Christian rock and roller Cliff Richard got involved in the machinations to stop The Hermetic Order of the Silver Blade Coven of Witches from buying Slack Chapel. The witch predicted weird consequences if her plans were thwarted, and that's exactly what happened...

The High Priestess of the Hermetic Order of the Silver Blade Coven of Witches

Ever since she was a child, Barbara Brandolani knew she was different, and so did the other children. She could, she claimed, do things just by willing them. Perhaps this was to be expected as both her grandmother and great grandmother had strange powers. An auspicious beginning for a career in witchcraft.[1]

Tragically, her father was killed on bomb disposal duty on the last day of the war and after her mother remarried she was brought up by her grandmother. This was when her powers really began to manifest themselves, if we are to believe what she told *The Guardian* in 1987. When she was 12, she accidentally smashed her grandmother's favourite vase, and knew she'd be in trouble. She drew on her magical powers and willed the vase back together again. The next day, she claimed, it was perfectly whole once more.[2]

Perhaps even stranger, one morning when she was 11 years old, she came downstairs and gave her grandmother the shock of her life: her face was completely black. Her grandmother went upstairs to Barbara's bedroom and saw huge bare footprints all over her pillow, too big, Barbara says, to have been hers. The incident so shocked her poor grandmother that she got rid of all the mirrors in the house.

Barbara left school at 15 and worked in a chemist's before becoming a laboratory technician for ICI. She got married to Marcio and had seven children.[3] She also developed the interest in witchcraft, which many years later, would bring her to the windy moors above the Calder Valley.

As Barbara's involvement in witchcraft grew, she eventually set up a shop in New Moston, Manchester, called The Witchery selling various occult and magical paraphernalia. This was where Paul Pearson, who was to become her scribe, first met her. In fact, he had visited the shop with the purpose of writing a magazine article exposing her as a fraud. In the end, they became lifelong friends and this led to the founding of their coven: The Hermetic Order of the Silver Blade.[4]

The coven met in Barbara's Manchester home. A short video exists on YouTube in which broadcaster James Whale interviews her in her front room temple. The walls and ceiling are mostly witchy black with astrological and magical symbols painted on them. Occult tomes and ceremonial goblets and candles abound and there is what appears to be an altar.[5] In the interview, Barbara disappoints James Whale by informing him that the rituals do not involve orgies.

So, what do the rituals of the Hermetic Order of the Silver Blade involve? Paul Pearson describes the practices as a unique 'melting pot' of pagan and magical traditions, including intuitive magic, elements of notorious occultist Aleister Crowley's work as well as some voodoo.[6] Describing what her coven does, Brandolani told the *Hebden Bridge Times*: 'People seem disappointed when I say we do not leap about naked and there are no orgies.'[7] She went on to say:

> People in the craft live better lives than the average Christian. Witchcraft is very womanly. Instead of praying to God and expecting everything to be done for you we turn to nature and the elements to help ourselves. It is like Christianity without the cross.

Just how much some local Christians disagreed with this interpretation of witchcraft would become apparent in the ensuing weeks.

During the coven's weekly meetings, they practised their rites and rituals, worshipped the phases of the sun and moon and cast their spells. 'We are white witches,' said Brandolani, 'and we do a lot of good helping to heal the sick.' She told the *Halifax Evening Courier* that she wanted to 'resurrect the pagan religion and restore it to its own grand form, from which we have been cheated for hundreds of years.'[8]

What about black magic? Barbara declares in the previously mentioned article in the *Courier*: 'We are not evil and we do not practise black magic.' Confusingly, she goes on to say:

> I am, however, not afraid to use black magic and will use it to fight against voodoo. One has to resort to black magic to fight this evil. There are times when I have cast bad spells as the only means to fight against something that is wrong or against a person who has wronged another and there is no punishment by law.

However, Barbara's Manchester home was too small for her large family and her coven, and in the summer of 1984, she found what she hoped would be a new base: a deconsecrated chapel on the moors near Heptonstall. 'I have cast a spell on my proposed purchase of the chapel,' she told the *Halifax Evening Courier*. 'The deal will go through and everything will be well and public reaction will be favourable. The tarot cards say that things will work out to my liking.'[9] The tarot cards, however, could not have been further from the truth...

Slack Chapel

Slack Chapel lies on a hilltop in the village of Slack, near Heptonstall. It stands by a crossroads, a magical place in much folklore, and in Barbara Brandolani's words, it is 'in tune with the elements.'[10] The chapel was opened in 1879 and replaced an older chapel on the same site.[11] In 1974 it was deconsecrated, and by the summer of 1984 it was up for sale for £17000. Brandolani and her coven had big plans for the former chapel. 'I intend to develop the temple in a classical mythical style as a place where we can be free to pray to the gods and restore them,' she told the *Courier* on 11 June 1984. She planned to tidy and maintain the graveyard and keep the outside of the building unchanged. Inside she planned an Egyptian style temple: 'The temple will be unlocked, not like the churches of today, and our most magical possessions in a case on the altar will be guarded by snakes,' she said in the *Hebden Bridge Times* of 13 July 1984.

However, forces were soon moving against the High Priestess. The *Courier* headline from the 10 July 1984 screamed: PAGAN TEMPLE PLAN ROCKS HILLTOP VILLAGE. The Rev. Stanley Kirby, minister of Hope Baptist Church, Hebden Bridge, said: 'We as Christian ministers are opposed to the powers of darkness.' Fractious local clergy and fellow Christians came together, buried the hatchet, and began making plans to thwart what they saw as a force for evil. The witch, though, would not give up easily, and vowed to use all the powers at her disposal to get her way…

Barbara Brandolani and pet (Photo: Evening Courier, Halifax)

Curses, Foiled Again!

The first spanner in the works occurred in early July when the owner of the former chapel, Bradford based John Parkinson, agreed to delay the deal and met with Hebden Bridge clergy and Barbara Brandolani herself. Brandolani offered her deposit of £100 but it wasn't accepted. Instead the owner decided to give the clergy first refusal.[12]

Meanwhile, the world's media were bewitched by the whole episode; it was, after all, a perfect silly season story. Brandolani and Fredrick Else (the last president of the chapel before it closed in 1974) were interviewed for radio and TV in Britain, Australia and America. It was around this time that Barbara's daughters returned home from school very confused one day. Their Religious Education teacher had told them that witches don't exist, yet their mother was probably the most famous witch on the planet at the time.[13]

One interview was particularly controversial. This was for Radio Manchester and was reported in the *Evening Courier* of 20 July 1984. Barbara was in the studio and had stated her case. Fredrick Else was to be interviewed over the phone, but the line mysteriously went dead, cutting him off in mid-quote from the Bible. A spokesman for Radio Manchester said there was a 'strange noise' before the line went dead, different from the usual noise when someone is cut off. It was not possible to reconnect the line, and Fredrick Else did not get to make his case against the plans. Brandolani denied casting a spell on the phone line, but the whole episode was a gift for the media. WITCH DENIES PHONE SPELL went the headline in the *Halifax Evening Courier* of 20 July 1984.

On the same day, villagers in the area met with local clergy in Heptonstall's Methodist chapel to discuss the developments. Bryan Green lived in the village at the time and I asked him about his memories of this bizarre meeting. He remembers it as being a lovely summer evening as he set off to the chapel early hoping to get a ringside seat for the spectacle. To his astonishment the hall was already heaving and more and more people kept turning up. During the evening many people got up and had their say and 99 per cent of opinion was against the property being sold to Brandolani. Bryan's most abiding memory of the night was of an elderly lady getting up and making an impassioned speech. She said that that very morning she had looked out of her window to find a dead blackbird and a dead hedgehog on her lawn. This proved, she went on to say, that there was evil in the valley and that the witch had to be stopped. There were some lighter moments too. After some people had claimed that Brandolani had been known to curse people who stood in her way, a local market trader said there was nothing unusual in that; he'd cursed plenty of people in his time!

Slack Chapel

The majority of people at the meeting were of one accord, however. The upshot of the discussion was a committee formed to stop the sale going through and to raise the money to buy the chapel themselves. Hebden Bridge parish priest Father John Gott told *The Catholic Herald* that 'Witchcraft was based on the powers of evil and we must stop this thing happening if we can.'[14] One week later this came to pass. MYSTERY BUYER ENDS CHAPEL STORM was the headline in the *Courier* on 26 July.

The mystery buyer turned out to be one Reverend Percy Nuttall, a retired Baptist minister from Burnley. Nuttall used his life savings to buy the building and planned to convert it to an outward-bound centre with accommodation, an information centre for walkers and also to keep some space for Christian worship.

A service of thanksgiving was held attended by over 250 supporters. Nuttall told the *Hebden Bridge Times* on 31 August 1984: 'It was the will of God that made me buy this church and the will of the people will make the plans for its future use successful.' The headlines in the *Hebden Bridge Times* reflected the feeling of the local Christian community:

THANKSGIVING FOR END OF PAGAN TEMPLE THREAT

JUBILANT CHURCHMEN CELEBRATE END OF PAGAN TEMPLE THREAT

Our witch may have lost the chapel, but the story was about to get even weirder...

The Lion, the Witch and Cliff Richard

'I have tried to turn my mind off the chapel now,' Mrs Brandolani told the *Halifax Evening Courier* on 28 July 1984, 'but cannot stop the forces which are present and have been activated by my plans to buy the chapel.' Supernatural forces set in motion by her will as she planned to buy the building now surrounded the chapel, she maintained. 'The forces will effect [sic] those who have been most against the plans to turn the chapel into a temple.' She denied casting a spell, and said that these magic forces 'will only find the demon within the person.'

Barbara Brandolani (Photo: Hermetic Order of the Silver Blade)

Meanwhile, Lancashire police were patrolling the moors above Rawtenstall. Geoffrey Dootson, a farmer from near Burnley, had found the carcasses of some of his sheep with the flesh stripped from them. Dootson had also witnessed a sable coloured lion like animal fleeing from the scene. This mystery big cat became known as the Rossendale Lion. Farmers and police patrolled the moors, traps were laid and the police warned the public to stay off the moors as there was a dangerous wild animal at large.[15] Although what seemed like tracks of a big cat were found, the Rossendale Lion remained elusive.

It was at this time that Barbara Brandolani made a sensational claim: *she* was the lion. She told a BBC Radio Manchester interviewer that she had turned herself into a panther and killed several sheep on the Lancashire moors. Next, she planned to visit

Heptonstall in panther form between midnight and 2 a.m. on August 18 in order to 'claim' the chapel. 'I will appear as a big cat in Heptonstall. People think it all belongs in books and so on but it does not. It is very real.'[16]

Two hours later Brandolani disappeared from her Morecambe holiday home. PANTHER THREAT WITCH VANISHES was the *Courier's* headline on 18 August. Her husband said he did not know where she was. In Heptonstall no panther was seen, but just after midnight an animal was heard shrieking in pain near the chapel. We are not told who heard the noise. Later Mrs Brandolani reappeared but the reason for her 'disappearance' was not revealed. She did, though, deny killing any sheep. In any case, an expert from Chester Zoo said the Rossendale lion tracks had been made by a dog.[17]

This wasn't the end of the strange goings-on. The chapel's new owner, Percy Nuttall, found a dagger pinning some snakeskin to the building's door. Inside, the number of the beast, 666, had been scrawled on the hymn board. Brandolani told the *Courier* that the dagger and the snakeskin were part of a ritual. 'The ritual will bind the chapel to me. There will be happenings during the phases of the moon and the property will come to me.' Some members of the local community who wished to remain anonymous told me they had seen people, presumably witches, dancing naked in the vicinity of the chapel in the moonlight. I asked Barbara's scribe Paul Pearson about this, and while he believed there may have been local pagans or occultists doing such a naked ritual (if that's indeed what it was), it certainly wasn't The Hermetic Order of the Silver Blades.[18]

In 1985 the building was exorcised to rid it of the witch's curse. The publicity that Mrs Brandolani was stirring up was actually helping the Christians' cause as donations flooded in to help pay for the expensive conversions necessary. Finally, congratulations and celebrations were the order of the day when Christian pop star Cliff Richard stepped in with a 'handsome' donation. It's been noted that Cliff had relatively little chart action in the decade or so after his donation and rumours were rife that he had been cursed. Unfortunately, the curse seems to have worn off by the time of his 1999 hit Millennium Prayer.

At last, in the summer of 1988, the former chapel was ready to open as an activity centre. Then tragedy struck. Days before the official opening, Reverend Percy Nuttall, the man who had saved the chapel from the witches' coven, died of heart failure, aged 73. After years of controversy and fund-raising, Nuttall died days before his dream was realised. The headline in the *Hebden Bridge Times* of 17 June 1988 was: MAN OF VISION MISSES FULFILMENT OF HIS DREAM.

Was he cursed? Paul Pearson is in no doubt that Barbara had the power to cast such a curse but is convinced that she would not use it to kill. Kevin Logan, in his 'Manifesto for Christian action' *Paganism and the Occult* wrote that it was more likely that 'the lord called home 73-year-old Percy for a good rest after a job well done.'[19]

Satanic Panic

There was, though, another story running through these events. It was a story of zealotry, intolerance and gullibility to the point of stupidity. This was the now seemingly forgotten story of the Satanic Ritual Abuse scandal that spread through the USA in the 1980s before crossing to the UK. Rumours circulated of an underground network of Satanists and occultists who indulged in orgiastic, murderous and cannibalistic rituals involving all kinds of depravity, including child abuse. The earliest evidence for the existence of these networks seem to be lurid autobiographical Christian misery memoirs such as the infamous *Michelle Remembers* by Michelle Smith and her psychiatrist Lawrence Pazder in the USA and *From Witchcraft to Christ* by Doreen Irvine in the UK. This latter book, which was popular enough to be reprinted six times in 1973, told the supposedly true story of how Doreen went from child to stripper to prostitute to dope smoker to heroin addict to black witch to Satan's High Priestess before turning to Christ while being pursued by demons.[20]

Soon a loose alliance of gullible fundamentalists, therapists, feminists and child agencies started reporting their concerns to the media. Discredited techniques such as regressive hypnosis were used along with leading questions to create false memories of appalling abuse and murder and many families were torn apart and innocent people imprisoned. However, virtually all the investigations into Satanic ritual child abuse in the USA, Canada and the UK eventually came to nothing. It was a myth.[21]

Although the peak of the Satanic Panic hysteria occurred towards the end of the 80s and early 90s in the UK, British pagans and occultists were likely aware of the coming storm and were feeling besieged. Many in the community felt they had to keep their heads down in order to keep their jobs, their liberty and their children. This approach was completely at odds with that of an out and proud witch like Barbara Brandolani who was perfectly willing to pose for photos surrounded by candles, snakes, magic circles and other occult accoutrements. This certainly led to some resentment of Barbara from others in the community as they thought she was needlessly provoking Christians. And buying a chapel to turn into a base for a coven, they thought, would play into Christian fears that there was a network of evil Satanists plotting all kinds of depravity. Indeed, Richard Bartholomew called Barbara's intended purchase a 'stupid unthinking provocation' that proved to credulous fundamentalists that their worst fears about Devil worship were well-founded and played a role in creating the Satanic Panic myth.[22] This allegation, though, seems unlikely to me as the sources of the Satanic panic myth were mostly fundamentalist 'literature', well-meaning but gullible social and charity workers and therapists' unprofessional uses of hypnosis and other leading techniques to create false memories. However, it may have been this simmering Satanic Panic as much as anything that put paid to Barbara's attempts to buy the Chapel.[23]

It's hard, though, to avoid the conclusion that had Brandolani attempted to buy a deconsecrated chapel today in our hopefully more tolerant times, it would not ruffle many feathers. Indeed, when Paul Pearson reflects on the whole saga today he notes a number of ironies. One is that witchcraft and paganism is now common in Hebden Bridge. Another is that the scandal of hysterical false accusations of child abuse did not affect Barbara, but did haunt Sir Cliff.[24]

Epilogue

After the Slack Chapel debacle, Brandolani certainly did not disappear. The following year, she appeared in the *Liverpool Echo*, on Halloween obviously, describing herself as being several hundred years old as well as detailing her coven's Halloween ceremony.[25] She appeared in a *Guardian* article in 1987 (again on Halloween) detailing some of her misadventures with Black Magic.[26] In 1988, she made headlines again after announcing she was setting up a trade union for witches![27]

She also registered a complaint with the National Council of Civil Liberties concerning false allegations about witchcraft made by a visiting Christian speaker in a Religious Studies lesson at her daughter's school. The speaker had said, apparently, that witchcraft was anti-Christian.[28]

After her husband died, Barbara moved to Tuscany and lived a hermit like life.[29] This was a surprise to many as (despite her Italian surname) she could not speak the language and was of Irish descent. She passed away after a short illness in February of 2015. In his eulogy for her, Paul Pearson describes Barbara as 'a force of nature, a woman who knew what she wanted and how to get it. She was a matriarch who ruled with a velvet glove and was loved for it.'[30] Paul also fondly remembers her irreverent sense of humour: she would often refer to the pagan god and goddess in rituals as 'The Gaffer' and 'The Matron'. Similarly, she told the *Liverpool Echo* that witchcraft rituals had been updated: 'That's a good thing too-it's a hell of a job finding heart of bat and tongue of lizard nowadays!' She was certainly a larger than life character that made a lasting impression on 1980s Hebden Bridge and who was capable of entrancing the media and offending both fundamentalists and pagans alike.

Graves around Slack Chapel

The Burning of Alice and Amy Kirby

'Then the light moved again to the window, and once more towards the door. Then I saw the child's hands through the flames…'

(Phoebe Ramsden, 1899)

In 1899, two Sowerby Bridge sisters were fatally burned in mysterious fires. The strange thing was that both sisters caught fire at the same time, despite the fact that they were living a mile apart in separate houses on the opposite side of the valley. At the time it was seen as a tragic coincidence, but some have suspected that it is a dual case of spontaneous human combustion…

The Burning of Alice Ann Kirby

Alice Ann Kirby (5) lived with her father and her grandmother in Wakefield Road, Sowerby Bridge and had been living there on and off for the last few years. Her father, John Henry Kirby, was a gas stoker for the Halifax Corporation and had separated from Alice's mother. Her mother, Sarah Kirby, lived in Hargreaves Terrace with Alice's sister Amy (4) and two younger siblings, on the opposite side of the valley about a mile away from Alice and her father and grandmother.[1]

On the morning of the 5 January at about 10.30, Alice's grandmother, Mrs Kirby senior, left Alice sleeping while she went to help one of her married daughters prepare her house for some building work. She was gone around three quarters of an hour.[2] Meanwhile, Miss Phoebe Ramsden, a neighbour who lived opposite was walking past the house when her attention was attracted by an unusual light in the window that seemed to be moving. At first, she thought Mrs Kirby (senior) was burning rags, though she noticed that the door was open. In her own words:

> Then the light moved again to the window, and once more towards the door. Then I saw the child's hands through the flames. Her nightdress was on fire. I afterwards thought the child had been trying to get to the door, and became blinded and could not see where she was going.[3]

Phoebe threw a rug over Alice and managed to put out some of the flames and then fetched another neighbour, Mrs Hollas, who also helped to roll the burning child in rugs, burning herself in the process.[4]

A neighbour rushed to tell Mrs Kirby (senior) about what had happened and met her as she was on her way home. Mrs Kirby arrived at the scene to see her granddaughter being rolled in the rugs by her neighbours. The neighbours told Mrs Kirby that Alice was dead, but the child seemed to come round and said rather pitifully: 'Let me drink a right lot.'[5]

The nearest available doctor was sent for; with horrible irony, his name was Dr Wellburn. He examined the child and sent for a horse drawn ambulance to take Alice to Halifax Royal Infirmary. Alice's injuries were horrific. She was 'fearfully burnt from her ankles to the top of her head, the flesh in many places seeming to be completely charred.'[6]

A messenger was sent to inform Alice's mother what had happened.

The Burning of Amy Kirby

At approximately the same time as the dreadful events were unfolding at Wakefield Street, Mrs Sarah Kirby, Alice's mother, went to fetch some water from a nearby well to wash the flag stones outside her house. Alice's sister Amy and two of Sarah's other children were left alone. Mrs Kirby was only gone for about two minutes. 'As I was going along,' she told the inquest, 'I heard someone screaming. I put the pail down and ran and looked through the window and saw Amy was on fire.'[7]

A neighbour, Joseph Barker, a foreman porter at Sowerby Bridge station, heard Mrs Kirby shout 'Our Amy is on fire!' and quickly grabbed some coats and ran to assist. When he entered the house, it was full of smoke and a flame a yard high was coming from the child. Two other children were hiding behind a chair. He wrapped the coats around Amy and with her mother's help put out the fire. Amy had serious burns to her face, neck and arms.[8]

Mrs Kirby ran to tell the girl's grandmother what had happened, but on the way was met by the messenger carrying the terrible news about her other daughter being dreadfully burnt. The shock and disbelief she must have felt from this cruel twist of fate is unimaginable,

Both girls were taken to hospital in the same horse drawn ambulance and arrived at around 1pm. Alice asked for a drink, but died later that afternoon from shock. Amy lingered a little longer, but died around midnight.[9] At the inquest, Mr Barstow, the coroner, summed up the 'very strange' case for the jury:

> CORONER: It is very strange that these two children should be burnt at the same time, one child living with its mother, and the other child lying with its grandmother, and the two children being sisters. However, if they believed the evidence they could come to no other conclusion than that death was accidentally caused. It was another instance of the danger of leaving children by themselves. These incidents were sadly too common.
>
> JUROR 1: We have no evidence to show how the fire occurred in either case.
>
> CORONER: No, there is nothing to show that. There is fire in the house, but beyond that, there is nothing. Death is due from shock, through burns. Are you satisfied that in each case the burns have been accidentally caused?
>
> JUROR 2: There is no doubt about it. They have been playing with the fire.
>
> JUROR 3: We have no evidence of that.

Accidental death was the verdict for both girls.[10]

Spontaneous Human Combustion?

Spontaneous Human Combustion (or SHC) is the mysterious and contested phenomenon whereby people for no apparent reason burst into flames and are often reduced to ashes, perhaps with surprisingly little damage to surroundings. At the time of the Kirby case, many people would have heard of this disputed phenomenon, especially as it featured prominently in *Bleak House* by Charles Dickens. In the reporting of the Kirby burnings, though, there is no consideration of the possibility of SHC which, to some authors at least, seems very odd. However, almost 100 years later the tragedy was revisited in the *Halifax Evening Courier* of 13 March 1985 under the headline: FIRE FROM HEAVEN, and SHC was offered as an explanation of the Kirby girls' deaths.[11]

The *Courier*, listed some of the risk factors for spontaneous combustion. The victims are often female and working class. It usually happens indoors and there may be little damage to surroundings. The victims are often extremely thirsty before they catch fire and cases often happen in close proximity to each other. It's clear that most of these factors fit the Kirby case.

A reader of the *Courier* recognised the names and realised that the family involved was related to him and that the tragedy had been a family secret for nearly a hundred years. The relative passed the story on to researchers Jenny Randles and Peter Hough who included it in their 1992 book *Spontaneous Human Combustion*,[12] where they expressed great surprise that SHC was not considered at the inquest and noted how the coroner was 'prepared to dismiss' the case as a 'shocking coincidence'.[13] Since then the Sowerby Bridge burnings have frequently been cited as one of the world's strangest and distressing examples of SHC.

Certainly, the coincidence of two sisters catching fire at approximately the same time in different houses is astounding. Add to this the fact that the cause of the fires was not determined, and it may be argued that a superficial case for SHC could be made. Indeed, some authors such as Damon Wilson have gone further and suggested that the Kirby case indicates that there may be a 'strange psychic connection' between the girls and from this considers that unnamed mental forces could be at play in SHC and speculates that poltergeist-like phenomena may be involved.[14]

The spontaneous combustion of Mr Krook: Illustration by Phiz from Bleak House

All this speculation, however, goes well beyond the evidence. It's true that we don't know how the fires started, but we can make some reasonable suppositions. Although Amy was cautious of fire and would smack the hands of other children if they got too near, Alice was actually very fond of playing with fire. At the inquest, her grandmother reported that Alice had been 'whipped' for playing with fire and her father said she 'would stir the fire up and throw paper in to make it blaze.'[15] A child of five with a penchant for playing with fire left alone in the house with a fire burning in the front room is obviously a huge danger. Damon Wilson describes Alice as spontaneously combusting in her bed,[16] though it's clear that she was actually downstairs when she was on fire. Mrs Greenwood (senior) thought that Alice had woken up, put a woollen shawl over her nightdress and then come downstairs and sat in front of the fire.[17] She may have tragically taken the opportunity to play with the fire. Or it could easily be the case that both girls happened to sit too close to the fire at the same time.

The coincidence of the sisters catching fire at around the same time is indeed remarkable. However, it's a sad fact that newspapers at the time were full of distressing stories of children left alone for a short time and then being discovered in flames.[18] Open fires, flammable clothes and unattended children made such tragedies inevitable, but it is difficult to ignore the horrible irony of the Kirby case.

Epilogue

The girls were buried in unmarked graves in unconsecrated ground in Sowerby Bridge Cemetery. It's not clear why this is. A relative of the two sisters told Malcolm Bull:

> The mother of the girls, Sarah Ann, was my maternal grandma. She died in 1949 at the age of 77. The two little girls would have been my aunts. When the church would not allow the girls to be buried in consecrated ground, this upset my gran as they were very religious and already owned a family plot.[19]

Haunted Skies ~
The UFOs that Time Forgot

'As I was walking in the Royd hills… to my intense surprise I saw, hanging in the heavens a glorious globe of green. This object was semi-transparent and moving from North to South… at a high pace, emitting a high-pitched whistle as it went…'

('Old Lydgatian', 1931)

Although Todmorden's best-known UFO episodes occurred in the 1980s, the historical records contain references to much older strange phenomena in the skies above the town and its surroundings. These include ghostly lights around Stoodley Pike, reports of ball lightening, mysterious airships, strange flying dark matter and a peculiar green globe. And all before anyone had ever heard the term UFO or Flying Saucer…

Stoodley Pike ~ Tomb of One Unknown

Stoodley Pike Monument stands 1310 feet above sea level on the windy moors between Todmorden and Hebden Bridge. It has long attracted walkers to the panoramic views gained after mounting its dark and scary spiral staircase to the spectacular gallery. However, the story of the Pike stretches back to long before the present monument was built, and even further back than the earlier structure which it replaced.

Stoodley Pike Monument

Local folklore suggests that the site of the present monument once housed the cairn of a prehistoric chieftain. In local poet William Law's 1832 poem 'Wanderings of a Wanderer' (which is the source of much of the folklore of this site) we are told that the monument was erected 'on the tomb of one unknown'. In the notes to his poem Law says that a heap of stones marked the grave, but if even one of these stones was out of place no one in the area could sleep.[1] Doors were said to slam shut of their own accord and strange noises were heard until the owner of the land had put the out of place stone back. We are also told that strange lights or flames were seen flitting around the cairn; this must be the first reference to UFOs (in the literal sense of unidentified flying objects) in the skies over Todmorden.

A Singular Electric Phenomenon

A terrible storm hit the Calder Valley and surroundings in early July 1881. The thunder and lightning were described as being of 'unprecedented severity'.[2] 'The lightning was fearfully vivid, illuming the sky with its unearthly glare,' like no storm in living memory. There was much storm damage and flooding in the area and several people were drowned or hit by lightning. The storm was so intense that one Accrington woman died of fright.[3]

During the storm, at about 10pm in Cornholme, two 'respectable and credible' witnesses saw something rather odd. They described 'five or six discharges of globular shape' that looked like 'immense shooting stars'. These strange globes travelled obliquely across the sky at huge speed.[4] Had these two unnamed respectables witnessed the rare and controversial phenomenon of ball lightning? Unfortunately, these are the only details we have about this 'singular phenomenon'.

Mysterious Dark Matter

The next encounter also took place in Cornholme, near Todmorden. Around midday on Wednesday 4 July 1906 'mysterious dark matter' was seen travelling over the valley towards Todmorden Moor.[5] The *Todmorden Advertiser* received several 'vague and somewhat confused accounts' of 'strange moving objects'. Some witnesses thought this 'dark matter' could be piles of hay picked up by a sudden wind, while others suggested it was smoke from a fire. Smoke sounds unlikely as an explanation as smoke from homes, chimneys and bonfires would be a familiar sight and wouldn't have caused such interest. In fact, one witness said the flying objects looked like lumps of peat. Some of these strange flying things were observed to land on the hillside leading to Todmorden Moor, though there was no clear explanation as to what was witnessed. It's also strange that these UFOs were dark objects seen during the daytime rather than flying lights in the night sky.

Phantom Airships

In 1909 a wave of phantom airship sightings swept the country.[6] These mysterious flying objects are often seen as precursors to later UFOs, a kind of steampunk flying saucer. Some of these flying objects appeared as mysterious lights in the sky, while others (witnesses claimed) had structures (often cigar shaped and zeppelin like) or beamed out light. Some even claimed to have seen people in the objects. It was often surmised that eccentric inventors were secretly perfecting new flying technology and then testing it at night to avoid detection, though this obviously didn't work. The *Halifax Evening Courier* at the time said there were too many reports by 'uncomical' people such as doctors and lawyers to dismiss the phenomenon as hoaxes or overactive imaginations.[7]

Perhaps inevitably, these mystery airships headed towards Todmorden, but in the two cases I could find, all was not as it seemed. The first case occurred during the nationwide 1909 flap. On the 31 July 1909, hundreds of people gathered in the Millwood area of Todmorden after rumours circulated that a mystery airship was hovering in the sky there. Everyone stared in amazement at the 'flying thing' and, with the aid of binoculars, some witnesses were convinced that they could see the forms of people on board the strange craft. Suddenly, the wind changed and dissipated the vision. It was, apparently, just a cloud. 'Further comment is needless,' ends the report in the *Todmorden Advertiser*.[8] It must have been a remarkable cloud to fool so many people.

The second phantom airship episode in Todmorden occurred several years later in the September of 1916. The residents of Walsden had become accustomed to strange sights in the night sky every evening at around 10pm, and had started gathering outside to watch the show. It was later determined that the strange lights were actually the shafts of searchlights many miles distant. However, the locals maintained that a mystery airship had floated over Walsden and had been witnessed by numerous people.[9]

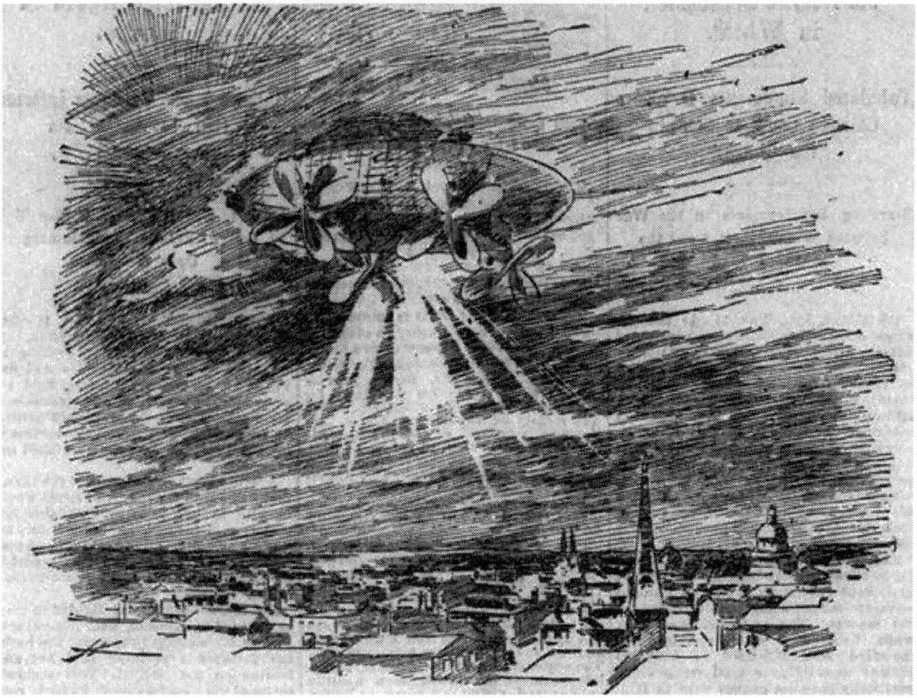

Illustration of mystery airship from San Francisco Call, 19 November 1896

A Gigantic Whirligig

This odd phenomenon was seen over Halifax in August 1909 by an anonymous witness and his friend. They were watching some lightening playing on the horizon in the evening, when they suddenly noticed a bright light in the sky, somewhat like a firework just after going off. The witness described it as a 'gigantic whirligig or some nebula within the atmosphere'. It was constantly throwing off bright sparks and was visible for around a minute. It started off very bright, but became fainter. It was not high enough, they believed, to be astronomical, and they assumed it was a 'freak of atmospheric electricity'.[10]

A Glorious Globe of Green

This experience can be found in a letter to the editor of the *Todmorden Advertiser* from 1932, and is perhaps the strangest of these pre-saucer era sightings. It is signed 'Old Lydgatian' and is reproduced below in full.

> A CURIOUS PHENOMENON
>
> Sir,- One day this year, in about the third week in September, I was witness of a curious phenomenon. As I was walking the Royd hills in the cool of evening I happened to lift up my eyes unto the hills (somewhere in the direction of Orchan Rocks), and to my intense surprise I saw, hanging in the heavens a glorious globe of green. This object was semi-transparent, and moving from North to South (i.e., from right to left) at a high pace, emitting a high-pitched whistle as it went. When it was - as far as I could judge – directly over an historic monument known as Stoodley Pike, it suddenly changed from

> green to yellow, and from yellow through all the remaining longer wave length colours of the spectrum. When it had reached a fiery glowing red, it hung for a moment motionless, and suddenly faded away as a tale that is told.
>
> Could any of your readers give me an explanation of such a curious – shall I say – manifestation?[11]

None of the paper's readers could explain this strange sighting, but it goes to show, like the other episodes described above, that strange things have been witnessed in the skies above Todmorden and its neighbouring towns for a long time.

A Curious Silvery Green Ball

This next episode was witnessed by multiple people from Halifax, Brighouse and even in North Yorkshire. It occurred at around 10.20pm on 18 August 1936 and resembles the previous sighting in some aspects. A Brighouse man described seeing a 'curious silvery green ball in the sky' which moved slowly until it passed out of sight over Southowram and Hove Edge. Witnesses from Highroad Well and King Cross also saw the strange light, comparing it to fireworks and saying it was visible for around 10 seconds. The most detail comes from a North Yorkshire witness, who described it as comet like and as 'a ball of fire, green in colour falling quite slowly towards the earth. It was almost circular in shape and about one quarter the apparent size of the moon.'[12]

~

Bars in the Sky

An unnamed air raid warden wrote a letter to the *Halifax Courier* describing his strange sighting above Halifax in the early hours of 30 March 1940:

> Sir,- Could any of your readers explain the curious phenomenon seen in the sky to the north-east at 5.10am this morning?
>
> The effect was as of 20-30 bars of light, almost like the beams of a searchlight spreading outwards from the apex to the horizon. No clouds were visible. The barred effect gradually merged into one broad beam with edges clearly defined and perfectly straight. It had disappeared entirely by 5.30am leaving no trace of cloud- yours, etc.
>
> AIR RAID WARDEN

As with most of the above sightings, details are lacking and witnesses are unnamed. But even before the famous American UFO sightings from the late 1940s onwards, there were strange things going on in the skies above Calderdale.

The Spirit in the Spire ~ Ghosts on Film

'I was gobsmacked when I printed off the photos. We'd been trying to get shots of the birds, but then this eerie figure appeared on one of them. I don't believe in ghosts but this is weird and in my twenty years as a steeplejack I've never seen the like.'

(Barry Done, 2005)

Builders working on the restoration of a Halifax church got more than they bargained for when an apprentice took a snap inside the ruined steeple. The photo seemed to catch a ghostly figure that some claimed to be the spirit of one of Halifax's most bloodthirsty vicars. It wasn't long before more spooky photos began to emerge...

An Eerie Figure in Halifax Square Church

All that remains of Halifax Square Congregational Church can be seen towering over the Piece Hall. The church, built in 14th century gothic style, was opened in 1857, and the spire, still one of Halifax's most recognizable landmarks, stands at 235 feet. At the time of building it was the second tallest spire in Yorkshire. The church held its last service in 1970 and in 1976 all but the spire and the foundations were demolished.[1]

Halifax Square Church Spire

The Ghost in the Spire? (Photo: Anthony Finnigan)

Restoration work on the spire carried out by Manchester firm Best was halted in early 2005 as rare birds, possibly kestrels, were thought to be nesting in the ruin. However, when 18-year-old apprentice Anthony Finnigan tried to take a digital photo of the 'lovebirds' on Friday 11 March he came out with something rather different. In the words of foreman Barry Done: 'I was gobsmacked when I printed off the photos. We'd been trying to get shots of the birds, but then this eerie figure appeared on one of them. I don't believe in ghosts but this is weird and in my twenty years as a steeplejack I've never seen the like.'[2]

The photo shows a long-haired figure in a purple robe with arms raised in a pious looking pose. It's not clear if the figure is male or female as the photo is too blurred and Finnigan claims he didn't see the 'ghost' at the time of taking the photo. Of course, as the apprentice didn't see anything at the time this means the ghost didn't appear on the digital camera's screen but magically imprinted an image of itself in the camera's memory. Unfortunately, (or suspiciously) the original photo was deleted, the apprentice obviously having thought that evidence of life after death wasn't worth saving. Anyway, who could possibly suspect an 18-year-old with a digital camera of perpetrating a hoax? In any event, the builders, the *Courier* informs us, were now too afraid to work in the spire alone.

The Bloody Vicar of Halifax

If the photo did depict a real ghost, then who could it be? Medium Linda Francis, aka the Ghostmistress, of Ovenden, believes she might know the answer. She says the ghost could be Dr John Favour, vicar of Halifax from 1593 to 1623.[3] Favour was a Puritan from Southampton who founded Halifax Grammar school and also found time to try, torture and execute Jesuit Priests, as detailed in his book *Antiquite Triumphing Over Noveltie.*

The main reason Linda thinks the ghost could be Dr Favour is the costume and the pose of the figure which is quite similar to a bust of the vicar in Halifax Minster. The bust shows the vicar with open Bible in front of him, his hand ominously resting on a skull. Unfortunately, as vicar Pauline Millward observed, many memorial busts show people in similar poses, and it's not even obvious that the 'ghost' is a male. Furthermore, as Favour died in the seventeenth century, it would surely be highly irregular for him to be haunting a Victorian building. Nevertheless, Linda Francis claims to have even more ghostly Halifax photos...

Bust of Dr John Favour in Halifax Parish Church

Ghosts in the Chapel

Next to the spire of Halifax Square Congregational Church is the Square Independent Chapel, now used as a theatre and art centre. The Chapel was finished in 1772 and held services until 1857 before becoming a Sunday school for the church next door. However, it was after an afternoon concert on 5 December 1998 that another ghostly figure appeared on film as if from nowhere.[4]

The Grim Reaper? (Photo: Haunted Truths)

A photo of a member of the audience chatting with a musician appears to show a hunched white figure in the background; perhaps, it is claimed, holding a staff. Nothing untoward was seen when the picture was taken, and Linda and her husband Ian took other photos in the chapel that they believe show manifestations. To sceptics these 'ghosts' look like flaws in the film or overexposures, but the figure with the staff has been 'authenticated' by the Ghost Research Foundation. This means, in the words of the evidence analysis report, that the photo 'is believed to be of paranormal origin and has been analysed by The Ghost Research Foundation for signs of camera malfunction, light influx, fogging, deliberate hoax or any other natural explanation.'[5] The negative, though, remains unanalysed. Ian Francis told me that the figure with the staff is the Grim Reaper or Soul Catcher.

Halifax Square Chapel

Unfortunately, when I asked The Ghost Research Foundation about the photos in the Chapel, they categorically refused to comment on anything to do with Linda Francis and her photos. However, the musician in the photo was later identified as Tim Bayley of the York Waits and the gentleman chatting to him is Dudley Hanson who created the period music group's recorders. Although Mr Hanson is now deceased, his death occurred over a decade after the picture was taken.[6]

Epilogue

Linda and Ian Francis believe that spirits are everywhere and that they turn up on photos all the time. Indeed, they showed me numerous pictures of buildings in the Halifax area many of which showed 'orbs'. Orbs are blobs of light that often appear on photos, especially those taken with a digital camera, and are usually unseen by the photographer at the time. Some believe that these strange lights are actually spirit manifestations. Photographic experts say orbs are particles of dust and other debris illuminated by the flash, especially when compact digital cameras are used as the lens and flash are in close proximity.[7] Linda and Ian disagree. If they are right virtually every photo album in the world is chock full of ghosts posing for the camera.

A 'Water Witch' Visits Hebden Bridge

'The evidence that Mr Mullins possesses the power to find water far outweighs anything that has been raised against him... the man does possess some unusual power, call it an extra endowment of animal magnetism, witchcraft, or anything else.'

(Todmorden and District News, July, 1890)

John Mullins was one of several celebrity dowsers or water-diviners known throughout Britain for their supposed prowess at locating underground water or mineral sources using only their trusty hazel twig. These v-shaped 'divining rods' would twitch in the diviner's hands as he crossed running water, or so their testimonials and many enthusiastic fans would claim, and the services of these 'water witches' were often in demand by farmers, mill builders, brewers or anyone else needing to locate a water source. Calderdale was no exception, and when the celebrated Mr Mullins visited Hebden Bridge at the end of the nineteenth century it caused much public interest but a great deal of controversy too. It led to a furious war of words in the letter columns of the local press. In the blue corner was James Moss, the fustian manufacturer who, with his brother, built Bridge Royd Mill in 1868.[1] In the red corner was science teacher, rationalist and sceptic, Samuel Fielding. It's unclear who won this nineteenth century battle of wits. But it is clear who had the last word...

John Mullins ~ Celebrity Dowser

John Mullins the master dowser was born in Wiltshire in 1838, one of eleven children. He worked as a mason as his father did until he witnessed a dowser called Adams at work while he was employed as a mason by Sir John Orred, a Gloucestershire landowner. Sir John was so impressed with this dowser that he got all the men in his employ to have try at it and they all failed miserably. They walked over the grounds clutching the hazel twig, but the wood just wouldn't move for them. However, when it came to the turn of young John Mullins, the twig jerked up so violently that it snapped! It was obvious he had the gift, and from that moment, so he tells us in his book, he was declared a water-finder.[2]

Mullins married in 1859 and fathered four daughters and two sons, two of whom had 'the gift'.[3] And Mullins was not any old water finder. The water he found was exceptionally pure and clean: 'The supply from such a source may be generally relied upon for its purity and wholesomeness, and from its freedom from risk of contamination.'[4] With this and his impressive list of endorsements and recommendations, Mullins was in demand around the country and this is what brought him to Hebden Bridge in 1889.

Mullins was employed by John Edward Greenwood to dowse for water at Stubbing Brink and he duly used his powers to indicate three places where water was to be found. Greenwood then employed some contractors to drill down to the water source. The first place selected by the water diviner was supposed to have a supply of water 100 feet below ground, though the contractors found it at 35 feet and stopped boring. The quality of the water was not considered good enough so they proceeded to the second spot indicated but found nothing. At this point the work stopped as the contractors and Mr Greenwood fell out about payment and broken verbal contracts resulting in a court case brought against Mr

Greenwood.[5] The results for Mr Mullins the 'water witch' were rather mixed, but it didn't stop his fame from spreading around the town and beyond. The following year he would make an even bigger splash in Hebden.

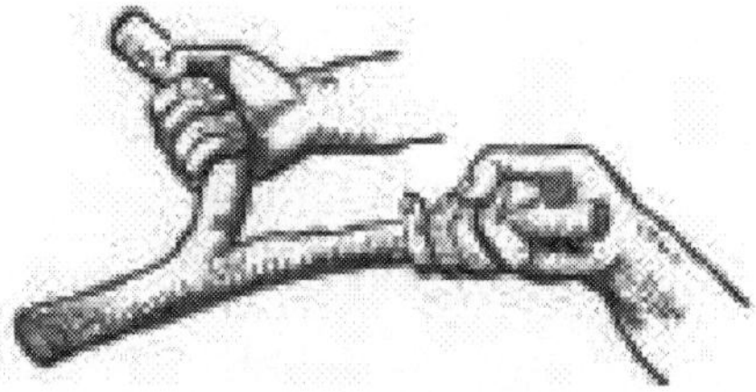

Hazel Divining Rod

John Mullins

Lying Imposters ~ A War of Words

However, local science teacher Samuel Fielding was no fan of celebrity water diviners like John Mullins. In fact, he was so vexed by the ignorance and superstition he saw in their practices that he took pen to paper and wrote a caustic essay about the matter and entered it into a competition for *Science and Art* magazine and won. His prize essay, 'The Divining Rod' was printed in the local paper and he did not pull any punches.[6]

Fielding's first argument is that newspaper accounts of celebrity water diviners celebrate their successes but ignore their failures. This would give a much better impression of their skills than was actually the case. His second argument is that trickery of some sort must be involved. His logic goes like this: if no trickery were involved in divining for water, then the hazel twig would twitch in *anybody's* hands, but it does not. It only seems to work in the hands of the dowser, which makes the twig the equivalent of a stage magician's magic wand: a blind to distract the audience from what's really going on. And what's really going on, according to Fielding, is the water diviner is taking his clients for a ride:

> I suppose, we dare not flatly say they are not lying imposters, or, on the other hand, dogmatically assert upon what bases of observations of the physical features of the district they become assured of the presence of water, although at the same time we may feel perfectly sure, in our own minds, what the real guides to such an assurance are. We should like some gentleman to be at the expense of paying wages for a few days, while we go about with a hazel twig in our hands.[7]

To be fair, Fielding is willing to concede that the dowser may have some acute but undiscovered sense that may be sensitive to water, but he concludes that the water-finder merely observes the geology, geography, flora and fauna of the area and makes conscious or unconscious judgements from these pointers. The prodigious book learning of the science teacher landed with a thud: the final word on water witches.

Or so he thought. Local mill owner James Moss, however, had other ideas. He wrote a stinging rebuke printed in the local press several days later. 'I may admire [Fielding's] floral language,' Moss begins, 'but not his arguments.'[8] As proof of the water divining abilities of Mr Mullins, Moss explains how the dowser had selected the best place to bore a well when Moss was constructing Bridge Royd dye works. Moss had also personally tested Mullins' skills with much success, once in a warehouse where there could be no geological or botanical clues. 'If we are to accept nothing but what we ourselves can fathom, to say the least it is very egotistical. If the Almighty is pleased to give certain individuals this gift,' Moss asks, 'what is there to doubt in it?' He signs off with a somewhat unclear point about how we are surrounded by inexplicable mysteries like the telephone and phonograph, yet it would be absurd to say that these marvels were just the product of instinct.

But Fielding was just getting warmed up. In his swift reply he began to wax metaphysical, explaining that 'every man must bow to the great fundamental laws whereby the earth and the universe is governed… These laws God himself obeys, not because he is beneath them, but because they are the expression of his natural way of working.'[9] Science, he points out, relies on 'constancy and universality of result', and this being so, if the hazel twig worked, it would work for everyone. Because it doesn't, as he wrote in his prize-winning essay, there must be some trickery involved.

~

Mr Mullins Returns to Hebden Bridge

Fielding's prize essay and subsequent letter column spat with Moss must have added an extra frisson to the atmosphere of Hebden Bridge when Mr John Mullins paid his next visit to the town just a few months later in July 1890. This time Mr Mullins had been invited by The Hebden Land Syndicate and Fielding's letter column nemesis James Moss to seek water sources behind Foster Mill and at a farm called Faugh Well, Wadsworth.[10] Mullins arrived by train and was taken to the Albert Hotel. His visit had attracted a great deal of local interest and crowds of both believers and Doubting Thomases would follow him, including a rather sycophantic journalist from the *Todmorden and District News*.

John Mullins is a 'good-looking man of some five foot four or five inches, broad set, and has much of the farmer look about him, a free and frank speaker' according to the local journalist who reported .his visit. He also seemed to be something of a showman, happy to give a demonstration of his power to the crowds of men filling the Albert. He walked around the pub holding his hazel twig until it suddenly shot up in his hands 'with unmistakable force'. We are assured that there was indeed water under the Albert's cellar floor. His demonstration seems to have been well-received and it caused many to wonder how it was possible. The journalist was in no doubt:

> The evidence that Mr Mullins possesses the power to find water far outweighs anything that has been raised against him... the man does possess some unusual power, call it an extra endowment of animal magnetism, witchcraft, or anything else.[11]

The following morning Mullins began work on some land behind Foster Mill, followed by a crowd of witnesses. Mullins did not seem fazed by the large gathering of onlookers and he 'entered heartily into all their chaff and banter'.[12] Starting in a three cornered field at Nursery Nook under the road to Hardcastle Crags he took his v-shaped hazel rod and 'fixing a frond between the second and third finger of each hand, and grasping them with his thumbs' he walked 30 yards when suddenly the twig seemed to take on a life of its own and jerked upwards. There was a ripple of applause, and no doubt with the prize-winning essay in mind, some wag shouted 'Where's Mr Fielding?'[13]

Mullins claimed there was water at this spot 130 feet below the surface, though not much. At this point, some sceptics in the crowd pushed the twig (still grasped by Mullins) back into a horizontal position, but as soon as their hands were removed the rod shot up again. Some tried to hold the rod down but the power was so great that the rod twisted and broke. Presumably, Mr Mullins had some spares with him. Others in the gathering tried their luck at the same spot but the divining rod remained resolutely motionless, except when Mullins grasped the audience member's wrists, for then the twig would obediently turn upwards. Some said they felt 'a slight dull electric sensation' running through their arms. Across Midgehole road the rod again twitched upwards 'pointing with mathematical exactness to where the water mains ran.'[14] After trying a few more places, Mullins settled on a high corner in the field as the place to dig for a well.

Next the party proceeded to Faugh Well farm, Wadsworth. However, as Mullins set to work, a sceptic in the crowd shouted that it was 'all bosh!' and insisted that the dowser do a blindfold demonstration. Although Mullins had been all too willing to demonstrate his powers previously, he declined the invitation to a blindfold trial citing lack of time. Instead, it seems he read out a glowing testimonial written by Spalding Conservative MP Murray Finch-Hatton which described how he had personally subjected Mullins to a blindfold test and Mullins had passed with impressive accuracy. The day rounded off with the dowser attending a private meeting where he again demonstrated his powers, though this time showing that his rod could detect coins.

How accurate Mullins was in his identification of water sources on that day is unknown. What is known, though, is that Samuel Fielding would not let matters rest. Five years later in 1905 he was still exercised about the whole business, as can be seen in his letter to the *Todmorden and District News.* He announces that there has been scientific proof that he was right about dowsing and that James Moss and (the now late) Mr Mullins were wrong. He cites an experiment carried out by scientist W.F. Barrett that Fielding claims vindicated everything he said. Professor Barrett had concluded that the dowser's twitching rod was caused by an 'unconscious muscular spasm' (or the ideomotor effect as it is sometimes called) possibly supported by an unexplained instinct or a power new to science like clairvoyance.[15] It's strange that Fielding the rationalist science teacher is so ready to accept clairvoyance as a possible explanation. But this still wasn't his last word on the matter.

Epilogue

In 1908, some nine years after the publication of his prize essay, Fielding again put pen to paper. This time he is celebrating the news of an 'automatic water finder', a machine that supposedly detected water scientifically. Fielding sees this as further proof that he had been right all along and that the (now also late Moss) and all who had doubted him were conclusively shown to be wrong. He gloated:

If any of my aforetime opponents are still living, and still retain the former correspondence- alas! The best of them have joined the immortals- let me ask them to reread the same and see how far I was right and how far I was wrong.[16]

The Todmorden Vicarage Massacre

'And all good people, oh, prey consider,
Where true-love is planted, there let it dwell,
And recollect the Todmorden murder,
Young Miles the weaver, and Sarah Bell.'

(Anonymous ballad 'Miles Weatherhill the Young Weaver', 1868)

In 1868, young Miles Weatherhill packed four pistols and a hatchet into a custom-made belt. He had sworn revenge on those responsible for separating him from the woman he loved, and his vengeance was furious and bloody. The awful reports of Miles and his sweetheart Sarah Bell held Victorian England transfixed by its horror and tragedy. This is the story of one of Calderdale's most notorious murder sprees: The Todmorden Vicarage Massacre…

Miles and Sarah

Miles Weatherhill was a 23-year-old cotton operative from Todmorden who lived in Back Brook Street with his sister and widowed mother. The *Courier* described him as 'above the usual working-class stamp, but in his countenance deep moroseness and passion are to be traced, and his eyes are peculiarly bright under excitement.'[1] While helping out at the local Sunday school Miles met his sweetheart, Sarah Bell, a 17-year-old cook working at Christ Church, Todmorden for the local vicar, the Reverend Anthony John Plow, and his wife Harriet.

Miles Weatherhill (PHDA © Todmorden Antiquarian Society)

Wanting to do the honourable thing, Miles asked Reverend Plow for permission to court Sarah, permission that Plow was reluctant to give. He said he would talk it over with his wife and provide a final decision after a couple of days.[2] Unfortunately for Miles, The Reverend and Mrs Plow decided that Sarah was too young and they did not want to have a long courtship going on in their house. They did, though, commend Miles for the honourable way he had sought their permission. Miles seemed to take the news well.[3]

Sarah Elizabeth Bell (PHDA © Todmorden Antiquarian Society)

However, the young couple were not to be kept apart so easily. Miles and Sarah were forced to meet in secret, unaware that one of the vicar's servants, Jane Smith, was spying on them and reporting their clandestine arrangements back to the vicar. Finally, to put an end to the situation once and for all, the Plows sacked Sarah and sent her back to her parents in Thirsk.

Miles continued to visit Sarah, trying to convince her to find a new position near Todmorden. He wrote to her on 7 November 1867:

> My dear, dear Sarah
> I am now at Todmorden once more, but with a very sad heart. You know how we left each other, and you may guess how I have been since. O Sarah, my true love, I do so long to see you... Sarah, it makes my blood boil to think of the wrong they have done to you. I will never forgive them, they have ruined our happiness. Oh, Sarah! That I could have died in your arms, I should have been thankful.[4]

In a further letter dated 18 November, Miles wrote to Sarah and referred to the Plows and their servant, the 'traitor' Jane Smith:

> He and his wife and the traitor has spoiled our happiness, and unless that happiness can be renewed, they shall rue it, for I shall open Jane's secret to all of Todmorden. No, I will not be the only one to suffer. No, the traitor shall suffer a little. I cannot forgive them for doing as they have done towards us.[5]

In one of these letters, Miles informed Sarah that he was planning to go to Manchester to watch the public execution of three members of the Irish Republican Brotherhood (IRB). The three men, William O' Meara Allen, Phillip Larkin and Michael O'Brien, had been found guilty of taking part in the ambush of a horse-drawn police van carrying two prominent members of the IRB in which an unarmed police officer was shot dead and the prisoners escaped. The execution was to take place outside the New Bailey Prison, Salford on 23 November 1867.[6]

When Miles arrived in Salford, he would have seen barricades manned with armed soldiers and police officers around the scaffold in case a rescue of the doomed men were attempted. The crowd was unusually small, so Miles would easily have found a good place to watch the grim proceedings. He would also have seen one of Britain's most notorious hangmen, William Calcraft, a man he would soon have the opportunity to meet face to face.

William Calcraft had been a professional executioner for close to fifty years by this time. He had sent hundreds of men and women (even a nine-year-old boy) to their graves with his notorious 'short-drop' method.[7] This short-drop method of hanging that Calcraft favoured meant that only his lucky victims died quickly; many would be slowly throttled as they desperately twisted and writhed on the end of the rope, and Calcraft, it was said, had the longest career and the shortest rope of any hangman. Calcraft would often resort to swinging on the legs of the unfortunates to hasten their demise. The long-drop method, where a longer rope and drop meant that the victim's neck would be broken causing instant death, may have been more humane, but sometimes led to the grisly spectacle of the victim's head being torn off.

Descriptions of Calcraft were not very flattering. One said after witnessing one of his executions that he would never forget 'that ghoul of a Calcraft, with his disreputable grey hair, his disreputable undertaker's suit of black, and a million dirty pinpricks which marked every pore of the skin of his face.'[8] On that miserable, freezing foggy morning in November 1867, Miles would have seen Calcraft the hangman looking nervous. He had received threats to his life should he go ahead with the execution, and he no doubt wanted to get the hangings out of the way as quickly as possible. Up on the platform, Calcraft would have been an easy target for an assassin.[9]

Miles and the rest of the crowd would have seen the three Irish men, their arms pinioned, led to the scaffold by Calcraft and his assistant. Priests accompanied the doomed men, praying and offering them comfort. The condemned men were led onto the scaffold and white hoods were placed over their heads, the nooses were positioned round their necks and their ankles were strapped together. Calcraft went below the scaffold and drew the bolt to send the three men swinging. Although the scaffold was designed so that the audience would only see the head and shoulders of the victims, it would have been very clear to Miles and the gathered crowd that something was terribly wrong. Although one of the men, Allen, had died quickly, the other two were straining and writhing in agony. Calcraft leaped onto Larkin's back to finish him off, but when he tried to do the same to O'Brien, the attendant priest refused to allow it. Instead, O'Brien, his hand holding the priest's, suffered forty-five minutes of painful strangulation before he eventually expired.[10]

Hangman William Calcraft

The following year, Miles received this letter from Sarah:

> My dear Miles
> Please do not come any more, because there has been such a row. My dear Miles, I am very sorry to disappoint you, but mother says it cannot be now for one thing. You must guess the rest, as I have to do, but I can tell you it is quite as great a disappointment to me as it would be to you. If it is convenient for you to be at the station on Friday morning at 7 o' clock, I should so much like to see you again. It is hard to part with you, my own dear boy, but you must not fret, for I shall love you as well away as here. You know it is hard-hearted long parted, so I must say goodnight, my dear, for it is bed time. With a kiss, I remain, yours ever,
> SARAH E. BELL[11]

There was no hope for Miles and Sarah. Sarah had found a place in York and her mother would not let their courtship continue. The lovers met to say their final goodbyes. As they parted, Sarah heard Miles utter in a low voice: 'Revenge!'[12]

On the evening of 2 March, Miles returned to Todmorden. He had a whisky in the Black Swan Inn and then headed towards the vicarage. Miles was armed with four pistols and a hatchet all held in a custom-made belt.

'Brutal Murder and Butchery'

Reverend Plow was about to go to bed at sometime between 10 and 11 o' clock when he was startled by a violent banging on the vicarage door. He went to see what the commotion was, and the servants told him they could not open the door more than a little. The Reverend ran outside by another entrance to see Miles

Weatherhill securing the doors with cord from the outside; no one was going to leave that house.

Rev. Anthony John Plow (PHDA © Todmorden Antiquarian Society)

Miles heard the vicar's footsteps and immediately drew a pistol and shot at him. The gun misfired. Miles rushed at Plow and dealt him a blow from his hatchet. Miles landed more blows about Plow's head and face with the hatchet as the two men struggled and wrestled with each other back into the vicarage, Jane Smith having managed to cut the string holding the doors closed. The three servants who were present, Elizabeth Spink, Mary Hodgeson and

Jane Smith, bravely tried to stop the assault and managed to hold Miles back long enough for the fearfully wounded and copiously bleeding Plow to stagger out of the door, clutching a pistol he had wrested from his attacker.

Christ Church, Todmorden

Next Miles turned his attention to the second object of his hatred, servant Jane Smith, the 'traitor' he had accused of spreading tales about his sweetheart. Miles went after her with his hatchet, but plucky Mary Hodgeson managed to grab the weapon and throw it to the floor. This gave Jane time to run to the dining room where she tried to shut the door, but Miles prevented her. On her knees, Jane begged Miles to show her some mercy. 'Where's my Sarah?' Miles asked before putting two bullets through her head and killing her instantly. At some point, he retrieved the hatchet and hacked away at Jane's body, all but severing her arm.

Miles then wandered up and down the corridors as he reloaded his pistols. All the time he said to himself: 'Where's my Sarah? Where's my Sarah?' before mounting the stairs. In the bedroom were Harriet Plow, her three-week-old baby and a nurse.

Harriet Plow (PHDA © Todmorden Antiquarian Society)

The nurse barred the door to the bedroom saying the people he wanted were downstairs, to which Miles replied: 'I have finished them, but you needn't be afraid, you haven't done me no harm.' He barged past the nurse and entered the bedroom while Mrs Plow hid under the bedclothes. He tried to pull the sheets off the bed but couldn't, so he lifted them up at the foot of the bed and fired under the covers. Harriet, though, had jumped out of bed in the nick of time and the bullet missed. Miles pursued his quarry round the room until he finally trapped her and set about beating her head and face with a poker breaking open her nose.[13] At first, she defended herself against the blows with her arms and hands, but this became too painful and she gave up and played dead. This ruse saved her life.[14]

Miles considered his work done and was heading downstairs when he was apprehended by some neighbours brought by the fleeing servants. He gave up quietly, offering no resistance, and calmly took a pipe from his pocket. 'I may as well have a smoke,' he said, 'it may be the last I have.' At this point Elizabeth Spink told him that the vicar was dead, at which news he laughed.

One of Miles' custodians was his former teacher, one Joseph Gledhill. 'I was one of your pupils, Mr Gledhill,' he told him, 'and you thought me a good grammarian. You didn't know it would come to this.' He said he had no desire to escape or hurt anyone who had not hurt him. When the police arrived, he said: 'I've done all I wanted to do. I'm only sorry the damned pistols did not go off better.'

However, Elizabeth Spink had been wrong: Reverend Plow wasn't dead. After fleeing the vicarage, and convinced that he was dying, he staggered to the house of his church organist, Mr Greenwood, clutching one of Miles' pistols, where he collapsed from loss of blood. A surgeon was called to tend the deep gashes in his face and head and about his body.

Trial and Punishment

The horrific attack was widely reported and shocked the nation. The headlines in the *Halifax Evening Courier* read: FRIGHTFUL TRAGEDY AT THE TODMORDEN VICARAGE: BRUTAL MURDER AND BUTCHERY. The *Courier* went on to describe what happened as 'a frightful drama, bearing features of the continental type of murder and outrage.'[15] The crime seemed to touch a nerve, perhaps because the attempted murder of a man of God in such a brutal fashion by one of his own flock was an outrage to Victorian morals, as was the murder and attempted murder of two defenceless women. But against this there was a tale of forbidden love, madness and blood lust. Hordes of ghoulish visitors flocked to Todmorden, which had gained national notoriety because of the crime.[16]

Miles was indicted before Mr Justice Lush on Friday 13 March 1868 at Manchester Assizes for the murder of Jane Smith. The case for the defence was that the nature of the crimes themselves was evidence that Weatherhill was insane.[17] Miles remained cool most of the time, though he apparently became animated when he disputed a number of trivial aspects of the murder. He denied saying 'damned' when referring to the pistols, and he also denied laughing on being told Reverend Plow was dead. The press at the time commented that it was hard to believe that this youth with his 'pale, boyish face' could be a brutal murderer.[18] The Reverend himself attended the trial, despite his terrible injuries. There could only be one verdict. Justice Lush donned the black cap and pronounced the death penalty. Miles Weatherhill was sentenced to be publicly hanged in Manchester.

On Saturday March 14 Reverend A.J. Plow died an agonising death from inflammation of the brain caused by his injuries. He was 37 years old. As a further tragic twist, their month-old baby, Hilda Katherine, died on the same day. It's not clear why the baby died; there is no mention of Miles physically harming the child, and we are only told that the mother's injuries required them to be separated while she recovered. Some sources say it was this removal from her mother that caused the infant's death.[19]

The inquest into Reverend Plow's death took place on Monday 16 March. Controversially, the coroner banned reporters from the proceedings. The coroner went on to say that the magistrates should not have allowed Plow to come face to face with his attacker at the trial, as the excitement was injurious to his health and contributed to his death.

That evening a service was held in the parish church in Todmorden in Plow's memory. The Reverend Blakelock castigated the congregation for being suspicious of Plow and his strict and supposedly dogmatic ways. He also told those present how, being mortally wounded, Plow had humbly lamented that it was his sin that had brought this evil about. Blakelock had previously visited Miles in his cell, and Miles had given the following message to be read to the congregation: 'Let me be a warning, but bid them beware the lusts of the flesh.'[20] This sermon was followed by another delivered by Plow's father, the Reverend H.A. Plow. He asked God to forgive Miles for his crimes.

The following day the Reverend Anthony Plow was buried with his baby in Todmorden, near the grave of his servant Jane Smith. It was a grim, stormy day with violent showers of hail and rain, but two thousand people came to see the funeral procession and shops, pubs and factories were closed as a mark of respect to the fallen priest and his infant daughter.[21]

Death Row

As Miles awaited execution in his Manchester prison cell, the letters he wrote were widely published in the newspapers.[22] The first letter was to his mother and his sister:

> My dear mother and sister-
> It must be very painful to you to know that I am in a prison, and what is worse, condemned to die. Well, you must bear it as well as you can. You will be allowed to see me once or twice more in my cell; then you must bid me farewell for ever. Undoubtedly it is now, and ever will be, a very great trouble to you when I am gone for ever from you; but you must

> remember we may all meet again in heaven if we only repent of our sins... You will be sorry when you hear I have not repented of my sins, but I will try my best to meet you both and Sarah in heaven. You must not think it hard of me because I write to Sarah more than you, you must know I look upon that good girl as my wife, though she is not, but I think she would if I was only free. I think that you will have found it out before now that she is a good girl, Ah she's too good for me... I will draw to a close, and hope that we may all meet in heaven.
> From yours, dear mother and sister, affectionately,
> MILES WEATHERHILL

The second letter was written to a friend:

> I suppose you know that I have been found guilty, and that I shall have to be hung. It is an awful and shameful death to die, but I have deserved it; and there is no chance left. I wish I could undo this shocking crime. I was very sorry when I heard that Mr. Plow and the babe was dead…

Miles went on to write that he wished he'd been allowed to see Sarah because then the tragedy would not have taken place. He would have found a better job and married his sweetheart. Miles continued in the letter to his friend:

> ...but when she left Todmorden, there was a turning point in me. Yes, I turned wild, I cared little what I did, I spent all my money, I saw nothing but poverty and despair, and now I am condemned to die. Ah, I was a changed man when she left me; I am sorry to say changed for the worse. I shall soon be parted

> from her for ever in this world, but I will try to meet her in heaven. But there is only poor signs yet of me, for my heart is quite hardened; but I will try and die a true penitent.

As Miles languished in jail, the media's fascination with the case continued, and more details about the central characters were revealed. Reverend Plow, it seems, was not popular with some sections of his congregation. He was too ritualistic, some felt, and had made too many changes. What is more, he had refused to let members of rival Saint Mary's church worship at Christ Church. As for Miles, he was declared a 'general lover' who had 'an especial affection for cooks who had a well filled larder'. He had also been expelled from the local Wesleyan Sunday School for 'irregular conduct'.[23]

The case was, perhaps surprisingly, used as an argument against capital punishment. The *Halifax Courier* reported that before the murders Miles had gone to Manchester to see a public hanging, referring to the execution of the three Fenians he had witnessed. If this is so, the argument went, hanging couldn't possibly be a deterrent to potential murderers if they are desperate enough. Miles, it seems, was well aware of what would become of him.[24] By this time, a waxwork effigy of Miles had been created and displayed in Madame Tussaud's Chamber of Horrors.

Miles' mother was allowed to visit her son in his cell a number of times, but each time she came, he refused to prepare himself for death until he was allowed a last meeting with Sarah. Miles did not in any way appear contrite for the murders, as was evident when he told the Reverend Caine to get out of his cell and take his books with him. But finally, a meeting with Sarah was arranged. This must have been a tremendously difficult time for this teenage girl as she found herself swept up in this brutal murder case, with her former lover about to be put to death. Miles somehow knew it was Sarah before his cell door opened to admit her, and leapt to his feet and clasped her in his arms a final time, crying 'my dearest Sarah'.[25] It was only on this final parting with Sarah that his full grief finally erupted, allowing him to show contrition and accept the justice of his doom.

On the eve of the execution a letter appeared in a Manchester paper saying that Miles Weatherhill suffered from hereditary insanity, and argued that the death penalty should be commuted. The author of the letter, who signed himself only 'a Todmordian', went on to give us a glimpse of Miles' family circumstances.[26]

Miles' father, Dick Weatherhill, was the 'most notorious character' to live in Todmorden in living memory. When Miles was a baby his father shut him in a drawer for a 'considerable' time and told his wife her son had been stolen by a tramp, just to see how she would react. Dick was also known to walk along the edges of high buildings threatening to kill himself in order to extort money from relatives. 'Never was there a fitter candidate for a strait-waistcoat than the well-known "Dick Weatherhill" of Todmorden,' the anonymous author continued.

The condemned man's mother was described as suffering from 'semi-intellectual imbecility' while his sister was 'nearly idiotic'. The author pointed out that nobody defended Miles at the inquest or before the magistrates, and if the jury had known the full facts about the accused's family history, they may have been inclined to mercy. The letter was written to redress this, so that petitions could be made to the home secretary to commute the death sentence. It was not successful. The execution was to go ahead at 8am on Saturday 4 April 1868.

Execution

Crowds began to gather outside the New Bailey prison, Salford in the very early hours. Some had walked for miles overnight to be sure of a good view, and were huddled in doorways trying to get some sleep before the execution. Refreshment stalls were set up to cater for the gathering throng, which by 8am had swelled to 20,000 people by some accounts,[27] though some reports estimated around 7,000.[28] According to the *Halifax Courier*: 'The behaviour of the crowd is said to have been very bad indeed. The very dregs of society were there. The lowest types of Lancashire and Yorkshire men were represented.'[29]

Miles had gone to bed at 10pm on his final evening and spent a restless night, disturbed by the noisy crowd which had even then started to congregate outside the prison. The noise was so great, that he got up at 2.30am and spent the rest of the morning praying with Reverend Caine and Thomas Wright, a prison philanthropist who had been visiting Miles.[30]

Finally, the time came. 'During the pinioning of his arms,' the *Courier* tells us, 'the convict's fortitude never forsook him; he even manifested a sort of cheerfulness, and conversed with the chaplain and Mr Wright without the least tremor or hesitation.'[31]

Outside the prison, the thick haze that had covered the street began to lift revealing the 20-foot-high gallows draped in black cloth. The crowd would also have seen the spidery figure of hangman William Calcraft inspecting the trap door, the mechanism and the nooses on his cruelly short ropes, and as the melancholy prison bell chimed eight times Miles Weatherhill appeared, accompanied by two chaplains and another prisoner who was also to be hanged that day.[32] Miles' companion in death was another notorious killer, John Faherty, the Droylsden Murderer, who had beaten the woman he loved to death with a poker on Christmas Day 1867 when she spurned his drunken advances.[33]

First, Faherty ascended the steps while Miles waited at the bottom of the platform. Calcraft, perhaps still nervous about the threats of death he had received for the hanging of the three Irish Republican Brotherhood members a few months earlier, was not quite ready, and the two condemned men had to endure an agonizing delay. Faherty was left standing on the trap door, the noose round his neck and the customary white hood over his face, unaware of what was happening. Miles was waiting at the bottom of the steps. A warder held Miles by the arm, but he shook him off saying: 'You need not hold me; I can stand by myself.'[34]

Finally, the hangman was ready. Miles ascended the steps and took his place next to Faherty. The noose and white hood were placed over his head and the executioner shook hands with both men. 'May God have mercy on my soul' were Miles Weatherhill's last words as the bolt was drawn. Both men were seen to struggle violently for a few moments after their short drop through the trap door.[35] At 9am they were cut down and buried in the prison graveyard at the New Bailey, Salford.

They were the last men to be publicly hanged in Manchester.[36]

Epilogue

In the aftermath of these terrible murders, it was only natural to seek explanations for Mile's bloodlust. In the august pages of the *British Medical Journal,* renowned physiologist Thomas Laycock wrote that Miles was suffering from 'erethism of the genital organs' and this had sent him mad with lust. Laycock believed that if Miles had happened upon his love Sarah Bell at the vicarage that night, he would have killed her too.[37] This is hard to believe. During the attack, Miles had plenty of opportunity to harm the two servants and the nurse who was with Mrs Plow if he had wanted. His attack was not indiscriminate and had clearly been planned, as can be seen in his letters to Sarah, his specially fashioned belt to hold his weapons and his grim visit to the public hanging in Manchester. He knew what his fate would be, and even watching the men twist and jig on the end of Calcraft's short rope did not deter him.

As opposed to the man of science's medical explanation, one man of God had a different answer. Reverend Caine had been with Miles in his condemned cell at the end, and he reported that Miles told him the crime was suggested by his reading of sensational novels.[38] It is true that the late 1860s saw the peak of the Victorian 'sensation novel', a genre mixing romance, crime, mystery and horror and often featuring extremes of emotion, melodrama, suspense, innocence and madness. Wilkie Collins' 1859 work *The Woman in White* kickstarted the genre, and there was a certain amount of handwringing and pearl clutching from some quarters about the effects these books might have on tender young minds. Although Miles may have read some of these books, it's hard to believe they played a role in his monstrous crime. After all, many people read these novels without going on murder sprees.

Illustration from the 1868 Broadside Ballad of Miles Weatherhill

Perhaps it was a fatal flaw in Miles' character, some speculated. An article in the *Manchester Guardian* noted that Miles often spent his free time in reading rooms, reading up on local and national affairs. He was well-read and knowledgeable and confident enough to best people of greater education and social standing in any dispute.[39] This may have led to 'inordinate self-esteem' to such an extent that when he was crossed by stuffy Reverend Plow, he exploded in murderous rage.

It's hard to discount the effect that Miles' family background and its history of mental problems may have had on his disturbed thought process. Yet, despite his father's apparent madness and his mother's supposed imbecility, Miles was an intelligent and sane young man. Or so it was thought until the night of the vicarage murders. Then, wise after the event, many who knew him said they had always known he was a dangerous young man.[40]

Whatever the case, this tragic story resonated with a sensation hungry Victorian public. An anonymous doggerel ballad telling the story was sold at the execution and was adapted and recorded by several folk singers, perhaps Nic Jones' 1977 version being the best known. The ballad ends:

At the early age of three and twenty,
In the shades below with the worms do dwell,
On the fatal drop, he cried, broken hearted,
'May we meet in heaven, my sweet Sarah Bell.'[41]

The Halifax Gibbet ~ The Last Cut is the Deepest

'... by the antient custom, and liberty of Halifax, whereof the memory of man is not to the contrary, the said Abraham Wilkinson, and Anthony Mitchel, are to suffer death, by having their heads severed, and cut off from their bodies, at Halifax Gibbet; unto which verdict we subscribe our names the thirtieth of April, one thousand six hundred and fifty...'

(James Holland, Constable of Halifax, 1650)

The beheading of Wilkinson and Mitchel in 1650 marked the end of the Halifax Gibbet's long career dispatching criminals. For centuries this crude guillotine had given Halifax a grim reputation for tough justice, even after such punishment was abolished elsewhere. Stealing goods worth thirteen and a half pence was enough of a crime to lose you your head. Not surprisingly, the Gibbet's rich history contains macabre tales of bouncing heads, dramatic escapes and melancholy ghosts...

The Origin of the 'Gin

The story of how Halifax got its 'gin' (engine) for decapitating criminals goes back to the time of King Henry I (1068-1135).[1] At this time, the story goes, materials such as kersey, the tough cloth often used for military uniforms, would be left stretched out to dry in fields around Halifax, a centre of the cloth trade. The drying cloth was easy pickings for enterprising thieves, and such theft was so concerning that the King of England gave a Mr Hodgekins of Halifax the privilege to hang thieves caught stealing the town's cloth. This tough new law seems to have worked and the townsfolk were pleased that their cloth was safe at night. So safe, in fact, they sacked the town's watchmen and slept easily in their beds.

There was, though, a notorious and daring thief who found the prospect of this unguarded treasure irresistible. His name was Mighty Wallis, called so because of his valour and his manhood. 'I would venture my neck for a pack of northern cloth,' he was heard to say, and he set about planning a daring robbery. As with all heists, the first part of the operation is putting the gang together, and this is what Mighty Wallis did. Eventually he persuaded two mates to be partners in the crime.

The next part of the operation showed Wallis's cunning. He and his men took their horses to a farrier's in the early hours of the morning and gave instructions that all of their horses' shoes should be put on back to front. The farrier was perplexed by this strange request and thought he was dealing with fools. The gang ordered him to do as was told and recited the proverb:

Be it better or be it worse
Please you the man that bears the purse

Finally, the gang were ready for their audacious heist, and headed off to Halifax.

It seems it was all too easy for Mighty Wallis and his comrades. They loaded their horses with stolen cloth before dawn and set off home with the loot. Soon the clothiers of Halifax realised they'd been robbed and the alarm was raised. Mr Hodgekins led the search for the culprits, and the thieves' tracks were discovered, though because of Wallis's ruse of having the horses shod backwards, the search party was sent on a wild goose chase and ended up back where they had started.

Unfortunately for the Mighty Wallis, the search party made up for the lost time and apprehended the gang. Now Hodgekins, it will be remembered, had been given the right by the King to hang cloth thieves, so Wallis and his men were facing summary execution. Nooses were placed round their necks and they prepared for death. Wallis gave a moving final speech in which he confessed his dissolute life and lamented his wrongdoing, before commending his and his partners' souls to God and their bodies to the grave. The crowd that had gathered to witness the proceedings were moved to pity.

Hodgekins asked a poor neighbour to be the hangman and carry out the execution. The incentive for doing this was the 'hangman's perk': the custom of the deceased felon's clothes going to the executioner. The poor neighbour refused. Then Hodgekins asked someone whose cloth had been stolen to do the deed, but he also refused. In fact, it turned out that nobody was willing to carry out the execution, and Hodgekins himself, though happy to order a hanging, was not willing to carry it out even though he had suffered most from the theft. Then he had an idea. The thief who agreed to hang the other two would go free; otherwise they would be held in prison until a hangman could be found.

But Mighty Wallis was a cunning rogue. 'My masters of the town of Halifax,' he told them, 'though your privilege stretch to hang up men presently that are stealing your goods, yet it gives you no warrant to imprison them till you provide them a hangman. Myself with these my fellows have here yielded ourselves to satisfy the law, and if it be not performed, the fault is yours and not ours, and therefore we humbly take our leave: from the gallows the 18th of August.' With this Hodgekins leapt off the ladder he was to have been hanged from and defiantly tossed the noose in Hodgekins' face.

The crowd of clothiers present had been moved to pity by the robbers' courage in the face of death, but now they began to realise that Wallis and the gang still had their cloth. They entreated the thief to return their property, but Wallis refused. 'A plague on you,' Wallis said to them. 'I made account to dine this day in heaven, and you keep me here on earth where there is not a quarter of that good cheer. The foul evil take you all. I was fully provided to give the gallows a box on the ear and now God knows when I shall be in so good a mind again.' And with that, Mighty Wallis departed along with his comrades and a sizeable pack of stolen cloth.

Hodgekins was powerless and distraught. His privilege from the King allowing him the power to execute cloth thieves was useless if none in the town were willing to play the role of hangman. However, while he was wallowing in his melancholy, a grey friar approached him. The friar went on to reproach the already despondent Hodgekins. 'What great cause of boldness have you given to bad livers by letting these fellows thus to escape,' the friar said. 'How shall you now keep your goods in safety, seeing that you fulfil not the law which should be your defence?' The friar had a point. When word got around that thieves need not fear death when stealing cloth from Halifax, there would be nothing to stop them.

The mysterious grey friar, though had a practical solution to the problem. This was not because he was concerned about the clothiers' profits, but rather due to his love for justice. The friar said to Hodgekins: 'Seeing I find you and the rest so womanish that you could not find it in your hearts to hang a thief, I have devised how to make a gin [engine] that shall cut off their heads without man's help.' Hodgekins was much comforted by this prospect, and would again ask the King for the privilege to behead thieves rather than hang them. The friar, meanwhile, employed a carpenter to produce the decapitation machine according to the friar's design.

Hodgekins sought an audience with the King and told him that the privilege to hang thieves was 'not worth a pudding' because no one was willing to be the executioner. Therefore, Hodgekins went on, if the King would allow it, there was a grey friar who could create a device which 'shall without the hand of man cut off the crags of all such rogues.' The King understood and the petition was granted. And this device came to be known as the Halifax Gibbet and gave rise to the town's infamous Gibbet Law…

This version of the Gibbet's origin is taken from Thomas Delany's sixteenth century novel *Thomas of Reading*. It's a good story, and perhaps there are elements of truth to it. It would indeed be hard to find a hangman in a small hamlet as Halifax then was because everyone would know each other and there would be fear of reprisals from the relatives of the executed. However, the association of Halifax with the cloth trade came later than the setting of this story, and as local historian T.W. Hanson pointed out, the gibbet custom may have been more related, at least in its early days, with the theft of cattle.[2] Nevertheless, the Halifax Gibbet and the Gibbet Law are an integral and macabre part of Halifax's story.

The Gibbet Law

The guillotine, of course, is most commonly associated with France and the French Revolution, but it is certainly arguable that the origins of this device lie in Halifax and that Monsieur Joseph Guillotine was inspired by the gibbet.[3] Between 1541, when records proper began, and 1650, when its use was discontinued, around 60 people met their death on the gibbet, though there were possibly more victims. The earliest recorded use was in 1286 on one John of Dalton.[4]

The Halifax Gibbet (Volume II of Thomas Allen's 'A New and Complete History of the County of York', 1829)

The use of the gibbet was enshrined in the town's gibbet law. The law states that if a felon is taken within the precincts of Halifax either 'handabed' (carrying stolen goods in his hands), 'backbarend' (with stolen goods on his back), or 'confessand' (having confessed to stealing goods) to the value of thirteen and a half pence, 'he shall after three markets... be taken to the gibbet and there have his head cut off from his body.'[5]

Imagine you had committed the crime of stealing something worth more than thirteen and a half pence. First, you would face a trial of sorts and locals of the 'most ancient, intelligent, and the best ability' would hear your case.[6] If you were found guilty, you would face some time in the stocks with the stolen goods arranged around you as a warning to others. Finally, your execution would take place on the subsequent Saturday market.[7]

So, Saturday comes and you are led to your place of execution. Originally the gibbet was at Cow Green but was later moved to the end of Gibbet Street. You see a raised platform with a few steps leading to the top which you must climb. On the platform you see the bailiff, the jury that convicted you and worst of all, the gibbet itself. The gibbet consisted of two tall wooden posts at the top of which was a blade held in place by a pin attached to a rope. Unlike the French guillotine, the Halifax gibbet's blade was not particularly sharp, but it was heavy; it will be the *weight* of the blade that will squash your neck and sever your head. To make matters worse, as well as the crowd of spectators there are psalms being played on the bagpipes. A minister prays with you for the last time.

Now you are made to lie with your head between the posts. The pin holding the blade in place was sometimes pulled out by the bailiff or sometimes by the jury themselves, along with anyone in the crowd who fancied lending a hand. Some sources say that everyone present would take part in pulling the pin and those who could not reach would stretch out their hands towards the gibbet to demonstrate, presumably, that they were happy to see such rough justice done.[8] But let's imagine that your crime was the theft of a horse. In this case the rope attached to the pin will be pulled by the very animal you had taken. The crowd giddy the horse up, out comes the pin and the hefty slab of metal plummets towards your neck. You would imagine that this would be the end of it, but you might be wrong.

Your heart might continue beating in your headless trunk for some time, but even worse than that, your severed head may remain conscious for a few seconds, perhaps even a minute.[9] It's recorded that when Mary Queen of Scots was beheaded, her lips continued moving in silent prayer for 15 minutes, and there are similar reports about victims of the French guillotine.[10] Someone picks up your rolling head and the last things you see are the crowd gawping, your friends and relatives weeping and a fountain of blood spraying up to six feet from your torso...

It's not entirely clear how many people were beheaded, but there are records that contain some names and details. John of Dalton, as mentioned above, bears the honour of being the first recorded victim in 1286. A 'strange harper' was executed in 1298, though what his crimes were and the relevance of his harp are lost to time. All we do know is that one Nicolase de Wyston has 'many times received' this mysterious musician and was ordered by the court to produce the harp that had been left at his house by this unnamed harpist.[11] Some of the records tell a rather mundane story such as the beheading in 1316 of Hugh of Cock Hill for stealing a cow from John of the Cliff. Some records are enigmatic, such as the execution of 'a certain stranger' in 1542. Others are tantalising in what details they do give. For example, on 23 November 1588 the vicar notes in the register that he has just buried one George Fairbanke, 'most depraved scoundrel, commonly called Scoggins, on account of his villainy and Anna, illegitimate daughter of this George, both most deservedly beheaded on account of crimes of which they were clearly guilty.' There were even some husband and wife double beheadings such as on 28 August 1630 when Henry Hudson and his wife of Ettal met their end.[12]

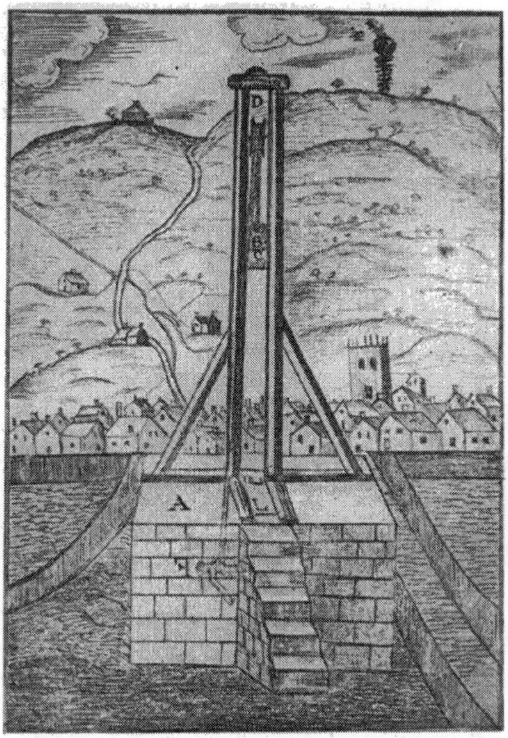

17th century engraving reprinted in The Saturday Magazine, 1834

Considering the Halifax gibbet was in use for centuries, there seem to be remarkably few victims on record. It's not clear why this is. Perhaps, as Hanson speculates, only the most well-to-do criminals with land or substantial property were recorded and that it was not considered worthwhile recording the executions of poorer felons. Calderdale folklore expert John Billingsley, on the other hand, suggests juries may have just been reluctant to find some of the accused guilty knowing that it would lead to their execution.[13] Indeed, perhaps if you were lucky, you might receive a lesser sentence such as that meted out to Frank Frankleton and an unnamed Heptonstall convict in 1649, who had their ears nailed to the gibbet's wooden post. They were given a knife and ordered to cut themselves free.[14]

Replica of the Gibbet, Gibbet Street

Gibbet Lore ~ Flying Heads and Running Men

Because the violence of the gibbet's blade falling was so great, the head would sometimes fly up into the air. One particularly tall tale about the gibbet concerns a lady visitor to Halifax who paused on her way to watch an execution. The gibbet blade fell with such force that the felon's severed head flew over the assembled crowd, landed in the lady's lap and gripped her apron with its teeth, refusing to let go. In another version of the story (or perhaps it's a different bouncing head) the head plops into the poor woman's shopping basket and she remains unaware of its presence until she gets to market and looks in her basket to find the grisly contents.[15] In his journey through Halifax, a sceptical Daniel Defoe of *Robinson Crusoe* fame was told the second of these stories, but commented that the tale was 'a little Yorkshire.'[16]

Another dramatic aspect of the gibbet story is the possible means of escape. The custom was that after the pin was removed, if you could pull your head out of the way and dash the short distance to Hebble Brook without being caught, you were free.[17] Amazingly enough, this was said to have happened on more than one occasion. These fleet felons are the Running Men.

A criminal known only as Dinnis managed to remove his head from the gibbet before the blade got it, jump from the platform and start running. As he dashed for the Hebble Brook and the parish boundary he met a number of people on the way to watch his execution who enquired of him if Dinnis was to be executed that day, not realising that they were speaking to the man himself. 'I trow not,' he replied. 'I trow [believe] not' became a local catchphrase to describe something unlikely: I trow not, quoth Dinnis.[18]

John Lacey was another running man. He too pulled his head out of the way of the blade in time and made a successful dash over the parish border. Unfortunately, Lacey believed his escape meant that he had been pardoned for his crime and seven years later he returned to Halifax where he was rearrested and taken straight to the gibbet. He wasn't as lucky the second time. John Lacey lost his head on 29 January 1623,[19] but at least he has a pub named after him: The Running Man on Pellon Lane. For many years, the pub's sign showed the wrong kind of gibbet. It showed a celebrating John Lacey, arms in the air in triumph, having just crossed Hebble Brook with the cheated executioner behind him. But the gibbet in the picture was a metal cage used to hang the bodies of executed criminals in, not the decapitation machine that was the Halifax gibbet.

The Running Man pub sign in 2004

Another Running Man story was related to Daniel Defoe on his eighteenth century visit to Halifax. It may be a variant on the Dinnis or Lacey episodes, or perhaps even a third escapee. In this daring escape, the cocky criminal paused in his dash for freedom to request the crowd throw him his hat before he continued. Then, on reaching Hebble Brook, he waited for the executioner to catch up with him and threatened to drown his pursuer in the river. The executioner decided better of it and stopped too. Defoe notes, having himself examined the gibbet's weighty blade and the scaffold, that it is unlikely a fellow could be so quick as to remove his head after the pin is pulled in time to save himself.[20] Indeed, perhaps these incredible escapes simply happened on or before the day of execution, rather than as the blade was falling. Whatever the case, these running men are a celebrated part of Halifax Gibbet Lore.

Sign outside the Running Man pub in 2021

The End of the Gibbet

The gibbet was in use in Halifax for much longer than similar machines were in use in other parts of the country. This is thought to be because of Halifax's lucrative cloth trade; the hills around Halifax would have been covered with cloth stretched out to dry in wooden frames called tenterframes. The gibbet, in theory anyway, would have been a brutal deterrent to those tempted by such easy cotton pickings.

The last two victims of the gibbet were Abraham Wilkinson and Anthony Mitchell of Sowerby. They were convicted of stealing cloth and horses and were beheaded in April 1650.[21] By 1650, the practice of beheading thieves for stealing goods valued at more than 13 pence must have seemed unduly harsh; that's about a fiver in today's money.[22] After the practice was abandoned, only the gibbet's platform remained. Local children played on it, as recalled by James Cook towards the end of the 18th century. He remembered how he and his friends would jump on and off the platform when they were teenagers. Slabs of sandstone were stolen from the platform as settings for ovens, and the platform eventually became lost, buried under a rubbish tip, known as Gibbet Hill.[23]

Ghosts of the Gibbet

As you might expect, the macabre history of the Halifax gibbet has its share of ghostly folklore. The ghost of John Lacey, the Running Man who'd made the mistake of returning to Halifax after miraculously escaping the gibbet's clutches, is said to haunt the pub that bears his name. It's hard to pin down an origin to this story, but local historian Kai Roberts considers it possible that the ghost is a rumour that was inspired by the name of the pub, or possibly even created and spread by previous owners to their patrons.[24] Another ghostly legend involves the Moot Hall (demolished in 1957) where many of the gibbet hearings took place. At one time there was a cruel judge called Jackson who apparently took every opportunity to condemn the guilty to the gibbet. Jackson gained such notoriety that the Moot Hall became known as Jackson's Court due to his terrifying reputation. He kept with him at all times a pet weasel, and the two of them haunt the streets of Halifax.[25] Roberts writes that Jackson and his pet are likely fictional figures, but the ghost of a fearsome gibbetting judge and his evil weasel are certainly colourful additions to Halifax's rich ghost lore.

Another story connected with the Moot Hall was described by local historian F.A. Leyland in 1852:

> There are people living who remember, in their childhood, old men saying [how] in times past many [convicted criminals] had been conducted from its portals to the scaffold and that in the long winter nights the misty forms of men without heads might be seen gliding through its gloomy precincts.'[26]

Epilogue

In June 1839 workmen made a gruesome discovery after digging through two centuries of accumulated rubbish on Gibbet Hill: two skeletons and their severed skulls. It was assumed they had unearthed the remains of the Halifax gibbet's final victims, Wilkinson and Mitchell. This would tie the story of the gibbet up nicely, so it's tempting to believe it, though there was no direct evidence for this identification. Soon afterwards, the platform itself was rediscovered too.[27] A replica of the gibbet stands on the platform that saw many a head roll (or perhaps bounce) during the gibbet's centuries long reign of terror.

End Notes

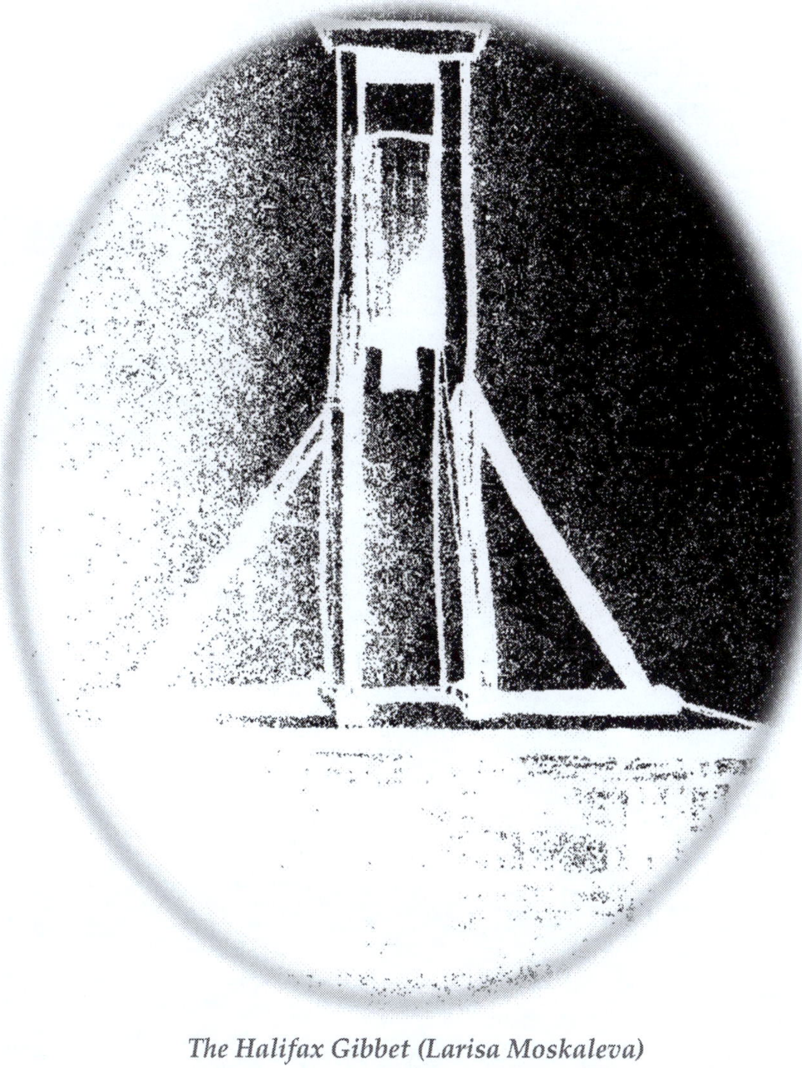

The Halifax Gibbet (Larisa Moskaleva)

1. The Halifax Slasher ~ Razor Blade Terror

[1] *Halifax Evening Courier* 17 November 1938
[2] *Halifax Evening Courier* 25 November 1938
[3] Ibid
[4] *Manchester Guardian* 26 November 1938
[5] *Yorkshire Evening Post* 15 December 1938
[6] *Yorkshire Evening Post* 26 November 1938
[7] *Yorkshire Evening Post* 28 November 1938
[8] *Yorkshire Evening Post* 16 January 1939
[9] *Halifax Evening Courier* 28 November 1938
[10] *Yorkshire Evening Post* 6 December 1938
[11] *Yorkshire Evening Post* 28 November 1938
[12] Ibid
[13] *Yorkshire Evening Post* 29 November 1938
[14] *Yorkshire Post and Leeds Intelligencer* 30 November 1938
[15] *Yorkshire Evening Post* 29 November 1938
[16] *The Guardian* 6 March 1997
[17] *Yorkshire Evening Post* 29 November 1938
[18] Ibid
[19] *Yorkshire Post and Leeds Intelligencer* 30 November 1938
[20] *Manchester Guardian* 29 November 1938
[21] *Halifax Evening Courier* 28 January 1939
[22] *Yorkshire Post and Leeds Intelligencer* 29 November 1938
[23] *Yorkshire Evening Post* 29 November 1938, 1 December 1938, 2 December 1938, 3 December 1938, 6 December 1938, 10 December 1938
[24] *Yorkshire Evening Post* 3 December 1918
[25] *Halifax Evening Courier* 1 December 1938
[26] *Manchester Guardian* 3 November 1938
[27] *Manchester Guardian* 11 January 1939
[28] *Western Morning News* 2 December 1938
[29] *Halifax Evening Courier* 15 December 1938
[30] *Yorkshire Evening Post* 3 December 1938
[31] *Halifax Evening Courier* 14 January 1939
[32] *Yorkshire Evening Post* 3 December 1938

[33] *Halifax Evening Courier* 14 January 1939
[34] *Halifax Evening Courier* 28 January 1939
[35] Ibid
[36] Ibid
[37] *Yorkshire Post and Leeds Intelligencer* 16 December 1938
[38] *Halifax Evening Courier* 21 January 1939
[39] *Yorkshire Evening Post* 27 March 1939
[40] *Halifax Evening Courier* 28 January 1939
[41] *Halifax Evening Courier* 27 September 1986
[42] *Halifax Evening Courier* 28 January 1939
[43] Michael Goss, *The Halifax Slasher: An Urban Terror in the North of England* (Fortean Times Occasional Paper Number 3, 1987)
[44] *Aberdeen Press and Journal* 26 July 1922
[45] *Halifax Evening Courier* 17 February 1927
[46] Heather Shore, 'Rogues of the Racecourse', *Media History*, 20:4, pp.352-367, (2014) doi: 10.1080/13688804.2014.949417
[47] *Yorkshire Evening Post* 31 October 1938
[48] *Manchester Guardian* 6 December 1938
[49] *Gloucester Citizen* 28 August 1943
[50] *Daily Mir*ror 13 May 1955
[51] Robert E. Bartholomew, *Little Green Men. Meowing Nuns and Headhunting Panics,* (McFarland & Co, 2001) p.14
[52] Robert W. Baloch and Robert E. Bartholomew, *Havana Syndrome: Mass Psychogenic Illness and the Real Story Behind the Embassy Mystery and Hysteria,* (Springer, 2020) p.1
[53] Ibid p.14

2. Haunted Valley ~ The Ghosts That Time Forgot

[1] Lucy Hamerton, *Olde Elland* (1901) p.104
[2] Ibid
[3] Kai Roberts, *Haunted Halifax and District,* (Stroud: The History Press, 2014) p.56
[4] Edwin Waugh, *Tufts of Heather* (1881)
[5] According to the garbled retelling of the legend in *Todmorden Advertiser and Hebden Bridge Newsletter* 22 November 1926
[6] Email from Pete Marney to author 7 April 2021
[7] *Todmorden and District News* 13 September 1889

[8] John Billingsley, *Head Hood and Hag* (Hebden Bridge: Northern Earth, 2011) p.86
[9] Roberts p.76
[10] *Todmorden and District News* 13 September 1889
[11] *Halifax Guardian* 24 April 1843
[12] *Halifax Courier* 3 June 1854
[13] *Halifax Courier* 27 November 1869
[14] *The Brighouse News* 29 July 1876
[15] *Halifax Courier*14 December 1880
[16]*Todmorden and District News* 17 August 1906
[17] *Todmorden and District News* 20 June 1890
[18] Jill Liddington, *Rebel Girls: Their Fight for the Vote* (London: Virago, 2008), p.104
[19] R. Thurston Hopkins, *Ghosts Over England* (London: Meridian Books, 1953), p.115
[20] *Leeds and York Mercury* 12 March 1907
[21] *Milltown Memories,* No. 9 pp.24-25
[22] *Burnley Express and News* 24 January 1953
[23] *Milltown Memories,* No. 9 pp.24-25
[24] Malcolm Gaskill, *Hellish Nell: Last of Britain's Witches* (London: Harper Collins, 2001)
[25] Ibid p.53
[26] Ibid p.110
[27] *Todmorden News and Advertiser* 14 December 1934
[28] Ibid
[29] Gaskill p.82
[30] *Todmorden News and Advertiser* 14 December 1934
[31] *Todmorden News and Advertiser* 7 June 1935
[32] Ibid p.139
[33] Ibid pp.155-156
[34] *Halifax Daily Courier and Guardian* 17 February 1955
[35] Ibid
[36] Ibid
[37] Ibid
[38] *Yorkshire Observer* 18 February 1955
[39] *Halifax Evening Courier* 28 June 1950

[40] *Halifax Evening Courier* 17 August 1953; *Yorkshire Post and Leeds Intelligencer*, 22 September 1953
[41] *Halifax Daily Courier and Guardian* 24 February 1955
[42] Ibid
[43] *Yorkshire Observer* 25 February 1955
[44] Roberts, p.65
[45] Ibid p.65
[46] https://greenhow-hill.org.uk/sowerbytown/old/history/ghosts/ghost59.html

3. The Adamski Mystery

[1] Alan Godfrey, *Who or What Were They?* (Oz Factor Books, 2017) p.69
[2] Ibid pp.69-70
[3] Jenny Randles, *The Pennine UFO Mystery* (London: Granada, 1983) p.16
[4] Randles, p.17
[5] Godfrey p.75
[6] Hanson and Sankey, *A Review Into The Mysterious Events Surrounding Mr. Zigmund Adamski*, p.6
[7] Stefnie Krzyszczyk (telephone interview, 2020)
[8] Hanson and Sankey p.2
[9] Randles p.18
[10] Randles p.19
[11] Randles p.20
[12] Godfrey p.82
[13] Randles p.20
[14] Godfrey pp.79-80
[15] Cats Protection League Talk, Hebden Bridge Arts Centre, 4 September, 2003
[16] John Sheard and Stuart Bonney, *Sunday Mirror* 27 September 1981
[17] Hanson and Sankey pp.3-4
[18] Mikael Rothstein, 'Hagiography and text in the Aetherius Society' in *Alien Worlds* ed Diana G. Tumminia, (New York: Syracuse University Press, 2007)
[19] Philip J. Klass, *UFO Abductions: A Dangerous Game,* (Buffalo: Prometheus Books, 1989) pp.25-37
[20] Klass pp.28-37
[21] John Sheard and Stuart Bonney, *Sunday Mirror* 27 September 1981

[22] Graham Birdsall, 'Unnatural Causes', *Unopened Files,* no.18 (October/November, 2000) p.35
[23] Randles p.26
[24] Godfrey p.89
[25] *Daily Mirror* 3 October 1978
[26] Madeleine Teahan, *The Catholic Herald* 26 July 2013
[27] *Birmingham Daily Post* 30 October 1962
[28] Birdsall p.79
[29] Stefnie Krzyszczyk (personal communication, 2020)
[30] Ibid
[31] Birdsall p.34
[32] Hanson and Sankey p.3
[33] Birdsall p.35
[34] Birdsall p.36
[35] Ji Xu, Hongyong Deng, and Xueyong Shen 'Safety of Moxibustion: A Systematic Review of Case Reports', *Evidence-Based Complementary and Alternative Medicine* (2014) p.7
[36] Hanson and Sankey p.3
[37] Godfrey p.72
[38] John Sheard and Stuart Bonney, *Sunday Mirror* 27 September 1981
[39] Hanson and Sankey p.5
[40] Email to author from Graham Birdsall, 1 September, 2003
[41] Stefnie Krzyszczyk (telephone interview, 2020)
[42] Hanson and Sankey p.2
[43] Marriage certificate
[44] Email to author from Graham Birdsall, 1 September, 2003
[45] Randles p.17
[46] Birdsall p.78

4. Invasion of the Bobby Snatchers ~ The Alien Adventures of PC Alan Godfrey

[1] Alan Godfrey, *Who or What Were They?* (Oz Factor Books, 2017) p.94
[2] Ibid pp.95-96
[3] Jenny Randles, 'A policeman's lot', *Flying Saucer Review* 27, 2 (1981) p.4
[4] Jenny Randles, *The Pennine UFO Mystery* (St Albans: Granada, 1983) p.124
[5] Randles (1981) p.5

[6] Ibid p.5
[7] Godfrey p.103
[8] Ibid p.105
[9] Ibid p.117
[10] Randles (1983) p.131
[11] Godfrey p.108
[12] Ibid p.110
[13] Ibid p.111
[14] Godfrey pp.115-116
[15] Ibid pp.143-185
[16] Randles (1983) p.148
[17] Ibid p.162
[18] Ibid pp.148-158
[19] Ibid p.158
[20] Ibid p.165
[21] Ibid p.153
[22] Godfrey p.179
[23] Randles (1983) p.148
[24] Ibid p.168
[25] *Dundee Courier* 29 November 1986
[26] *Liverpool Echo* 1 August 1986
[27] *Dundee Courier* 29 November 1986
[28] *Dundee Courier* 6 December 1986
[29] *Dundee Courier* 29 November 1986
[30] Michael Heap, 'Tony Gibson (1914-2001)', *The Skeptical Intelligencer*, 4, (2001) p.24
[31] Hamilton Bertie Gibson, 'Hypnosis and Flying Saucers', *The Skeptical Intelligencer*, 4, (2001) pp.25-27
[32] Ibid p.25
[33] Ibid p.26
[34] Ibid p.26
[35] Ibid p.26
[36] Ibid p.27
[37] Robert A. Baker, *They Call it Hypnosis* (Buffalo: Prometheus, 1990) p.198
[38] Stuart Appelle, 'Alien Abduction Experiences', in *Dissociation, trauma, memory and hypnosis series. Varieties of Anomalous Experience: Examining the*

Scientific Evidence ed. by E.L. Cardena (Washington DC: American Psychological Association, 2014) p.334
[39] Richard Ofshe and Ethan Watters, *Making Monsters: False Memories, Psychotherapy and Sexual Hysteria* (London: Andre Deutsch, 1995) p.28
[40] Elizabeth Loftus and Katherine Ketcham, *The Myth of Repressed Memory: False Memories and Allegations of Sexual Abuse* (New York: St Martin's Griffin, 1994)
[41] Godfrey pp.133-141
[42] Todmorden UFO Meet, Golden Lion, Todmorden, 24 September, 2019
[43] Randles (1983) p.128
[44] Randles (1981) p.6
[45] Randles (1983) p.129
[46] Godfrey p.115
[47] Randles (1981) p.6
[48] Randles (1984) p.129
[49] Godfrey p.115
[50] Randles (1981) p.1981
[51] Randles (1984) p.129
[52] Godfrey (2017)
[53] National Institute for Neurological Disorders and Stroke, available at: https://www.ninds.nih.gov/Disorders/Patient-Caregiver-Education/Fact-Sheets/Narcolepsy-Fact-Sheet, accessed 1 March 2021
[54] Godfrey p.178
[55] Randles (1983) p.148
[56] Ibid p.166
[57] Ibid p.216
[58] Ibid p.217
[59] Brian A. Sharpless, 'A clinician's guide to recurrent isolated sleep paralysis', *Neuropsychiatric Disease and Treatment* ,12, (2016) pp.1761-1767 (p.1762)
[60] Randles (1983) pp.226-223
[61] www.youtube.com/watch?v=4PXYrflN-a4
[62] Godfrey (2017)
[63] Alan Godfrey, Talk for Cats Protection League, 4 September 2004

5. Tom Bell ~ The Exploding Outlaw of Hebden Bridge

[1] William Broadbent, 'A Rural Walk on a Summer's Day' in *Miscellaneous Poems,* (Todmorden, 1840), pp.53-55

[2] William Dearden, *The Vale of Caldene*; (Halifax: Walker, 1844)

[3] Dan Thomas Wilcock, *Stories from Hardcastle Crags and Heptonstall No.1,* (Heptonstall, 1919)

[4] Broadbent (1840)

[5] Dearden p.229

[6] Ibid p.229

[7] Ibid p.230

[8] Wilcock (1919)

[9] *Stories and Folkore from the District Called Hardcastle Crags,* Hebden Bridge

[10] Dearden p.234

[11] *Todmorden Advertiser and Hebden Bridge News* 25 March 1894

[12] *Hebden Bridge Times* 13 October 1899

[13] *Hebden Bridge Times* 27 October 1899

[14] *Hebden Bridge Times* 10 October 1899

[15] *Hebden Bridge Times* 13 October 1899

[16] *Todmorden and District News* 12 October 1900

[17] *Todmorden and District News* 15 August 1902

[18] *Hebden Bridge Times* 2 February 1900

[19] *Burnley Express and Advertiser* 21 October 1899

[20] Personal communication, 2005

[21] *Todmorden and District News* 15 August 1902

[22] *Todmorden and District News* 26 January 1900

[23] *Todmorden and District News* 12 October 1900

[24] Ibid

[25] *Halifax Daily Courier and Guardian* 16 June 1958

[26] *Halifax Daily Courier and Guardian* 10 February 1967

[27] https://www.youtube.com/watch?v=9SLFjimPJMs

[28] G.A. Gilks, 'The human skull from Tom Bell's Cave, Hardcastle Crags, West Yorkshire and its relative date', *Hunter Archaeological Society,* Vol 17 (1993), pp.60-62

[29] *Todmorden Advertiser and Hebden Bridge News* 25 March 1894

[30] *Halifax Daily Courier and Guardian* 20 May 1960

[31] *Halifax Daily Courier and Guardian* 10 February 1967

[32] J.A. Heginbottom and J.A. Gilks, 'A Note on the History and Archaeology of Tom Bell's cave, Hardcastle Crags', *Transactions of the Halifax Antiquarian Society 1989*
[33] John Mayhall, *The Annals of Yorkshire From the Earliest Period to the Present Time,* (J. Johnson, 1800), p.158
[34] http://hebdenhey.org.uk/tombell-theman.htm

6. Magic on the Moors ~ The Hunt for the Mixenden Treasure

[1]James Raine, 'Proceedings connected with a remarkable charge of sorcery, brought against James Richardson and others, in the Diocese of York, AD 1510', *Yorkshire Archaeological Journal* 16 (1859) p. 75
[2] Ibid p.79
[3] Ibid p.79
[4] Reproduced in full in Raine (1859)
[5] John Billingsley, *The Mixenden Treasure,* (Hebden Bridge: Northern Earth, 2009)
[6] Raine, p.80
[7] Billingsley, p.13
[8] Raine p.81
[9] Ibid p.75
[10] Billingsley p.21
[11] Ibid p.38
[12] Raine, pp.77-78
[13] Ibid p.76
[14] Ibid p.76
[15] Ibid p.76
[16] Billingsley p.42
[17] Ibid p.49
[18] Ibid pp.50-51
[19] T.W. Hanson, *The Mixenden Treasure,* Halifax Antiquarian Society (1926)
[20] Billingsley p.71
[21] Hanson (1926)
[22] *Halifax Daily Courier and Guardian* 18 April 1949
[23] Ibid
[24] *Yorkshire Observer* 14 May 1949
[25] *Yorkshire Observer* 14 May 1949

[26] *Halifax Daily Courier and Guardian* 13 May 1949

7. Prophet of Doom ~ The Halifax Astrologer

[1] C.E. Mitchell, *Foretold by the Stars,* (Manchester: Two Worlds Publishing, 1940) pp.15-16
[2] *Halifax Daily Courier and Guardian* 8 November 1937
[3] Mitchell pp.15-16
[4] Ibid p.3
[5] Ibid p.5
[6] Ibid p.18
[7] *Halifax Daily Courier and Guardian* 8 November 1932
[8] Mitchell p.1
[9] *Halifax Daily Courier and Guardian* 24 July 1933
[10] Mitchell, p.2
[11] Ibid, p.13
[12] *Halifax Daily Courier and Guardian* 29 August 1935
[13] Ibid
[14] *Halifax Daily Courier and Guardian* 23 January 1936
[15] Mitchell p.13
[16] Ibid p.14
[17] *Halifax Daily Courier and Guardian* 31 August 1935
[18] *Halifax Daily Courier and Guardian* 26 June 1931
[19] *Halifax Daily Courier and Guardian* 2 September 1935
[20] *Halifax Daily Courier and Guardian* 2 November 1939
[21] *Halifax Daily Courier and Guardian* 6 November 1934
[22] Mitchell p.23
[23] Ibid p.73
[24] *Halifax Daily Courier and Guardian* 30 July 1941
[25] *Halifax Daily Courier and Guardian* 22 August 1958
[26] *Halifax Daily Courier and Guardian* 30 August 1952
[27] *Halifax Daily Courier and Guardian* 5 November 1952

8. Bewitched ~ Witches, Wizards and Cunning Folk

[1] William Henderson, *Folklore of the Northern Counties,* (1879) p.209. Available at www.wikisource.org.
[2] *Todmorden and District News* 15 March 1935
[3] *Todmorden and District News* 8 January 1904

[4] Dan Thomas Wilcock, *Stories from Hardcastle Crags and Heptonstall* No.1, (1919)
[5] James Raine, *Depositions from the Castle of York Relating to Offences in the Northern Counties in the Seventeenth Century* (1861) p.8
[6] Ibid p.7
[7] Owen Davies, *Popular Magic: Cunning-Folk in English History* (London: Hambledon Continuum, 2007) p.108
[8] Raine, p.8
[9] Ibid p.7
[10] Ibid p.7
[11] Ibid p.8
[12] *Todmorden and District News* 11 March 1898
[13] *Todmorden and District News* 16 May 1913
[14] T. Hawkins, *The Iniquity of Witchcraft, Censured and Exposed: Being the Substance of Two Sermons, Delivered at Warley, Near Halifax, Yorkshire,* (1808)
[15] Ibid p.32
[16] *Halifax Guardian and Huddersfield and Bradford Advertiser* 10 February 1844
[17] This account and the heading are taken from *Leeds Mercury* 25 February 1858
[18] Davis (2007) pp.147-148
[19] *Todmorden and Hebden Bridge Weekly Advertiser* 9 August 1862
[20] *Bradford Daily Telegraph* 18 November 1879
[21] *Keighley News* 22 November 1879
[22] *Bradford Daily Telegraph* 18 November 1879
[23] *Bradford Daily Telegraph* 21 July 1880; *Leeds Times* 24 July 1880,
[24] *Brighouse News* 24 July 1880
[25] *Bradford Daily Telegraph* 21 July 1880; *Leeds Times* 24 July 1880,
[26] *Bradford Daily Telegraph* Tuesday 24 April 1883
[27] *Sheffield Independent* Saturday 10 March 1883
[28] Ibid
[29] *Wakefield Free Press* 28 April 1883
[30] *Yorkshire Evening Post* 2 December 1891
[31] *Yorkshire Post* 21 March 1892
[32] *Bradford Daily Telegraph* 28 November 1886
[33] *Halifax Daily Courier and Guardian* 8 December 1932

[34] Davies (2007) pp.187-188

9. Close Encounters of the Tod Kind ~ Disco Lights in the Sky

[1] *Todmorden News; Hebden Bridge Times* 23 April 1982
[2] Ibid
[3] *Hebden Bridge Times* 30 April 1982
[4] Ibid
[5] http://news.bbc.co.uk/1/hi/magazine/4789887.stm
[6] Ibid
[7] *Hebden Bridge Times* 30 April 1982
[8] https://www.space.com/23315-lyrid-meteor-shower.html
[9] Personal communication from Sowerby Bridge firefighter, 2005
[10] *Hebden Bridge Times* 30 April 1982
[11] Jenny Randles, *The Pennine UFO Mystery*, (Granada: St Albans, 1983) p.229
[12] *Hebden Bridge Times* 30 April 1982
[13] Andy S. Rogers, *Analyzing Sonic Boom Footprints of Military Jets*, Available at: https://proceedings.esri.com/library/userconf/proc01/professional/papers/pap284/p284.htm, (Accessed 26 February 2021)
[14] *Hebden Bridge Times* 30 April 1982
[15] *Fortean Times* 19, p.21
[16] *Fortean Times* 23, p.29
[17] *Fortean Times* 19 and 23
[18] *Hebden Bridge Times* 21 August 2008
[19] *Halifax Evening Courier* 1 September 2008
[20] *Fortean Times* 255 and 256

10. Snow Booth ~ The Farm That Dripped Blood

[1] I first heard this story from musician and friend Steve Lacey-Marsden
[2] *Todmorden Advertiser* 14 July 1933
[3] Ibid
[4] *Todmorden Advertiser* 30 June 1933
[5] Ibid
[6] *Yorkshire Post* 23 July 33
[7] *Todmorden Advertiser* 14 July 1933
[8] *Todmorden Advertiser* 14 July 1933

[9] *Lancashire Daily Post* 29 June 1933
[10] *Todmorden Advertiser* 30 June 1933
[11] Ibid
[12] *Yorkshire Post* 23 July 33
[13] Ibid
[14] *Illustrated Police News* 3 August 33
[15] *Yorkshire Post* 23 July 1933
[16] *Todmorden Advertiser* 25 August 1933
[17] *Yorkshire Post* 23 July 1933
[18] *Todmorden Advertiser* 14 July 1933
[19] *Illustrated Police News* 6 July 1933
[20] *Yorkshire Post* 23 July 1933
[21] Ibid
[22] *Leeds Mercury* 25 July 1933
[23] *Yorkshire Evening Post* 25 July 1933
[24] Ibid
[25] Ibid
[26] Ibid
[27] *Daily Independent* 26 July 1933
[28] *Todmorden Advertiser* 25 August 1933
[29] *Western Daily Press* 19 August 1933
[30] *Daily Herald* 23 August 1933
[31] Simon Webb, *Execution: A History of Capital Punishment,* (Stroud: The History Press, 2011)
[32] Ibid
[33] *Todmorden Advertiser* 4 August 1933
[34] *Todmorden Advertiser* 25 August 1933
[35] Ibid
[36] www.blackkalendar.nl
[37] *Todmorden Advertiser* 11 October 1935

11. Merlinus Rusticus ~ Todmorden's Wizard Priest

[1] John Birch, *Henry Krabtree: Curate of Todmorden,* (Paper Portal Publishing, 2019) pp.8-36
[2] Ibid p.41
[3] Ibid pp.50-52
[4] *Todmorden Advertiser and Hebden Bridge News* 10 July 1898

[5] Birch p.107
[6] Ibid p.71
[7] Ibid p.67
[8] John Billingsley, *Folk Tales from Calderdale Vol 1,* (Mytholmroyd: Northern Earth, 2007) p.22
[9] Birch p.226
[10] Henry Krabtree, *Merlinus Rusticus 1685,* reprinted in Birch (2019) pp.249-300
[11] Birch (2019) pp.102-104
[12] Lieut-Col Fishwick, 'The Lancashire Demoniacs', *The Historical Society of Lancashire and Cheshire,* volume 35, (1886) p.139
[13] Thomas Jolly, *The Surey Demoniack,* London (1697)
[14] Fishwick (1886) pp.40-41
[15] Jolly (1697) p.32
[16] Ibid p.40
[17] Birch p.112
[18] Jolly p.3
[19] Birch pp.140-141
[20] Ibid pp.116
[21] Ibid p.114
[22] Ibid p.114
[23] Jolly (1697)
[24] Zachery Taylor, *The Surey Imposter,* Manchester (1697)
[25] Ibid p.20
[26] Ibid p.19
[27] I am indebted to the work of John Birch for this chapter

12. Haunted Streets ~ The 'Rippers' That Time Forgot

[1] *Todmorden Advertiser and Hebden Bridge Newsletter* 19 October 1888
[2] Paul Begg, *Jack the Ripper: The Definitive History,* (Pearson Longman, 2004) pp.269-278
[3] *Todmorden Advertiser and Hebden Bridge Newsletter* 19 October 1888
[4] *Halifax Evening Courier* 12 January 1899
[5] *Todmorden Advertiser and Hebden Bridge Newsletter* 18 November 1892
[6] *Todmorden and District News* 24 March 1893
[7] *Halifax Evening Courier* 6 February 1892
[8] *The Halifax Evening Courier* 7 January 1899

[9] *The Halifax Evening Courier* 14 January 1899
[10] Ibid
[11] Ibid
[12] John K. Walton, 'Mad Dogs and Englishmen: The Conflict over Rabies in Late Victorian England', *Journal of Social History*, Vol. 13, No. 2 (Winter, 1979), pp. 219-239
[13] *The Halifax Evening Courier* 14 January 1899
[14] *The Halifax Evening Courier* 21 January 1899
[15] Ibid
[16] Ibid
[17] *The Halifax Evening Courier* 28 January 1899
[18] Ibid
[19] *The Halifax Evening Courier* 11 February 1899
[20] Ibid
[21] *Halifax Courier* 27 February 1899
[22] *Halifax Courier* 18 August 1899
[23] Walton (1979)
[24] https://www.dailymail.co.uk/news/article-2987859/Second-dog-reported-dead-Crufts-murder-mystery-poisoning-victim-Jagger-Irish-setter-cremated.html
[25] https://www.examinerlive.co.uk/news/west-yorkshire-news/dogs-death-poison-holmfirth-cliff-16925645
[26] *Yorkshire Evening Post* 5 November 1908
[27] *Todmorden Advertiser and Hebden Bridge Newsletter* 6 November 1908
[28] Ibid

13. Robin Hood's Grave and the Kirklees Vampire

[1] Kai Roberts, *Grave Concerns: The Follies and Folklore of Robin Hood's Final Resting Place,* (Devon: CFZ, 2011) Press, p.18
[2] Robin Hood's Death (Percy Folio).
[3] Ibid
[4] J.C. Holt, *Robin Hood,* (London: Thames and Hudson, 1982) p.16
[5] Ibid p.50
[6] Ibid p.40-61
[7] Ibid p.40-61
[8] Roberts (2011) p.19

[9]www.bbc.co.uk/nottingham/features/2003/10/shooting_the_final_arrow.shtml
[10] Holt (1982) p.41
[11] Roberts (2011) p.43
[12] Holt (1982) pp.41-42
[13] Roberts p.45
[14] Holt p.42
[15] Roberts (2011) pp. 25-32
[16] Ibid pp.28-29
[17] Ibid p.30
[18] Ibid p.59
[19] Roberts p.123
[20] Steve Hill, email to author, 12 March 2003
[21] Barbara Green, *The Mystery of Robin Hood's Grave,* (Palmyra Press, 2001)
[22] Thanks to Barbara Green for forwarding Roger Williams' accounts to me
[23] Roberts pp.132-133
[24] Sean Manchester, *The Vampire Hunter's Handbook,* (London: Gothic Press, 1997), p.15; Roberts, p.99
[25] Bill Ellis, 'The Highgate Vampire Hunt', *Folklore,* 104, 1-2, (1993) pp.24-32
[26] Ibid p.32-33
[27] Green (2001) p.40
[28] Roberts p.121
[29] *Liverpool Echo* 4 January 1989
[30] Manchester pp.19-22
[31] Ibid p.33
[32] Ibid p.34
[33] Ibid p.34
[34] Roberts p.127
[35] This account comes from Green (2001) pp.94-96
[36] Green (2001) p.91
[37] Ibid p.95
[38] Quoted in Roberts (p.131)
[39] Personal communication 11 July 2003
[40] Roberts p.136
[41] Email from Vampire Research Foundation 4 February 2005

[42] Telephone interview with David Farrant, 2004
[43] Email from Bishop Sean Manchester 30 January 2005
[44] Ibid
[45] Roberts p.140
[46] Ibid p.138
[47] Ibid p.138
[48] *Brighouse Echo* 2 May 2005
[49] Alan Murdie and Gareth J. Medway, 'Necrolog', *Fortean Times*, 383, (2019) p.30
[50]https://davidfarrantobituary.blogspot.com/?fbclid=IwAR3C66NxUYzY7GdenpySDsPczllq4LXA3-p9SrwWTFq89IZsyLrbwOVf-4w
[51] Email from Barbara Green 25 January 2021

14. Season of the Witch ~ The Lion, the Witch and Cliff Richard

[1] Dennis Thorpe, 'Dagger in the Mind', *The Guardian* 31 October 1987 p.11
[2] Ibid
[3] Ibid
[4] Paul Pearson and Tallis Harrill, *The Mountain and the Stream: Rural Animism and Pagan Practice* (Windgather Publishing, 2017)
[5] https://www.youtube.com/watch?v=yws8vlbH8wU
[6] Paul Pearson, 'The Hermetic Order of the Silver Blade', *Greenmantle: A Pagan Journal,* Beltane, (2015) p.31
[7] *Hebden Bridge Times* 13 July 1984
[8] *Halifax Evening Courier* 11 July 1984
[9] Ibid
[10] *Hebden Bridge Times* 13 July 1984
[11] http://www.calderdalecompanion.co.uk/qq_83.html
[12] *Halifax Evening Courier* 14 July 1984
[13] Paul Pearson, email to author
[14] *Catholic Herald* 27 July 1984
[15] Andy Roberts, *Cat Flaps: Northern Mystery Cats,* (Bideford: CFZ Press, 1992) p.24
[16] *Halifax Courier* 17 August 1984
[17] Roberts p.25
[18] Paul Pearson, email to author
[19] Kevin Logan, *Paganism and the Occult,* (Eastbourne: Kingsway Publications, 1988) p.205

[20] Doreen Irvine, *From Witchcraft to Christ,* (London: Concordia, 1973)
[21] Rosalind Theresa Waterhouse, *Satanic abuse, false memories, weird beliefs and moral panics.* (Doctoral thesis, City University London, 2014)
[22] Richard Bartholomew *Barthesnotes.com*
[23] Paul Pearson, email to author
[24] Ibid
[25] Keith Kendrick, *Liverpool Echo* 31 October 1985
[26] Dennis Thorpe, 'Dagger in the Mind', *The Guardian* 31 October 1987
[27] *Liverpool Echo* 7 March 1988
[28] Ibid
[29] Pearson and Harrill (2017), p.68
[30] Pearson (2015) p.31

15. The Burning of Alice and Amy Kirby

[1] *Halifax Evening Courier* 6 January 1899
[2] Ibid
[3] *Halifax Evening Courier* 7 January 1899
[4] Ibid
[5] Ibid
[6] *Halifax Evening Courier* 6 January 1899
[7] *Halifax Evening Courier* 7 January 1899
[8] Ibid
[9] Ibid
[10] Ibid
[11] *Halifax Evening Courier* 13 March 1985
[12] Jenny Randles and Peter Hough, *Spontaneous Human Combustion,* (New York: Dorset Press, 1992) pp.29-30
[13] Ibid p.30
[14] Damon Wilson, *Strange but True: Spontaneous Human Combustion,* (New York: Sterling Publishing, 1997) p.79
[15] *Halifax Evening Courier* 7 January 1899
[16] Wilson (1997) p.75
[17] *Halifax Evening Courier* 6 January 1899
[18] See for example *Sowerby Bridge Chronicle* 2 April 1897, 20 August 1897, 31 December 1897
[19] http://www.calderdalecompanion.co.uk/mmk69.html

16. Haunted Skies ~ The UFOs That Time Forgot

[1] E.M. Savage, *Stoodley Pike,* (Todmorden Antiquarian Society, 2001)

[2] *Todmorden Advertiser and Hebden Bridge Newsletter* 8 July 1881

[3] Ibid

[4] Ibid

[5] *Todmorden Advertiser* 6 July 1906

[6] *Halifax Evening Courier* 18 May 1909

[7] Ibid

[8] *Todmorden Advertiser* 6 August 1909

[9] *Todmorden and District News* 8 September 1916

[10] *Halifax Courier* 23 August 1909

[11] *Todmorden Advertiser* 18 December 1931

[12] *Halifax Daily Courier and Guardian* 19 August 1936

17. The Spirit in the Spire ~ Ghosts on Film

[1] www.calderdalecompanion.co.uk/qq_4.html

[2] *Halifax Evening Courier* 15th March 2005

[3] Interview with Linda Francis, May 2005

[4] Ibid

[5] Ibid

[6] https://www.facebook.com/TheYorkWaits/posts/uncanny-tales-of-the-unexplained-no-94-the-haunted-waits-bandif-you-are-of-a-ner/1315245195200827/

[7] See, for example, Phillip Carr, 'The Riddle of the Orbs', *Ghost Club Winter Newsletter,* (2000), http://www.ghostclub.org.uk/winter2000.htm#Orbs

18. A Water Witch in Hebden Bridge

[1] Charlestown History Group (2009) http://www.hebdenbridgehistory.org.uk [accessed: 25 February 2021]

[2] John Mullins and Sons, *The Divining Rod: its History, Truthfulness, and Practical Utility,* (Corsham, Wilts: J. and H.W. Mullins, 1864), pp.1-2

[3] Ibid p.3

[4] Ibid p.5

[5] *Todmorden and District News* 17 May 1889

[6] *Todmorden and District News* 16 May 1890

[7] Ibid

[8] *Todmorden and District News* 23 May 1890
[9] *Todmorden and District News* 30 May 1890
[10] *Todmorden and District News* 11 July 1890
[11] Ibid
[12] Ibid
[13] Ibid
[14] Ibid
[15] *Todmorden and District News* 3 March 1905
[16] *Todmorden and District News* 10 April 1908

19. The Todmorden Vicarage Massacre

[1] *Halifax Evening Courier* 7 March 1868
[2] *Whitby Gazette* 21 March 1868
[3] *Norwich Mercury* 18 March 1838
[4] *Whitby Gazette* 21 March 1868
[5] Ibid
[6] Geoffrey Abbot, *William Calcraft: Executioner Extra-ordinaire,* (Kent: Eric Dolby Publishing, 2004) pp.122-123
[7] Ibid p.15
[8] Ibid p.14
[9] Ibid p.122
[10] Ibid p.123
[11] *Halifax Evening Courier* 7 March 1868
[12] *Whitby Gazette* 21 March 1868
[13] *Halifax Evening Courier* 7 March 1868
[14] *Halifax Evening Courier* 21 March 1868
[15] *Halifax Evening Courier* 7 March 1868
[16] *Manchester Guardian* 16 March 1838
[17] *Norwich Mercury* 18 March 1868
[18] Ibid
[19] Ibid
[20] *Manchester Guardian* 16 March 1868
[21] *Illustrated Police News* 24 March 1868
[22] *Halifax Evening Courier* 21 March 1868
[23] Ibid
[24] *Halifax Evening Courier* 21 March 1868
[25] *Frome Times* 8 April 1868

[26] *Halifax Evening Courier* 4 April 1868
[27] *Walsall Free Press* 11 April 1868
[28] *Frome Times* 8 April 1868
[29] *Halifax Evening Courier* 11 April 1868
[30] *Walsall Free Press* 11 April 1868
[31] *Halifax Evening Courier* 11 April 1868
[32] *Frome Times* 8 April 1868
[33] Abbot (2004) p.126
[34] *Halifax Evening Courier* 11 April 1868
[35] *Frome Times* 8 April 1868
[36] Abbot (2004) p.127
[37] Thomas Laycock, 'Contributions to a new chapter in the physiology and pathology of the nervous system', *British Medical Journal*, 13 June (1868) p.577
[38] *Manchester Guardian* 27 October 1868
[39] *Manchester Guardian* 16 March 1868
[40] Ibid
[41] 'Miles Weatherhill the young weaver and his sweetheart Sarah Bell' (1868) Broadside ballad

20. The Halifax Gibbet

[1] This account is taken from an episode in a 16th century novel, *Thomas of Reading* by Thomas Deloney. I have modernised spelling in quotations.
[2] T. W. Hanson, 'The Halifax Gibbet Custom', *Transactions of the Halifax Antiquarian Society* (1948)
[3] Christopher Jennings, 'The Halifax Gibbet', *The Yorkshire Journal* 1 (2018) p.33.
[4] Ibid p.27
[5] William Camden, *Britannia*, pp.853-854
[6] John Watson, *The Histories and Antiquities of Halifax* (Lowndes, 1775) p.216
[7] Ibid p.215
[8] Ibid p.223
[9] Simon Webb, *Execution: A History of Capital Punishment in Britain* (Stroud: The History Press 2017)
[10] Nigel Cawthorne, *Public Executions from Ancient Rome to the present Day* (London: Arcturus, 2006)

[11] E. W. Crossley, 'A Halifax Gibbeting', *Transactions of the Halifax Antiquarian Society* (1908)
[12] Jennings (2018) p.34
[13] John Billingsley, *Hood, Head and Hag* (Northern Earth: Hebden Bridge, 2011) p.67
[14] Edward Armitage, 'Halifax Gibbet Law', *Transactions of the Halifax Antiquarian Society* (1948)
[15] William Bentley, *Halifax and its Gibbet Law Placed in a True Light.* (1708)
[16] Daniel Defoe, *A tour thro' the whole island of Great Britain, divided into circuits or journies*, letter 8, part 3, (1724) available at: www.visionofbritain.org.uk/travellers/Defoe/31
[17] Watson p.220
[18] Watson p.220
[19] Ibid
[20] Defoe (1724)
[21] Watson p.216
[22] Jennings p.36
[23] T.W. Hanson, 'A Gibbet Miscellany', *Transactions of the Halifax Antiquarian Society* (1952)
[24] Kai Roberts, *Haunted Halifax and District* (The History Press: Stroud, 2014) p.7
[25] Ibid p.8
[26] Ibid. p8
[27] *Bradford Observer* 20 June 1839

Robin Hood's Grave (Larisa Moskaleva)